THE
DAY
THE
CHARIOT
MOVED

THE
DAY
THE
CHARIOT
MOVED

HOW INDIA GROWS AT
THE GRASSROOTS

SUBROTO BAGCHI

PENGUIN
BUSINESS

An imprint of Penguin Random House

PENGUIN BUSINESS

Penguin Business is an imprint of the Penguin Random House group of companies whose addresses can be found at global.penguinrandomhouse.com

Published by Penguin Random House India Pvt. Ltd
4th Floor, Capital Tower 1, MG Road,
Gurugram 122 002, Haryana, India

First published in Penguin Business by Penguin Random House India 2025

Copyright © Subroto Bagchi 2025

All rights reserved

10 9 8 7 6 5 4 3 2 1

This book is a work of non-fiction based on the personal experiences, observations and interpretations of the author. It does not claim to provide an exhaustive or definitive account of the topics discussed. The author has made every effort to ensure accuracy, but errors or omissions are unintentional. The views and opinions expressed are those of the author alone and do not reflect the stance of any government, corporate entity or third party. The book is not intended as professional advice, and the publisher, editor and author shall not be held liable for any interpretation, reaction or action taken by the reader based on the content. The publisher and author disclaim any liability arising from unintended harm, defamation or misidentification. This book is not intended to malign, disparage or offend any individual, group, community, institution or government entity, nor to show bias toward or against any country, person, political party, business, region, caste, society, gender, territory, nation or religion.

Please note that no part of this book may be used or reproduced in any manner for the purpose of training artificial intelligence technologies or systems.

ISBN 9780143471257

Typeset in Sabon Lt Pro by MAP Systems, Bengaluru, India
Printed at Thomson Press India Ltd, New Delhi

This book is sold subject to the condition that it shall not, by way of trade or otherwise, be lent, resold, hired out or otherwise circulated without the publisher's prior consent in any form of binding or cover other than that in which it is published and without a similar condition including this condition being imposed on the subsequent purchaser.

www.penguin.co.in

For Niti,
In partial redemption of all the love loved

Contents

Why This Book   ix

Part I: Crossing the Chasm

1. In the Service of the State   3
2. Of Platform and Purpose   7
3. Free to Go   16
4. Do You Speak the Language?   23
5. In the Rank and Status of a Cabinet Minister   32

Part II: Where Does the World Live?

6. 30 Days, 30 Districts, 3000 Kilometres   45
7. Ten, Six, Four, Two   59
8. Muni Tigga   67
9. Where Is the 'Two' in the Equation?   72
10. Balasore to Bahadurgarh   78
11. Knitting the Pieces Together   88
12. Basanti Pradhan   93

Part III: Living in a Bubble and the Enemy Within

13. They Cannot Even Read or Write!   101
14. The Non-Performing Asset   108
15. Manjulata Bhukta and the Nursing Skill Gap   114
16. The Plumber of Santa Clara and the Barber of Bhubaneswar   123
17. Information Asymmetry   130
18. But They Are Not Our Children   137

Part IV: A Time to Act

19. The Success Managers   145
20. The Day the Chariot Moved   153
21. My A-Team   159

Part V: Flowers Wait to Bloom

22. Doing More by Doing Less   173
23. Fix the ITI   178
24. The Buried Aircraft Engine   187
25. Girls Can Do Better   196
26. A Skill Anthem, a Boy Rapper and the Caravan   211
27. Bringing the Opera to the Rainforest   216
28. Zheng HE and the Art of Collaboration   222
29. Changi, Here We Come   228
30. Tilting the Scale   232

Part VI: Things Fail, Things Work

31. Mission Aborted	245
32. Nano Unicorn	251
33. 100, 300, 1000	259
34. And Then Flowed the Narratives	263
35. The Change Agents	272
36. Everyone Loves a Competition	285
37. Creating Wonder	296
38. Something Too Large to Ignore	302
39. World Skill Center	307

Part VII: Leading Transformative Change

40. How Far Can We See?	323
41. Crossing Over, Making It Work	329
42. Managing Change	344
43. The Transformative Leader	352

In Closing	361
Acknowledgements	369

Why This Book

It was towards the end of October 1976, two months into my master's in political science, that I decided to quit my studies at the Utkal University in Bhubaneswar. There were two reasons for it. One, I was not enjoying what was being taught; it wasn't the place I wanted to be. Two, I did not want to depend on my family for higher studies. My father had retired when I was in Class VIII, and ever since, I had been a drag on my eldest brother, Debi Prasad Bagchi, who was the only family member with a steady income at that time. Hence, I decided that pursuing an MA at a place that did not challenge me enough was a waste. I decided to grab the only job available in a small town like Bhubaneswar of 1976 and wait until I would turn twenty-one, the minimum age at the time for writing the civil services examination to join the Indian Administrative Service. The day after I told my professor at the university that I was leaving, I learnt that there was a recruitment test at the State Secretariat for the temporary position of lower division clerks. I showed up for it and, to everyone's dismay, on 1 November 1976, I was appointed as a lower division clerk with the Government of Odisha's industries department for a salary of Rs 350.20. By 2024 standards, after adjusting for inflation, that would be the equivalent of Rs 10,000. I lasted in the job for less than a year. I wasn't going to wait around at the State Secretariat for two long years to be able to write my civil services examination. In 1977, my real professional life began when the DCM Group, India's seventh-largest conglomerate at the time, selected me as a management trainee.

At the time of writing this book, I am sixty-seven.

In the intervening years, I have lived through multiple identities: a private-sector professional turned IT entrepreneur, an author of several business books and, later in life, a public servant.

As an entrepreneur, the pinnacle of my achievement was co-founding Mindtree in the year 1999, where I started as the chief operating officer. When I stepped down in 2016, after seventeen eventful years, I was the executive chairman.

In 2019, Mindtree was acquired by Larsen and Toubro (L&T). After its merger with L&T's own IT subsidiary, it became LTIMindtree. In June 2024, the combined entity reported sales of USD 4.3 billion, hit a market cap of USD 17.84 billion and employed 81,000 people worldwide. This made it the 1018th most valuable company in the world.

In 2006, I debuted as a published author. Since then, I have written many books on a variety of subjects, such as entrepreneurship for startups, organizational leadership, building scale and becoming a true

Why This Book

professional. Each book became a bestseller when it was published. Some titles such as *The High Performance Entrepreneur, Go Kiss the World* and *The Professional*, written two decades ago, are still popular and continue to sell. *Go Kiss the World* became an evergreen and iconic book. My books have been translated into all major languages in India; some have been translated into Chinese and Korean.

In 2016, at the behest of Naveen Patnaik, then chief minister of Odisha, my home state, I took on the role of chairman, Odisha Skill Development Authority. Along the way, I was also the chief spokesperson of the government on Covid-19. In 2024, I transitioned to a new role as the chief adviser to the government on institutional capacity building. Here, my aim was to envision the transformation of the twenty-odd civil services training institutions of Odisha in anticipation of 2036, by which time the state would be a hundred years old. However, on 5 June 2024, my stint with the government came to an end when people voted out the Naveen Patnaik-led government. Through all these assignments in the state, I worked simultaneously at the policy and implementation levels. I saw the functioning of public institutions from within in the process. This gave me a rare, engine-room view that the layperson never gets to see.

Between the very first toehold of a job at the Odisha Secretariat and where I am today, it has almost been fifty years. Reflecting on my recent stint one day, I thought it would be interesting to chronicle my experiences of working within the government, and to write about the people and places and the lessons learnt along the way. These could serve professionals in the private sector, non-profit organizations and the government sector well. The lessons I learnt would also be valuable for the new breed of politicians who are increasingly making their voice heard.

The essence of leadership does not change across any of these profiles. Nor do some of the inherent challenges leaders often face.

* * *

This is primarily a book on leadership, but not my leadership. While forty years in the corporate sector gave me the chance to study leadership of a different kind, my work with the government brought me up close, on a daily basis, with leaders among ordinary people, whom we invariably miss in the crowd. These are the people who keep the world moving on its axis so that we can go seeking our name, fame and fortune. Yet they do not write memoirs, much less speak about who they are and what they do. In the course of my stint with the government, I was more inspired by them than by many of my previously held idols. I worked with and learnt from political leadership and some truly outstanding bureaucrats, both of whom are often objects of awe and vilification that shroud their real stories.

This is a book by a crossover. In heeding Chief Minister Naveen Patnaik's call to come work with the government, I was the quintessential crossover. The ability to cross over is particularly important in today's world where one job, one employer, one career is losing its shine. More and more young leaders I meet want to have multiple identities; they want to cross over from the private sector to the public, from the government to the non-profit, from consulting to the setting up of their own enterprises. Some are quitting the security of a well-paying government job with its power and perks, to enter active politics. The list gets longer every day. It is a global phenomenon fuelled by a new reality that presents malleability of competences and new global opportunities. But the act of crossing over, from weighing the decision to making it work, needs thinking through. We do not have many frameworks to do that. It is in that context that I hope mine is a useful, lived script and a template that might serve young leaders.

It is true that this book is built on my eight years of working with the Government of Odisha, largely in the domain of skill development. But Odisha is a major state among twenty-eight Indian states and eight union territories. Most of the things I got to see, feel and experience are relevant to any other place in India. And skill development, as you will find in the pages that follow, is truly about human transformation. Seen in that light, this is a book on the unfolding saga of human development in India, about how India is growing at the grassroots. The layered narrative of aspiration, achievement, failures, frustrations and eternal hope are universal. The lessons I learnt on development hold true across domains and geographies.

Why This Book

This is a book on the kind of governance that most people are unaware of. Karl Marx romanticized a day when the state (and perhaps the government) would simply wither away. A good century and a half after, it is very much alive and thriving. Our lives would be chaotic without the existence of governments. However, I am yet to meet anyone in the world who loves the government. Governments across the world are characterized by stereotypes of unreasonableness, sloth and arrogance. All of it wrapped in corruption and personified by a crafty politician and a conniving bureaucrat. Yet, these are stereotypes. Our lives function because there are some politicians and government servants who are different. They work. They routinely take more risks than their counterparts in the private sector. They experiment and innovate in ways that CEOs of Fortune 500 companies can only dream of.

This is also a book about transformative change. All transformative change follows a certain trajectory. Managing that process is even more critical so that the sheer intent and the instruments of change that we may deploy are effective. In public life, we deal with people. Real people. Each story matters as does the collective will. True leaders respect both. They do not let aggregated data drown the individual narrative. Data is important. But it does not give people dignity. Transformative change takes place when we respect the story of each person, one at a time. White Paper, policy and plan often lose sight of the fact because they dehumanize the idea of citizenship.

My hope is that the reader will begin to appreciate that the story of human development is an unending process. It is rewarding and punishing at the same time. It is not an 'event' even as sometimes we like to see it that way, given our obsession with the so-called success stories and impact assessments. In reality, it is a process. That process asks us to embrace it, rise above mere success and failure and take a hard, dispassionate look at ourselves. It asks us to feel privileged to be able to serve fellow beings. In turn, it gives us an unbelievably massive platform to stand on and an even larger canvas to paint.

Finally, this is a book for those who want to be inspired by their own lives and see themselves as instruments of change. In every chapter that follows, they will see a reflection of their own yearning and hopefully learn a few new things. These will sometimes fill them with hope and sometimes despair. We need both.

Before I finish, I must tell you what this book is not: it is neither a self-help book nor a typical memoir. The ability to be observant, to be a keeper of useful memories are important qualities for those who are responsible for creating a beneficial future for others. I see this as imperative for leadership.

In this book you will meet many people. You will get to know their stories. You will hear their voices. All of them are real people. They exist. Their names are real. Their situations are real. No one wears a mask here.

The Day the Chariot Moved is presented in seven distinctive sections. Part I, titled 'Crossing the Chasm', tells you my own intergenerational story of becoming a crossover.

Part II, titled 'Where Does the World Live?', is my discovery of Odisha after forty years of being away from the state. The stories narrated in this part are set in Odisha, a microcosm of India. In reading this chapter, you will begin to see the country through a different set of eyes.

In Part III, 'Living in a Bubble and the Enemy Within', I share the stories of people at the bottom of the pyramid. Through these, most readers will find how much we, the educated, city-dwelling people, live in a country but in reality, journey through a parallel universe. They will also see a stark part of the development narrative of the world's most populous nation and largest democracy in how social systems and deep-rooted stigma foil government initiatives and forces of transformative change.

Part IV titled, 'A Time to Act', is how my team and I responded to the set of realities narrated in the previous sections. This is the section that tells you how we built strategic perspectives for moving the chariot.

In Part V, 'Flowers Wait to Bloom', you will be elevated to another level. You will be filled with joy, witnessing how inert systems respond to an involved call to change and how real people, at the bottom of the so-called hierarchy, lead when appreciated, armed and empowered to take destiny into their own hands.

In Part VI, 'Things Fail, Things Work', you will see some tempering of that spirit. It will take you through stories of derailment, of failed dreams and, then again, of green shoots arriving and the return of dreams, albeit packaged differently. This is a significant section in which you will meet the real stars of the story—ordinary people who achieved extraordinary success. Their journey will inspire you to expect more of yourself.

Part VII titled, 'Leading Transformative Change', is a step back. I recommend that you read this part of the book slowly, one chapter at a time. Pause. Reflect. Go to the next chapter the next day. As the title suggests, Part VII pulls back the entire narrative and begins to guide you towards the qualities of a transformative leader. It talks about the need for maximalism when moving the needle for the generationally disenfranchised. It tells you why things happen the way they happen and why certain things worked for me. It offers an experiential template that you may find useful in charting your own course one day.

Part I

Crossing the Chasm

1

In the Service of the State

I must begin with a story. This tale has its origin more than a century ago, sometime in the very early 1900s. At that time, my grandfather, Dr Jogesh Chandra Bagchi, was the civil surgeon to the King of Seraikella. Never mind if you have not heard of Seraikella. It is a small part of Jharkhand today, one of its twenty-four districts that carries the name Saraikella-Kharsawan. But at that time, it wasn't just a district. It was a kingdom, though a vassal of the British Empire. The king, Udit Narayan Singhdeo, did not have a doctor or a hospital in his land. He had gone to Calcutta, as it was known then, and headhunted my grandfather around the year 1902. After joining the king's service, my grandfather moved to Seraikella, where he worked all his life until he died. He had nine children of whom my father, Makhan Gopal, was the third.

During my father's growing up years, my grandfather would often say '*Chakri jodi kortei hoy, rajar chakri korbe*. (If you must seek a job, go serve the king.)'

The old man, a widower, died when my father was still in college in Calcutta studying engineering. By then, King Udit Narayan had also passed away, leaving the kingdom to his heir Aditya Pratap. At the suddenness of Dr Bagchi's death, King Aditya Pratap called for my father and his elder brother. Most of the other siblings were still in school. The king asked the two brothers to leave their studies and take charge of the family. He then asked my father to go to a place called Dhenkanal, a kingdom in erstwhile Orissa. The king wrote a letter of recommendation to the King of Dhenkanal; he had given his daughter's hand to his son. He asked my father to take the letter and meet the King of Dhenkanal who would perhaps give him a job in his *durbar*. My father did as he was told and thereafter, he too served a king.

After India became independent, the princely states were abolished. People like my father transitioned into employees of the government. I was born ten years after India got independence. We were a brood of five sons and during our growing up years, it was the duty of my father to pass on the exhortation of the doctor to his children who would someday take charge of their lives. The message from Dr Jogesh Chandra Bagchi to his own son to serve 'the king' had to be now reinterpreted in the context of a free India and delivered to us.

* * *

Post 1947, the king meant the Republic of India. Makhan Gopal Bagchi told his five sons that if a Bagchi did not work for himself, he could only work for the Republic. This was the Bagchi Rule.

While growing up, we were given further elucidation of the Bagchi Rule. As part of career guidance at home, we were told that we had two options of employment to choose from. Either we could join the Indian Administrative Service or we could opt to serve the defence forces. Right from high school, we were told to remember the office and its postal address from where the application forms could be obtained in due time. It was the Union Public Service Commission, Dholpur House, Shahjahan Road, New Delhi.

By now, you can surely imagine the kind of conversations our family had at the dinner table. In time, my eldest brother joined the IAS and the second brother joined the Indian Air Force. The third brother opted not to serve anyone and was exempted from obtaining forms from the UPSC. He became a lawyer and that was perfectly acceptable. The fourth one joined the Indian Army, but when it was my turn, I turned out to be the black sheep. In 1977, I joined DCM. It was the private sector. In doing so, I had crossed over to the dark side. I had sought employment from a 'company' and not the king. The Bagchi Rule had been violated.

Starting with DCM, my stint with the private sector lasted four long decades, mostly with the Indian Information Technology (IT) industry. The defining period in these forty years was co-founding Mindtree in 1999 where I rose to be the executive chairman.

On 31 March 2016, as part of a well-thought-through succession plan, I stepped down. At that time, I was fifty-eight.

As it turned out, destiny had other plans for me. Without giving the remotest hint, it was getting me drafted into the services of the state that I had so neatly escaped for forty long years.

I too was meant to serve the king.

And now the real story begins.

It is the end of 2015. We are still a few months away from my eventual stepping down as executive chairman of Mindtree. There is one last official trip planned to review the progress of the second phase of construction at the Mindtree Kalinga Campus in Bhubaneswar. It is my baby. I have raised it. It is also perhaps my final gift to the state that gave me my first breath and my first drop of water.

2

Of Platform and Purpose

Sometime in 2015, I was visiting Bhubaneswar, where Mindtree Kalinga, Mindtree's Global Learning and Delivery Centre, had commenced its operations. The process of setting up the meticulously designed centre spread over a twenty-acre campus brought me to the city quite frequently. It was an institute that the state government, in its eagerness to attract tech companies, was also justifiably proud of. In the course of all this, I got to interact with a few senior bureaucrats of the state.

One day, Ranjana and Sanjeev Chopra, both senior IAS officers, invited me over for dinner. The only other guest that evening, they said, would be Raju Balakrishnan, principal secretary, Finance, and development commissioner of the Government of Odisha. Apparently, he had expressed a desire to meet me.

At dinner, Raju Balakrishnan told me that he had read my book *Go Kiss the World*. He could deeply identify with the narrative at many levels. Like me, he came from an ordinary background. He had studied in Tamil-medium schools and eventually made it to the civil services. Upon joining the IAS, he was allocated the Odisha cadre, and ever since, the state had been his home. In the course of his long and successful career, he became deeply fascinated with the history, culture, literature and, in particular, the tribal heritage of Odisha. He was also a serious scholar of the Indus Valley civilization. The reason he had requested the Chopras to make the introduction to me, was to invite me to address something called the Odisha Knowledge Hub (OKH). His brainchild, the OKH was a platform where the entire top brass of the civil services periodically gathered to listen to an eclectic set of speakers from the outside world. In the past, he told me, speakers like Nachiket More and Raghuram Rajan had addressed the forum.

He wanted me to address the OKH's third edition on 2 April 2016. The date was chosen to commemorate the birth centenary of Biju Patnaik and it was also the eightieth year of the formation of Odisha as the first linguistically organized state in India. I agreed to the idea immediately. It would be an honour. But which topic would I speak on for a group of civil servants? He said, 'Speak on leadership.' That was obviously a huge canvas. Though leadership as a subject is very close to my heart, I had never really spoken to bureaucrats before. I told him I would think about the specific subject in the days to come.

In the ensuing weeks, I considered many aspects of leadership that I had worked upon in the past and zeroed in on the idea of 'Platform and Purpose', which I had developed through three decades observing high achievers from different fields of work.

The genesis of the concept of platform and purpose went back to the 1990s when I was chief executive of Wipro's newly formed Global R&D (research and development) division. In the decade prior, it was the core of Wipro's computer business and a driving force behind its success in the emergent Indian hardware industry. Then came the economic liberalization of the 1990s and suddenly, the Indian economy opened up. Global competition arrived and many Indian businesses that had thrived in a protected economy, wobbled. At that time, the future of Wipro's R&D became uncertain as it was a domestically focused cost centre. Now, Wipro had to compete with multinational giants such as IBM and Digital. These companies built their products at a global scale and their R&D investments and costs were many times higher. It was going to make less sense for Wipro to design and make its own hardware. Perhaps global sourcing of hardware to compete with global giants made more sense. Given that uncertainty, questions arose. How could Wipro's R&D stay relevant? Should it be closed down?

At that juncture, the company took a bold decision. Instead of shutting it down, Wipro decided to reposition its R&D as a global lab-on-hire. That is when I came in, first sent to set up Wipro's beachhead in the Silicon Valley and later, upon my return to India, to be chief executive of Wipro's Global R&D. There, more than the exhilaration of heading the business unit every day, I derived great joy in seeing the geeks, nerds and other life forms in the R&D up close. These were high calibre individuals with great dreams, real fears and an uncanny ability to solve complex problems but sometimes, with follies that defied common sense. I was working with a bunch of high achievers.

As I worked with them, my fascination with the idea of high achievement began. I saw how some of these individuals, the best India had produced in information technology, women and men from Indian Institute of Science, Indian Institutes of Technology, BITS Pilani and similar ilk, made it to the top. Some shot through the sky and then simply coasted and some who burnt out and fell apart midway. I saw their professional and their personal sides evolve. They faltered sometimes and clashed on other occasions, but a small number eventually succeeded in creating significant impact over a long period of time.

After Wipro came Mindtree. Here, I had the opportunity of working with many such outstanding people on a larger scale. Once Mindtree went public, I opted out of the role of the chief operating officer. Now, I was going to be titled *gardener*. The idea was to give my full time and attention to groom and mentor the top 100 Mindtree minds to take on larger responsibilities. Mindtree could grow only if its leaders yearned to grow themselves. These were the people who would lead Mindtree beyond the co-founders.

As part of my assignment as the gardener at Mindtree, I spent thousands of hours working with these 100 leaders. They let me into the deep recesses of their mind. As I listened to them, engaged with them and sometimes followed them at work like a fly on the wall, I slowly began to shape the paradigm of platform and purpose in my mind.

Let us start by looking at the platform. Every professional stands on a distinct platform that defines the individual. It broadly consists of six attributes: education, experience, network, net worth, family and finally, health. These six things, taken together, pretty much shape an individual's identity and self-worth at any point in time. Look at anyone. Look at yourself for that matter.

Where you studied and what you studied become a core part of your identity. Someone may say, I am from IIT Madras. I studied mechanical engineering there. Someone says, I am from IIM-Ahmedabad, batch of 2010. A doctor would perhaps say, I did my MD from PGI Chandigarh. It sticks to you. Or rather, you stick to it.

The next thing is your experience. It is amazing that within minutes of introducing yourself to a stranger aboard a flight, you find yourself talking about all you have done. 'Oh, I started as a sub-editor at so-and-so newspaper, and then I moved to Delhi where I worked for a magazine for eight years before shifting to my current job at this news company, where I have been working as a social media content producer for the last six years.'

With your education and experience, you build a portfolio of sorts. But that combination works only up to a point as you progress through a career.

Two individuals may start with very similar education and experience but quite often, as they move through leadership assignments, what differentiates one from the other is the network of the leader.

It is a resource that can be tapped in a jiffy. Who knows who becomes critical when the leader's personal education and experience are inadequate in a given situation. Take two equally competent professionals: the quality of their network and the ability to tap into it can create very different outcomes and consequent impact. Every bureaucrat seeks out a batchmate in another cadre. Every corporate employee does the same thing. This is exactly why LinkedIn is such a big success.

You want to fix a problem at work that you have not previously encountered or you want to get a referral for a bid you are unsure of winning—and in a flash you know whom you should be turning to for advice, critical input or help. Someone who can open the door and clear the path for you. A person's network can deliver formidable power.

For many professionals, this combination of education, experience and a solid network makes a great difference but this applies up to a certain extent in life. As people grow into their forties and the fifties, quite often, another thing comes into play. This is the net worth of an individual. It may sound rather crude but how many assets or how much money a person has in the bank go beyond just ensuring their comfort. Often, they determine an individual's risk-taking capability. Think of a single-income individual with a lot of domestic commitment and another who has good savings and a spouse with a well-paying job. Which of the two individuals is more likely to quit their job at the age of forty and become an entrepreneur? How much money you have in the bank can determine your sense of safety and your risk appetite.

I have seen many great professionals—who have received excellent education, gained great experience, carefully cultivated a valuable network and have built up substantial net worth by the time they are in their forties—slow down and even opt out of bigger possibilities. The determining factor is the quality of their relationships at home. Our spouses or partners make a huge difference, as do our children and other loved ones. A lack of understanding with a spouse, constant nagging and false comparisons with other people, a separation, a teenage child gone out of control or the protracted illness of a loved one can all take the wind out of the sails of any high-performance individual. Your family can make you, slow you down or break you.

If your family competes with you, that is the end of a professional dream. It doesn't matter how competent you are.

Many hitherto outstanding people, often enviably gifted on all fronts we have discussed so far, sail through their forties; they tick all the factors like education, experience, network, net worth and family support and yet, perhaps by their fifties, their health suddenly fails. The doctor says, 'I have bad news for you, you have a malignant tumour.' Or 'You need a stent in your heart.' Maybe an autoimmune disorder that will perhaps get worse over time announces itself. Now, you need to exit the high-speed lane, slow down and veer off the highway. You have little choice. That's when you realize, your health is everything. You can deal with the lack of all the other contributing factors of your platform only if your body lets you succeed. And when your body says no, it is a really tough call.

In our lives, the platform we stand on, the place from which we launch ourselves, the springboard from which we can make a lasting impact, is a combination of these six factors. Yet, the interesting thing is that the so-called platform does not solely determine your impact as a leader. Two leaders may start with comparable platforms, but their impact over a period of time could vastly differ. This is because their sense of *purpose* is different.

Only when you put purpose to a platform can you make a difference. The interplay between platform and purpose becomes very interesting when you look at the two as a XY graph with purpose plotted on the X-axis and platform on the Y-axis. The result is a 2x2 matrix with four quadrants. Professionals invariably fall into one of these four quadrants.

Some individuals fall into the 'low platform', 'low purpose' quadrant. Some are in the 'low platform', 'high purpose' one. Some are in the 'high platform', 'low purpose' box and the leader among leaders are those who operate from the 'high platform' and 'high purpose' quadrant.

Of Platform and Purpose

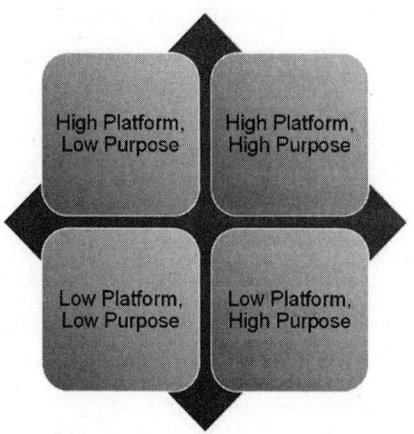

Each quadrant brings its own driving characteristics, vulnerabilities and trade-offs. As a result, the kind of impact one has over time depends on which quadrant the person operates from.

Most civil servants have very comparable *platforms* at the beginning of their career. Yet, the impact they have over time, can differ greatly because their *purpose* can be entirely different.

The interplay between platform and purpose has many cascading implications in the way a civil servant's outlook evolves over time on matters like probity and efficiency. There are people who end up neither corrupt nor efficient. There are some who are highly corrupt and highly efficient. There are the ones who are reasonably efficient and not corrupt, and then there are those few who are highly efficient and incorruptible.

For the theme of my address at the Odisha Knowledge Hub, I decided to present my paradigm of platform and purpose, contextualized for leadership in the bureaucracy.

3

Free to Go

31 March 2016. Susmita was ecstatic; it was my last day at Mindtree. She and I had first met when I was eighteen. She wasn't even sixteen then. She had just entered college and I was graduating the same year. We courted each other for four years and decided to get married when she was nineteen and I was all of twenty-two. Soon our babies came along and, to build our respective careers and raise a family, both of us worked really hard to keep everything in place. Now, it was time to let go, decompress and do all the things that were important to us that we never had the time or resources for. We told ourselves that, going forward, we would only do four things: travel, teach, read and write. Except, of course, one last official commitment I had already made—to deliver a talk at the Odisha Knowledge Hub.

That is how both of us reached Bhubaneswar on 1 April. The next day, using the four-quadrant idea of platform and purpose, I engaged my audience on the theme of transformative leadership in the government.

The talk was extremely well received. In part, because I was the proverbial son of the soil, the boy next door who had made it good. While many had only heard about my work in the IT industry, quite a few had read some of the books and now wanted to hear me in person. And because the subject I spoke on was based on my lifelong research on high achievers, the audience could relate to everything I said.

The auditorium at the State Secretariat was full to the brim. In addition, I could see that the collectors of all the thirty districts of the state had joined via video conference links along with their senior colleagues. The format of the OKH was that the speaker had the floor for forty-five minutes followed by an additional fifteen minutes for questions and answers.

It was a very uplifting experience for me. Coming back after four decades of mostly being away from my homeland to the adulation of an entire system felt special. After the talk got over, there was the usual shaking of hands, the media interaction followed and then, I became my own free man. It was time for me to fulfil my promise to Susmita that from this day, we were free to go. This was going to be our time. No more getting up to run in the morning, no meetings, no resolving issues and conflicts, no chasing targets, deliverables and deadlines.

Everything seemed to be on plan.

Except that I had no clue that Chief Minister Naveen Patnaik had been listening to the entire talk at the OKH via a live feed from his own office on the third floor of the Secretariat.

He never attended OKH events, even though he was the sponsor, because he wanted his officers to freely engage with the invited speaker. This time, however, for whatever reason, he had asked for a live feed in his chamber.

On 4 April 2016, exactly four days into my free-to-go plan, the phone rang. The caller at the other end said the Honourable Chief Minister of Odisha wanted to speak to me. It was dramatic. Naveen Patnaik came on the line.

'Mr Bagchi,' he said, 'we will be very grateful if you come and help us with skill development for our youth. This is something extremely important for us.

'I hope you will consider my request and say yes. The state needs you. We want you to consider joining us as chairman of Odisha Skill Development Authority.

'We will give you complete freedom and whatever resources you may need. You can bring in whoever you choose from outside for the assignment.'

I was caught completely off guard for a few moments. Then, very politely, I told him how humbled, how deeply honoured I was to receive his call and asked for some time to think it over.

Susmita knew something was happening, and I told her about the conversation as soon as it ended. Now it was her turn to be startled. Both of us were very confused. I had left Odisha four decades ago. What did the running of a government programme and I have in common? What did I know about skill development for youth, mostly school dropouts? It was one thing for the chief minister to tell me something flattering in that moment of induced importance and quite another to get accepted by the system without which one just cannot work in the government.

What if I failed to make any difference?

What if I got mired in the labyrinth of a potentially dangerous system?

What about the politics and corruption that have pervaded public life in varied measures across states?

It was all very nebulous, enticing, dangerous, yet somewhat beautiful in its allure. For starters, I needed to know more.

Following that short call, several parleys followed with the chief secretary of Odisha, Aditya Padhi, Raju Balakrishnan and the chief minister's private secretary, Karthikeyan Pandian.

The Biju Janata Dal, the party in power in Odisha, had made an electoral promise in 2014 to provide employable skills to 1.5 million youth, mostly school dropouts. Every other government department was involved in some form of skill development and training.

These had produced vastly varied results, and there was no unified vision. Skill development on the whole was unglamorous. No officer wanted to do it.

In that backdrop, the top leadership of the state felt an urgent need to find a solution. They realized a different approach was required in order to bring in a sense of purpose, vision and urgency to their mission. Within the government framework, like in every other state, skill development was not glamourous. It was perceived as a low platform, low purpose activity within the system. That sense of poor self-esteem cascaded down to skill training institutions. I was being asked to step in and move it to the high platform and high purpose quadrant. To that end, they were offering me the office in the rank of a cabinet minister reporting directly to the chief minister, freedom to decide the charter of the Odisha Skill Development Authority and their commitment to make resources available.

Following the initial conversations, I started reading up on everything I could find on the subject. This took me beyond the bubble of the IT industry to a world I had not known before. It was a world where millions of young people in India faltered in their ways. These young people fell off the traditional educational system for whatever reason and could not get skilled in any vocation but now desperately needed employment. These were the people who became welders, mechanics, plumbers, electricians, cab drivers, security guards, sales associates in malls, janitors at airports and bedside attendants in hospitals.

I soon realized that on the one hand, everyone had been speaking for long about the proverbial demographic dividend. On the other hand, we were lagging behind every developed country in creating opportunities for vocational training.

The demographic dividend could mean that we could be a global provider of skilled, employable workforce that the developed yet ageing countries needed. They had the money, we had the youth. Yet, the world did not just want hands—it needed expert, trained hands. As I delved deeper, I learnt many new things.

Previously, I had no idea that a staggering 96 per cent of the entire workforce in India was in the unorganized sector with undocumented workers and subsistence wages.

On the one hand, India seemed to be hurtling forward to become one of the top economies of the world, and on the other hand, there was increasing wage disparity, forced migration and, despite the ubiquitous smartphone, an enormous story of digital divide.

Women, half of India, were receding in percentage terms when it came to wage participation, while the same number was surging forward even in a country like Bangladesh.

Yet, there were opportunities everywhere. I read a report from the year 2011, put together by Ernst & Young, on skill gaps commissioned by the National Skill Development Corporation (NSDC), set up by the Government of India.[*]

It projected mind-blowing numbers between demand and supply. The report made my head swirl. Only 2 per cent of the population under the age of twenty-nine had ever received any formal skill training

---

[*] Ernst & Young. 'Skill Gap Assessment for the State of Odisha: A district wise analysis.' Available at https://nsdcindia.org/sites/default/files/files/odisha-skill-gap-report.pdf.

and only 8 per cent had some form of informal skill training.

Yet, across the twenty sectors that the report covered, the country needed more skilled workers than the entire population of many countries.

By 2022, it said, the construction and real-estate industry in India would need an additional 47 million people! That was almost the entire population of a state like Odisha.

The auto and auto-component industry needed 35 million people.

The logistics and warehousing sector had a demand projection of 17 million.

The textile sector needed 16 million.

On the services side, the organized retail sector alone needed 17 million.

The burgeoning financial sector called for 4.2 million new jobs that had to be staffed.

The healthcare system of the country projected an additional demand for 2.2 million nurses.

Suddenly, my life in the IT industry seemed small and insignificant. A whole new world was beginning to unfold; its allure was dizzying and dangerous.

4

Do You Speak the Language?

The allure of this new world caused Susmita and me a high degree of uncertainty. What if crossing over to the government—an area I had no previous exposure to—did not work out? My four decades of great work in the IT industry would simply be washed away because of a foray into something that could fall between naivety and foolhardiness. What about dealing with politicians and corruption? What if the Indian bureaucracy refused to accept an outsider like me? And, of course, what would happen to my resolve of stepping into the second springtime of life, of smelling the roses with Susmita?

I was indeed at a fork in life.

One path was a simple, lyrical, romantic road: to read, write, teach and travel. I had rehearsed it so much that it looked familiar. Also, at fifty-eight, I was dangerously close to the couch.

And the other one? Unscripted, seemingly glorious, but with no guarantees.

When confronted with the dilemma that every unusual decision entails, the human brain sides with the familiar. What was I to do? Turn to what looked familiar? Or go seek the unknown? And what may look like downright dangerous, may actually be life's door to the magic quadrant of high platform and high purpose for me.

Either way, I needed to take a decision quickly and convey it soon, because at the other end was a man like Naveen Patnaik who was no ordinary politician.

At critical junctures in life, when the stakes are high, data serves a limited purpose. One needs opinions. Solid opinions. Not necessarily from people in the same domain but from those who have the ability to connect the dots. These are well-wishers without a vested interest in the outcome and must be people you have enormous respect for. Further, these people should bring an eclectic set of perspectives. When you do find them, you must go to them with an open mind. Any confirmation bias makes the whole process infructuous.

At the greatest crossroads of my professional career, I decided to seek advice from four people who qualified the above criteria. Since the stakes were going to be high for me, I decided that I must err on the side of caution. All four had to say yes. A single contrary vote would be the proverbial red signal, deterrent enough for me to reject the offer from Naveen Patnaik.

The first person had to be Susmita. Up until Mindtree went public, she had to run the house on a budget. At every stage in life, our gratifications were postponed for one reason or the other. Now our daughters had grown up. Mindtree had grown up. It had been an intense partnership of decades and she had never denied me whatever I had wanted; she had let me take the big risks in life, underwriting me at every leap. She was my partner of many decades but she was also my biggest critic. I respected her independent voice each time I heard it. When I had repeated the message from Naveen Patnaik, she too was quite stunned. That night, we did not sleep, but ended up discussing the pros and cons. Over the next few days, we stopped and started the conversation many times over and, finally, I asked her what she really thought. I was completely at ease with whatever she might say. The next ten years of my life were meant to be hers. She had the first right of refusal.

Quite surprisingly, she said, 'You should go ahead. Retirement can wait. How many people get such an opportunity? You were born in that land and you owe it to your people.' She had no vacillation. A steady, calm yes.

The second person I turned to was Manish Sabharwal, the Wharton-educated founder of Teamlease—one of the largest employers of semi-skilled and skilled workers in India—and an authority on the skill-development narrative. Manish had made Bengaluru his home, where he had earlier founded a company named India Life that Hewitt had acquired. I met him in his office in Koramangala. He was almost always dressed in a khadi kurta and pyjama. His small, quirky office room had shelves filled with all kinds of books. Among the many things that fascinated me about Manish was an unexploded grenade that he kept on his table. His father was a celebrated top cop who was once posted in Jammu and Kashmir. The grenade had been tossed at him. It fortunately hadn't exploded and the man decided to keep it as a souvenir; this was now a decoration in his son's office.

Whenever I had met Manish in the past, I was invariably drawn by his maverick persona. He spoke well, often rapidly, in a knowledgeable voice. He was opinionated when it came to core issues. And he made sense. Manish and I had a long conversation. At the end of it, he said, 'You should do it. There is so much to be done in the world of skill development, particularly in a state like Odisha. You have been an entrepreneur; you are an institution builder. What if you have never done this stuff before? You can do it. You have nothing to lose.'

Next, I called my eldest brother, Debi Prasad Bagchi. The man who had made my father proud by adhering to the Bagchi Rule. Our age gap was a good fourteen years. When he started his life as a lecturer at Utkal University, in Bhubaneswar, I was being homeschooled in a place called Koraput because there were no schools nearby. I was seven at that time and my father had packed me off to be under his care. He had taken me to my first school in the university campus and thereafter had raised me like a father and a friend.

When he got selected for the IAS, he was allocated the Odisha cadre. He retired as chief secretary of the state in 2001. I was his prodigy during my growing up years. But when I had chosen not to write the civil services examination, he had been quite disappointed. In the years that followed, I made many career choices, but I never consulted him. But this time, I decided to for two reasons. One, my brother had served the state all his life. Two, he had been chief secretary of the state when Naveen Patnaik, the man who I was going to work with, was in his first term as chief minister. Who else would know matters of statecraft better than Debi Prasad and who else, other than Susmita, would be more invested in my welfare? After his retirement, he had settled down in Delhi. I gave him a call, told him about the unfolding development and asked him for his opinion. The opinion came wrapped in rebuke. 'You private-sector folks, you are always critical of the government. Now here is a challenge for you. If you are any good, go out there and prove yourself.' It was his admonishment to me for not writing the IAS way back in 1977. So that was a yes.

Now, I was left with the last man: (I met) Nandan Nilekani, co-founder of Infosys and more importantly, a man whose words inspired the author Thomas Friedman to title his global bestseller *The World Is Flat*.* Later, Nandan authored the book *Imagining*

---

* Friedman, Thomas L. 'It's a Flat World, After All.' *New York Times*, 3 April 2005. Available at https://www.nytimes.com/2005/04/03/magazine/its-a-flat-world-after-all.html.

India.* To implement an idea from his book, Dr Manmohan Singh, then Prime Minister of India, had invited him to join the Central government in the rank of a cabinet minister to set up the Unique Identification Authority of India (UIDAI) to give the Aadhaar number to a billion people. This revolutionary idea was to change India forever.

Nandan and I went back to his early days in Infosys and my early days in Wipro. I had a lot of admiration and respect for him. It was also interesting that his vision of creating an open-source software engine for Aadhaar was built by Mindtree. But most importantly, in the entire Indian IT community, he was the first and, at the time, the only one to join the government. Nandan was a crossover.

Our meeting took place over an extended cup of tea at his Koramangala residence in Bengaluru even though he was now spending most of his time in Delhi. By then, I had done some more research. I could articulate what the assignment could entail and what perhaps was expected by Naveen Patnaik. Nandan is a very patient listener and heard me out. Then, he just had one question for me. 'Do you speak the language?'

I paused for a moment.

I told him that as children, our parents always told us that we had two mother tongues, Bangla and Odia, and we needed to be equally proficient in both. Then of course, I studied in government schools where the

---

* Nilekani, Nandan. *Imagining India*. New Delhi: Penguin, 2008.

medium of instruction was Odia. So yes, I could read, write and speak Odia quite fluently.

'Good,' he said. 'You should not take up an assignment like this if you do not speak the language. If you speak to people in English there, however smart and capable you may be, they will simply chew you and spit you out before you know it.'

Then, Nandan added a few more invaluable pieces of advice. Some were quite obvious but one was very counter-intuitive.

The first one, he told me, was to negotiate access. It is one thing to be invited with warmth and fanfare, he told me. But in public life, memories are short-lived. Any serious, transformational work would take many years to be accomplished. Given that, you need assured and visible access to the sponsor throughout the assignment. It was non-negotiable and not settling it upfront can seldom be remedied. When Manmohan Singh invited him to come to Delhi to set up the UAIDI, Nandan had made it clear that people who handled Dr Singh's calendar would never make him wait.

He did not have to explain the agenda to the gatekeepers, far less get it pre-processed. 'Look,' Nandan coached me, 'you may seldom need to exercise this, but the fact that you have priority, gets notified to the world. It is a matter of messaging. It signals the gravity of the purpose for which you have been brought in. In an assignment like this, your legitimacy must be writ large.'

And then came the counter-intuitive thing: 'Do not land there and start creating brand new physical infrastructure as your very first priority. You would be quite surprised how much infrastructure a government already has. Incumbents think the easy thing to show results is to make buildings, buy equipment and spend big money. Even if these could be important, you need to put them on the backburner. Start with what is already on the ground. First sweat out the existing assets.'

Four ticks. A fortnight after the call from Naveen Patnaik, I flew down to Delhi where a meeting with him was arranged by his private secretary, Karthikeyan Pandian. Pandian belonged to the Indian Administrative Service and was the chief minister's closest aide. Gita Mehta, Naveen Patnaik's sister who was visiting from New York, was the host. She was clearly invested in the outcome of the meeting even though she never interfered in the official world of her brother. Naveen Patnaik, in any case, kept family out of statecraft. She was a well-known author and her renowned, charismatic publisher husband Sonny Mehta lived in New York. She was extremely fond and protective of her brother. Characteristically, Naveen Patnaik spoke very little, while Gita was lively and kept the conversation going.

Naveen Patnaik knew I had come to say yes. Over sandwiches and tea, he basically delivered the same message to me: 'The state needs you. You will be given a complete free hand. Thank you for accepting the invitation.' But then he added something else. 'We know this will be a great personal sacrifice for Mrs Bagchi, for her to leave everything behind in Bangalore and come all the way. We are very grateful for that.' After an hour, we shook hands and Karthikeyan Pandian saw me off.

On 29 April 2016, Chief Minister Naveen Patnaik read out the announcement on the floor of the Assembly that the Odisha Skill Development Authority would be set up and I had been invited to head it as chairman in the rank and status of a cabinet minister.

The next day, Susmita and I packed four suitcases, locked the house in Bengaluru and flew down to Bhubaneswar. On the flight, my mind floated back to forty years ago when I had first seen a particular portrait of the Mother at Auroville, Pondicherry. Below it, in her own signature style, were written the words, *'Blessed are those who take a leap towards the future.'*

5

In the Rank and Status of a Cabinet Minister

The first trapping of being appointed in the 'rank and status of a cabinet minister' became evident to me when I arrived at the Biju Patnaik Airport in Bhubaneswar. The principal secretary to the government, L.N. Gupta, a senior IAS officer and director of the State Employment Mission, G. Rajesh from the Indian Forest Service and two of his deputies were waiting right inside the airport arrival area with bouquets in hand. This was a huge departure from the IT industry where you arrived at whatever airport, picked up your own bag, hugged loneliness, hailed a cab and went to a hotel. The sole exception was Azim Premji, whom the local head of business would pick up and then be subjected to a formal review of operations during the car ride. To Premji, every minute mattered. And no bouquets please. They were an avoidable expense.

It was pre-arranged that on our arrival, Susmita and I would first travel to Puri, seek the blessings of Lord Jagannath and then return to Bhubaneswar to call on the chief minister before formally taking charge. After the very pleasant welcome, as we stepped out of the airport, there was a host of television crew at hand. The work had not even started but the media had arrived! I spoke to them briefly and got into the waiting car. It was then that I realized there was a police car parked directly in front that was going to escort us to Puri. When a cabinet minister travels outside the precincts of Bhubaneswar City, he gets a police escort vehicle. The rank and status start there.

And that is not all: the car he travels in has a red beacon on top and, whenever he arrives at a new district, he receives a ceremonial guard of honour by an armed constabulary. That courtesy is repeated when it is time to leave. Mercifully, after a few months of being there, the red beacon and the guard of honour, one a modern and the other a colonial trapping of power, were dropped at the behest of the chief minister, who did not like unnecessary pomp and ceremony. But there were many other things that went with the rank of a cabinet minister, and a brief commentary is in order.

* * *

Soon after I joined, Pinaki Patnaik, my officer-on-special duty (OSD) reported for work. He was a pleasant young officer from the Odisha Administrative Service (OAS), personally handpicked for me by Aditya Padhi, the chief secretary for the role. The OSD in the government could make or break your career. That person was your confidante, aide, gatekeeper, bouncer, walking encyclopaedia and Man Friday. Pinaki became indispensable to me for the next seven years. He had done his master's in science at the Indian Institute of Technology in Kharagpur. What on earth was he doing in the OAS? Well, I was soon to learn that Pinaki was not alone. It amazed me how many highly qualified individuals who could be pursuing practically any career anywhere in the world, chose to work in the government in their home state instead. Pinaki was my first encounter with a new breed of civil servants who defy the stereotype many people carry about the bureaucracy.

But the stereotype is also true sometimes.

Manoj Rout, my personal assistant (PA) was from the State Secretarial Service. An amiable man with a contended demeanour, he had a perpetual big smile on his face, red stain of paan on his lips, shirt outside his trousers and chappals for footwear. On day one, I called him aside and told him that he needed to fix three things from the next day if he were to work with me. One, he was to tuck in his shirt. Two, he had to wear shoes. Three, he could not chew paan.

Manoj was no servile guy. He immediately agreed to the first two conditions but, on the spot, made a counteroffer on the third condition. He said he had chewed paan for as long as he could remember. He could not stop that simple pleasure of life. Why don't we settle for this: he would not chew when he was in the office but during lunchtime, he could step out, be his own man, have his joy and return to his desk.

I loved his audacity and found the counteroffer reasonable. I accepted it with a rider. He had to rinse his mouth.

The next day, Manoj reported with the same big smile on his face with his shirt tucked in, but the chappals were where they had been earlier. I called him in again and told him to go with my driver to a shoe store, buy new shoes and bill me for it.

From the next day on, Manoj came to work in shoes every day till he worked with me.

As was my standard question to anyone who had newly joined, I asked Manoj where he was posted before landing on me. He said he was working in the 'res office' of a minister. The government thrives on abbreviations and anything that can be said with less is reduced in size. Res is shorthand for residence. Ministers and senior officers often have official meetings at their residence. Hence, their residences have an attached office. This is the res office. In case of politicians, it is an extension of their constituency with a constant flow of unannounced visitors for an inexhaustible number of reasons.

The PA played a seasonal role there because the ministers seldom stayed at their residence, except when Assembly was in session and any other official reason.

But when they were there, the PA was part of the crowd-handling apparatus and needed to blend with the politician's personality, understand their priorities and preferences. Coming from that background, I was as much an alien to Manoj as he was to me.

What a PA does in the government offices is often indeterminate and fungible. In olden times, when the boss 'dictated' letters, the PA was the one who wrote it down in shorthand, made a draft and returned it with many errors. Then, the boss had to pore over it and make corrections for the PA to go back and retype it. This created activity that was often confused with work for both the boss and the subordinate. But then, the PA also fulfilled other important tasks such as picking up the phone for the boss (thereby blocking undesirable people) and telling lies when the boss did not want to take a certain call or did not want to meet someone inconvenient.

The PA also picked up valuable contextual knowledge, gathered intelligence and curated gossip. None of that was useful to me. Instead, I told Manoj to go learn Odia word processing software and how to make PowerPoint slides in Odia. He did both remarkably well. We worked well enough despite his occasional attempts at overt friendliness which needed reining in. Overall, he was a sweet fellow. However, on one occasion, I got truly angry with him. It gave me regret all night and the next morning, I called him and apologized for my behaviour. Manoj told me not to worry about it, though he still looked a little sad. Then he said, 'I went home last evening and told my wife that Sir was very angry and shouted at me.' She told me, 'It serves you right. Knowing you, you must have done something very stupid to make Sir so angry.' Looking back, Lilibala Rout, Manoj's better half, would be such an ally for any boss anywhere, and I am so grateful till this date that she was on my side.

The third staff member to report to work was Santosh Dakua, a hefty man in a safari suit with cop written all over him. If you did not get it fully, a revolver bulged from under his belt. He was the personal security officer or the PSO in short. This man was carefully chosen from a cadre of police that hover around their charge like hawks and keep unwanted people out of range to prevent bodily harm to them when they are in public. Santosh's job was also to liaise with the Police Control Room whenever I was to travel outside Bhubaneswar for the escort vehicle. One day, I asked Santosh what he did before being assigned to me. It turned out that he was an intelligence decoy gathering information on someone inconvenient to the government. I told him it made him a dangerous man who could potentially snoop on me. In a deadpan voice, he replied, 'No, Sir. The only thing I have to do is inform the control room, just three times a day, on where you are.'

Speaking about the police escort vehicles, they served many useful purposes. Thanks to it, the journey time was always cut by half when I travelled to the districts. They made way through congested roads, took detours when there was any problem and of course provided overall security based on what is called 'threat perception'. Whenever they moved through habitations, they blew the siren. It irritated stray dogs who matched the siren with mournful howls, and the brave ones sometimes chased the cop cars. On one occasion, I had a somewhat hilarious experience when the sudden appearance of the convoy and the siren startled a three-year-old boy mindfully doing his number two by the roadside. The little guy jumped up in the air and quickly put both hands together at the right place to save his honour as the motorcade rushed past in a haze of dust, leaving me in splits.

As part of the rank and status, I was also allotted a man called Routray who was to be my peon. He came from the proud and characteristically belligerent clan of Odias known as *'paika'* who fought every invader including the British with different degrees of success but unquestionable valour. But Routray was the meekest man I have ever met. His job was to ensure that I was always hydrated and fed. He also remained in attendance at the portico of the office when my Toyota Innova arrived or departed. He and Santosh Dakua competed on who would open and close the car door for me. Cabinet Ministers never opened and closed their own car doors.

Along the way came Sujit Toppo, who was going to be my driver. He was a tribal man from Sundargarh. He spoke very little and inaudibly but was one of the most punctual people I have ever known. He was a great driver who never complained of fourteen-hour workdays that had no overtime allowance. Often, holidays meant work. On long trips, he could drive non-stop for eight hours and overnight too. Soon after joining me, he had a strange question. He had a whole bunch of white Turkish towels that were standard issue for the Innova. Where should he be storing them? In the government, the boss's chair in the office and the official car seats, must be covered with a white towel. It signified authority. I told him to take the towels to his home and keep them in the bathroom. That was where towels should be. Sujit heard me with a deadpan look. He had seen many weird bosses in his life.

Between Pinaki, Manoj, Santosh, Routray and Sujit, my flotilla was complete, and I was good to go. But there were a few other trappings that are worth mentioning.

In the government, there must be an office order for everything. The knowledge of when and by whom the last office order was issued and from where it can be pulled out determined how competent and valuable an officer was. Office orders worked like iron shields that could protect you at the opportune moments. Upon my joining, Aditya Padhi had someone pull out the office order on the rank and status of a cabinet minister from the General Administration (GA) department that listed my entitlement.

First, I would be given a rent-free, furnished, official residence with a telephone. Secondly, the government would reimburse 40 per cent of my electricity bill.

Thirdly, I would be delivered four newspapers of my choice every day. Fourthly, I could bring in four persons of my choice as personal staff, like a private driver, gardener, cook and so on. These people are called political appointees. Their salary is paid by the government but their job is 'co-terminus' with the cabinet minister.

A cabinet minister was also entitled to a salary of around twenty lakhs a year, travelling allowance while on tour and a small amount of money as entertainment allowance to offer tea, biscuits and the mandatory cashew nuts to visitors. The government also picked up all medical expenses and leave travel assistance.

A cabinet minister was entitled to air travel on official business and, on such occasions, was allowed to take an 'attendant' who could be anyone ranging from the spouse to a faithful flunky who carried the briefcase and official files. In the service of the state, a truly senior person never carries anything on his being other than his mobile phone. The higher you go, the lighter you travel. That is the rule.

To me, what truly mattered were the official residence—it was a massive house with a beautiful garden spread over an acre, located exactly five minutes from the airport—and the white Toyota Innova (with the red beacon gone after a few months). I soon realized that a white car with a government licence plate holds more gravitas than the most expensive car in the world. The four free newspapers mostly brought bad news and kept me grounded. The co-terminus political appointees held me and Susmita up so we did not have to worry about housekeeping. I did not take the salary as per the entitlement, settling instead with the chief minister that I would take Re 1 per year.

Every year, the cheque arrived dutifully. Over the eight years, I collected and framed those cheques. They are proud memorabilia that are hung up on the wall in my study.

Oh! I forgot to mention the most important thing. When you are a cabinet minister, no one calls you by name. You are always addressed or referred to as 'Honourable So and So'. The 'Honourable' prefix is followed by the office you occupy and not your name. Thus, I wasn't Honourable Subroto Bagchi. You had to call me Honourable Chairman, OSDA. If Pinaki or Manoj had to convey anything to someone outside, they said, Honourable Chairman wants this or wants that.

Wiping out the name serves a huge purpose. While individuals may come and go, the office continues. The essence of all government is the assurance to citizens that it will be there irrespective of who occupies the office.

Within days of crossing over, I was beginning to forget the world I came from—where an entry-level IT engineer called you by first name, ignored you in the hallway and generally made you to feel like a monkey atop the totem pole while sharing a cafeteria table during lunch. The government, on the other hand, required a certain level for formality that was meant to be taken seriously.

Part II

Where Does the World Live?

6

30 Days, 30 Districts, 3000 Kilometres

Starting off on the new assignment, having left behind four decades of corporate life to jump headlong into the government, I had three asks of the chief minister, who was now my boss.

One, that he would not see me for the first thirty days of my joining.

Two, he would let me meet the leader of the Opposition, one on one, to brief him about my early impressions even before I presented them to the chief minister.

And three, contrary to his offer of a free hand to bring in 'experts' of my own choice from the outside, I would work with the existing system even though that might take longer to see results.

He said, yes, yes and yes.

I signed my joining letter on 1 May 2016 and set out on perhaps the most memorable journey of my life. It was going to keep me on the road for the next thirty days. Odisha is extremely hot during the months of

May and June. In many districts, the mercury hits the high forties. My goal was to visit all thirty districts of the state by road over the next thirty days to assess the ground reality. What kind of skill development was going on, who the players were, the challenges they faced and the opportunities ahead. Above all, I needed to sense where the 'energy force', the hidden hand of destiny, wanted me to go.

One thing the government machinery knows perfectly is drawing up tour programmes. It is a non-trivial affair that people from the private sector cannot fathom. Imagine you get a forty-eight-hour notice to plan the prime minister's visit. The sheer stress of it can age you by ten years.

But Pinaki, my OSD knew the art and science of it all. He drew up the detailed tour programme: who would travel with me, where the entourage would stop, who would meet me where, where the lunch would be served and what the food would consist of, where exactly we would head to after lunch and where we would halt for the night. I was contrasting this elaborate planning to my IT industry days where you pretty much did everything yourself, balancing desire with the official entitlement limit set up by an HR guy. And incidentally, the person meeting you the next morning for breakfast generally thought they were doing you a favour and that you were a pain. In contrast, this thirty-day trip became something of a celebration for everyone. No one in the state had ever undertaken such a thing. No minister. No officer.

The state had about a few hundred ITIs and polytechnics, taking both the government and private sector into account and an equal number of short-term skill development centres of various hues. The tour programme was detailed in a way that I could visit three to four skill development centres in a district, meet district officials, stop at an industry somewhere en route, speak with school students and teachers at each place and drive to the next district to spend the night at a government circuit house and repeat the same routine the next day. The entire trip was to be a little more than 3000 kilometres. Just as a point of reference, the length of India from the north to the south is 3214 kilometres and the breadth from the west to the east is 2933 kilometres.

While the primary purpose was to know the ground reality, there was also a subtext. I needed to deliver the message to everyone that going forward, it wasn't business as usual. I was not a glorified adviser to the government who would conceptualize plans and policies while sitting in the comfortable office allocated to me at Rajib Bhavan, an extension of the State Secretariat. I was not going to be a light touch guy, airdropped for symbolism. It was my signal to the political system that had not yet fathomed whether I was fish or fowl.

As it turned out, I did not need thirty days to understand the ground reality.

We started with the government's own Industrial Training Institute (ITI) in Bhubaneswar, in a prime location right behind the Raj Bhavan. The plaster on the walls was falling off, and the ceilings had black mold. There was debris and dilapidated machinery everywhere. Right next to the office of Principal Jeetamitra Satpathy, there was a corridor where, among other things waiting to be removed but pending due permission from the top, was an upside-down commode. Jeetamitra Satpathy was one of three women principals to head an ITI in Odisha. A computer science engineer by education, she had taught at a Government Polytechnic before taking on the role of the principal of the third-largest ITI in the state. She gave me a tour of the place. Uninspiring classrooms. Lacklustre labs. I saw very few girls among the students I met. Why so? I asked her. She said employers were reluctant to offer jobs to girls. It was a huge disappointment for a girl who had trained there for two years to not get a job afterwards. It made sense that, with those prospects, girls were reluctant to join the institute.

She did not recall any senior official ever visiting the ITI, far less the Governor of the state whose expansive estate shared a boundary with her institute. I made a mental note that one measure of my success would be to get the Governor—who happened to be the chancellor of leading universities—there someday; an ITI was, of course, not for the plenipotentiary.

From there, we drove to the adjoining district of Cuttack. The collector of Cuttack and his team received me at the border between the districts of Khordha and Cuttack. Bhubaneswar, the state capital, falls in the former. After the pleasantries, instead of getting back to my car, I got into the collector's Bolero, little realizing the problem I was creating. Seating arrangement in an official vehicle is earmarked and bound by protocol. When you suddenly get into someone's vehicle, you create chaos regarding who sits where. Besides, it is very stressful for a government officer to be trapped with someone very senior, with whom there is no prior familiarity. Anyway, he settled down somewhat and we went to see the nearby short-term skill development centre run by L&T for training construction workers. The campus spread over forty acres, the large training centre and a hostel building had been constructed at government expense. It had fewer than 200 trainees. I was doing the math in my head on what the cost of forty acres of land right next to Cuttack City would be and wondered about the input-output ratio. Such a campus should be churning out trainees by the thousands and not hundreds. While L&T's computer-based learning and other training material were excellent, the number of trainees did not make sense. Neither the L&T top brass nor the government bothered about it. The trainees were tribal youth who were learning skills like bar bending and minor electrical work. The man in charge was competent and enthusiastically showed us around.

Before setting out that day, while reviewing the tour plan, I had noticed that lunch was being organized at the circuit house in Cuttack and there was time afterwards for some rest before continuing onwards.

I told Pinaki that wherever we went, there were to be no circuit house lunches. I wanted to eat lunch with the students and trainees. After the classrooms and lab walk-around at the L&T training centre, I went to the canteen. At the canteen, I stood in queue with the students. While waiting to fill my tray with food from the buffet counter, I attempted to talk to those next to me. They spoke in monosyllables and did not make eye contact with me. Their discomfort was palpable. They were scared.

After lunch, I wanted to see the hostel where they were housed. This was not on the 'minute-by-minute' programme given to the hosts and put everyone in a tizzy. Once we arrived at the hostel building, to my utter dismay, I found rows of bedrolls on the ground. The trainees obviously slept on the floor. I asked the centre head why there were no cots for them. He was clearly caught off guard. No one had given it a thought. Realizing that he had to say something, he mumbled, 'Sir, after the forty-five days of training here, when they go to the worksites, they will need to sleep on the ground. They better acclimatize from right here anyway. That is why there are no cots.'

Now I was fuming.

Why then were we housing them in a proper building with a concrete roof? Keep them in a shanty.

The two dozen accompanying officials from Bhubaneswar and Cuttack stood in silence. I told the centre in-charge that I was coming back after thirty days and did not want to see a single trainee sleeping on the floor just because they did not protest. This was simply unacceptable.

The next stop was a happy little place run by the Bansidhar and Ila Panda Foundation where young girls, again mostly tribal, were being trained to operate high-speed sewing machines. After a two and a half month residential training under a programme called Deen Dayal Upadhyaya Kaushalya Vikas Yojana (DDU-GKY), they were to go to faraway Tiruppur in Tamil Nadu, where work awaited them. Tiruppur is the capital of the garment industry in India, particularly knitwear.

Unlike the boys at the L&T Centre, the girls were very excited to see a visitor. This was going to be a pattern in most places I visited for the rest of my trip. Girls were always a happier lot to see a visitor come by. The trainees I met spoke to me with enthusiasm about where they came from, what family compulsions brought them there and what their expectations were. With every girl, more or less, it was the same story.

Father is old, he has stopped working.

How old?

Well, I can't really say. But perhaps fifty.

Fifty in a village is old.

My mother is very sick. My family is in a lot of debt. We have no land to work on.

Do you have siblings?

Yes, I have an older sister. She is married. I have a younger brother but he doesn't do anything.

Why is *he* not in skill development?

I don't know. He just wants a bike and a new mobile every now and then.

What will you do with the money you earn after your training?

I will send money home.

And so went the conversation.

My handlers were clearly getting restless. We had to travel ahead, but the girls would not let go of me. When it was time to go, they implored us to stay a little longer. 'When will you come again?' they asked me. I was touched by the simplicity of these girls, mostly school dropouts after Class 8 or 10—children of deprivation and denial with eyes full of hope.

Before leaving, I asked them if there was something I could do for them.

'Buy us ice-cream,' they chorused.

The caravan moved on.

Another day. Another place. Average temperature? 45 degrees Celsius so far, except when I was inside the car with the air conditioner running on full blast and the vents all open. But the frequent stops to see various training centres, as well as the meetings and interactions, had to happen in the blistering heat. Pinaki was getting worried by now. In a week, we would be hitting western Odisha and the temperature there would cross 45 degrees. Susmita called every so often to ask if I was drinking enough water.

The next day, we were on the outskirts of Dhenkanal. This was the place where Makhan Gopal Bagchi had come with a letter from the King of Seraikella for a job and placed it before King Shankar Prasad Singh Dev Mahendra Bahadur. This is where my mother Labonya

Prova Moitra had come as a young bride. This is where her three oldest sons grew up as babies. Even though I had grown up in Odisha, I had never come to Dhenkanal before.

By the time I was born, the family had moved to Balangir but I had heard names of places like Dhenkanal, Kamakshya Nagar, Parjang and Angul from my mother; from her I knew their stories.

We stopped at a skill development centre where a group mostly consisting of young girls and a few boys were being trained by an outfit called Indigram—set up by Gnosis, a hospital in Kolkata—to become 'bedside attendants'. These are people who are in between nurses and janitors in a hospital. They move patients around, change linen, clean and feed the patient. We only think of doctors and nurses when we think of a hospital, but the bedside attendant is as critical. At this centre, they were learning the basics of first aid and patient care. A cheap mannequin was their patient and a plastic skeleton hung alongside the anatomy chart. There was a stethoscope, a blood pressure machine and a few such medical trinkets that passed for training material. I went through the syllabus, learnt about the background of the trainers, which was not impressive at all, and interacted with the trainees. Soon it was midday. I sat down to eat lunch with them on the floor. There, I found something strange. Some of the trainees had stainless steel trays from which they ate their food. Others had all kinds of disparate utensils. I asked the people running the centre why it was that way. They hesitated, then sheepishly explained that during the last batch of training, many of the trainees had run away with the stainless-steel trays. 'Why not give them two trays each,' I asked. 'One to eat here and one to take home after the training ended?' No answer. By now I was beginning to understand where in the pecking order the trainee in the world of skill development stood.

From there, we went to the government-run ITI of Dhenkanal. It was off the main road in an unimpressive building. There were a few boys there but most had gone home as it was summer and no classes were held in the hot afternoons. I saw no girls at the institute. I asked the principal why there were no girl students. The man, his teeth darkened with incessant paan chewing for decades, said it was a big challenge. Parents did not want to send girls to an ITI because they could not wear sarees there. Unless a girl wore a saree and moved in a group of other girls, she drew unwanted attention in small places. Later, I sat down with a few students who were still there. While chatting with them, one of the boys asked me why classes could not be held regularly. I was taken aback and looked at the principal. He said meekly that the place was running with half the sanctioned strength of instructors. He had to make do mostly with part-time guest faculty (PTGI). These were basically locally available diploma holders with questionable technical knowledge and teaching capability. That day, I learnt a new term, PTGI. They were ad-hoc trainers, sometimes cronies of a local politician, who came and went when it suited them and pocketed some money with no accountability for their task. The principal had little control over them.

After the visit, as we were walking back to my vehicle, I asked the principal how old the ITI was. He fumbled for a moment, did the math in his head and then replied, 'Sir, it was set up twenty-four years ago.' I stopped in my path. That means, this institute would be a quarter of a century old next year? What plans did he have to celebrate the glorious milestone? He was completely blank. It hadn't struck him at all that until this ITI turned fifty, this was going to be the greatest milestone to be celebrated so far, a big opportunity to draw everyone's attention and in the process, get funds to make substantial upgrades to the existing building and machinery and garner goodwill for the institution. But then an ITI was a place of drudgery, not celebrations.

Over the next few days, I went to many training centres in the other districts. The narrative was a mix of what I had seen in Bhubaneswar, Cuttack and Dhenkanal. There was one place I will never forget—Pattamundai on the coast. If you meet an outstanding plumber in Dubai or Delhi the next time, ask him where he is from. There is a 99 per cent chance that he will say Pattamundai.

They are the gold standard of plumbing. It was no surprise then that the local ITI, named after the legendary Biju Patnaik, was a 'centre of excellence' (CoE) in plumbing and taught no other trade.

I walked around the building. Its walls and corridors were sprayed with paan stains and gutka spit. The ITI had a huge campus, overgrown with ipomoea weed, debris and filth everywhere. I asked the principal why he did not get these cleared with the collective effort of teachers and students.

'No, sir. You do not know the local media guys. They will take videos, pictures and report that we are forcing children into manual work.' He had the conspiracy theory nailed. I admired his creativity and sharp intelligence.

'Okay, can I see the hostel where the students stay?'

The man froze in his steps. He did not want me to go there. There was a lot of hesitation but I persisted. Once inside the hostel building, I went straight to the toilet. After all, a toilet is where all the plumbing is. If the ITI was a plumbing CoE, surely, they had to have good toilets? The toilet block, as expected, was a mess. It was dark, smelly and had broken plumbing and non-functional taps. Water dripping in places, dark smears of moss over broken tiles, shattered glass on windows that had not been repaired for years—this was it, the plumbing centre of excellence. I was deeply disturbed by the pervasive apathy and yet, the conditions were challenging me in a way that said, your purpose is unfolding.

Next, I went to ITI at Anandapur in Keonjhar district. In the otherwise uninspiring institute, they showed me the newly constructed 'smart classroom', which was a room full of computers, a projection system, internet connection and an electronic whiteboard. How was it being used? Not yet, they were waiting for the digital content to come for the past few months. 'Why are you not using You Tube in the meantime to show students all the millions of videos in every possible skill area?' No answer. They did not know such things existed. I sat down at a computer, opened YouTube and showed them. How do you put a thread into a needle? Videos popped up. How do you build a nuclear bomb? Videos came up. Well?

Over the next few days, whenever I stopped to see an ITI, the routine was predictable. To my horror, I would invariably find two rows of boys and girls waiting outside the campus in the blazing sun, along with a bunch of trainers and the principal, with wilting flowers in hand to ceremonially welcome me. God knows how long the kids were kept waiting like that. Then, I would be taken to the principal's office, usually the only decent place in an ITI campus.

Certainly, the only place with a clean toilet. The principal, usually a timid, fidgety guy, petrified as if he was going to be roasted, would usher me in and show me to his chair, covered with a white Turkish towel. The principal would want me to adorn his chair. That was the expected courtesy. After all, you never sit like a lord when someone higher on the totem pole visits. The best seat had to be his. After some tussle, the principal would finally accept that I was going to sit across on the visitor chair, bereft of the white towel. I would firmly say, more for the benefit of onlooking district officials, that only the head of the institution could sit in the principal's chair. But the nervous man would keep standing. More tussle would ensue, and then he would finally sit in his own chair with great discomfort, as if it was now laced with a hundred needles. Thereafter, I was handed out a clumsily stapled printed report, kept ready for me—word had gone around by now that this guy was an IT corporate type. It was better to give him a written report with graphs and charts.

The reports too were predictable. How many acres of land the ITI proudly stood on, how many lathe (or whatever other) machines it had and, in some places, with great satisfaction, the fact that there was three-phase power. After that, columns of whining. Faculty posts were vacant. There were no trainers. Most importantly, there was immediate need for more clerks without whom the principal had to do all the paperwork. No time for any academic work. And yes, the place needed three peons. The last one had retired three years ago. There was no watchman or boundary walls. Bad elements trespassed at night.

There was hardly any conversation on the students or their demographic profile. No academic achievement was highlighted. No discussion on practical training, industry visits or post-training placement efforts. No plans for the institute's future. No sense of pride.

The futility of the entire effort, partly comic, but mostly tragic, was sinking in rapidly.

It was time for change.

7

Ten, Six, Four, Two

After a week or so into the road trip, I called Pinaki aside and told him to inform the principals that from now on, I did not want to know how many acres of land and how many lathe machines they had, and the vacant positions of clerks and peons in the ITI were of no interest to me. In every review from this point on, I wanted to hear a different story and see a different set of data altogether.

From now on, each time I visited an ITI, we would focus on just four things. I explained to Pinaki what the four things were going to be.

Upon arrival, I would first want to know the names of ten past students the ITI was truly proud of. By names I did not mean just names. I wanted to know the socio-economic profile of these people. I wanted to know how these people came to know of the ITI, who brought them here, what they studied here, what they were good at, where they were right now, who they were working for and how much money they were making.

Of these ten past students, as the next point in the review, I wanted to know the names of six who had made it big outside the state of Odisha, because to me that was the true test of calibre.

Then, of the ten, I wanted to know the names of four girls who had studied at the institute.

Finally, of the ten, I wanted to know the names of two past students who did not seek a job after finishing their training and instead chose to start a small business somewhere nearby. Maybe a welding shop, a two-wheeler garage or perhaps an electrical goods outlet. Whatever. Not a job seeker but a micro-entrepreneur.

Pinaki immediately informed the principals what their meeting with me would entail. It is quite surprising how rapidly word spreads and how magically people rise to a new challenge.

Technical training institutions have been around in Odisha for longer than people know. To give you a perspective, one of the oldest technical schools was set up by the British in 1906 and it still functions as the Balasore Technical School. It has the reputation of being one of the best-run private ITI in the state. The Cuttack Survey School, set up by the British in 1876, was renamed Orissa School of Engineering in 1923 and produced technical hands during and after World War II.

Then came the Purnachandra ITI in Mayurbhanj. This ITI was started by the Queen of Mayurbhanj in memory of her husband with a personal grant of Rs 1 lakh way back in 1931. It was a magnanimous amount for those times. But what is amazing is the fact that the Queen had the foresight to sight up a technical training institution for girls! Post-Independence, when the Government of India came out with the idea of the modern-day ITIs, many newer ones arrived. In a state like Odisha, in 2024, there are twenty-four ITIs that are a quarter of a century old.

Given how long they have been around, it wasn't a big ask on my part to want to know the names of ten students the ITI was proud of.

The legacy of an educational institution cannot be its physical infrastructure. Its reputation is its alumni. There are no other determinants of the success of an educational institution. But sadly, most principals had a hard time naming ten ex-students who stood apart. On the other hand, I had a hilarious experience where one principal said, 'I do not know, sir, I am very new here; I was sent just six months back.' And worse, one person said, 'Sir, I will retire soon. I do not know.' Impending retirement exonerates most deficiencies for a government servant. You are not supposed to be harsh with people who are about to retire; it doesn't matter if they were effectively just furniture their entire life. It was a huge cultural contrast for me. Four decades in the private sector had made me internalize elaborate annual performance appraisals for employees, quarterly feedback for non-performance, an obsession with the bell curve to place who stood where and messaging to non-performers to move up or simply move out.

* * *

While the rationale behind naming ten outstanding students was understandable to many, some wondered why call out six students who had made a name for themselves but *outside* the state? It is simple. When you go outside the state, there is no one to cover for you. You cannot hide your incompetence. Whether you are a Zomato delivery guy or a software engineer, you must compete with the best people from everywhere. And there is a fascinating thing about skill development that is quite unlike mastering physics or economics. In case of the latter, it takes some time and effort to fathom the extent of your knowledge. But when it comes to skills, determining how skilled you are takes seconds. For example, the moment a nurse puts the needle into you, right that millisecond you can tell how competent the person is. The way a welder holds the torch even before starting to weld will instantly tell you how skilled they are. Unlike proficiency in physics or economics, skills are visible to the naked eye. If a boy or a girl is doing well in an advanced industrial city like Coimbatore or Pune, it is a ready reckoner of that individual's competitiveness and technical worth.

Thus, every ITI needed to tell me about six students who had made it good in a discerning place like the Defence Research and Development Institute (DRDO), Sundaram Clayton, Tata Steel or Schneider Electric. That one index was enough for me to work backwards and figure out how good, bad or ugly the alma mater was.

Now, let us come to four. I needed to know the names of four girls from that list of ten students. Girls who they were proud of. They needed to tell me their story, the full story. Who brought them to the ITI? What trade did they pursue? Who influenced their choice? What were some of the real challenges they faced while they were studying there and how did they persist instead of dropping out? Where were they now? When did they visit the ITI last and if they did, what was done to fete them and what did they do during their visit? For example, did they address the present flock of girls? Did they share their stories with the present batch of trainees?

Finally, the number two in the equation. God in heaven did not say an ITI must only produce job seekers. India needs thousands of flourishing small entrepreneurs to be a truly developed country. At the core of enterprise is self-confidence. At the core of self-confidence is a skill. That is why I needed to know how many small business owners existed in the vicinity who were able to stand on their own legs and perhaps employ one or two people because they had studied at this ITI.

Numbers have magic in them. For very interesting reasons.

They simplify things by cutting to the chase. You can bullshit me for hours with narratives but numbers seldom lie. The job of a leader is to simplify things so that people can rise above the bullshit, the clutter and the maze. That makes it easier for them to comprehend the leader's strategic intent. When they understand that, they rally around and participate whole-heartedly in the efforts.

Numbers are easy to remember. Remembering is critical to followership. People follow a leader only when they can *remember* what a leader wants. Followership is a function of memory.

Finally, numbers create clarity on the next steps in any endeavour. For example, if you do not have ten names, you go find them. If you do not have six names of your past students who have made it big in an alien city, you ask what we need to do to get there.

If you have names of four girls, you say, wow, let us bring them back and showcase them to nearby high schools, have them interact with the girls there who are in the ninth grade so that we improve female enrolment in the coming year. And if you do have names of the two micro-entrepreneurs, you say, how do we multiply that number? Numbers can more easily lead to actionable outcomes.

The concept of *ten, six, four, two* suddenly humanized the entire skill development narrative. It put people at the centre of everything. When we put a name and a face to the work we do, suddenly everything becomes aspirational, uplifting and worthwhile. Work finds purpose.

One of the greatest lessons I had learnt from management guru Peter Drucker was to always focus on the best people in any situation. He believed that at any institution, anywhere you go, the gap between the best and the average is always fixed. When you focus on the best 5 per cent, they rise further because they respond to the attention and inputs. When they rise, the average ones automatically improve because the gap between the best and the average remains fixed.

The idea behind *ten, six, four, two* appealed to the minds of every official, teacher and leader involved in the skill development. Slowly at first, and then rapidly, the floodgates had opened. When I visited the ITI in the steel township of Rourkela, predictably, the principal failed the test. Then, an old teacher who had been there all his life came forward. He said, 'Sir, many years ago, there was a boy here named Nunaram Hansda. His parents were tribal folks in the interior forests of Simlipal.' For readers who do not know, Simlipal is one of India's largest biospheres. It is a dense forest inhabited by many tribal groups. 'Nunaram's parents could not afford to raise him. He was sent off to an Ashram School when he was small.' Ashram Schools are run by the government's Scheduled Caste and Scheduled Tribe department, where children are often left behind as babies and the government pretty much becomes a foster parent, taking care of food, lodging and education right up to the high-school level. Nunaram studied in one such school and when he finished high school, he did not know what to do next. Somehow, his parents learnt about ITI and he was sent off to Rourkela. At ITI Rourkela, he studied for two years. Every month, invariably, he ran short of money, and his teachers always pooled together the deficit from their own paltry salaries and helped him pay his hostel dues.' I was very touched by the story, particularly how teachers had come forward to help the boy.

'Okay, but where is Nunaram Hansda?'

'Sir, he works in a company called Biocon in Bangalore.'

'What? Did you say Biocon? Biocon as in Biotechnology? That Biocon?'

'Yes, sir.'

I almost fell off my chair.

'What does he do there?'

'We do not know, sir.'

I looked at Pinaki. He knew me well by now. He asked someone for Nunaram's coordinates. By the time the review was over, he told me that Nunaram had been contacted. He ran the insulin manufacturing line at Biocon.

After visiting ITI Rourkela, we moved on to ITI Bargarh. Bargarh is one of the newly created districts of Odisha. Carved out of Sambalpur, it was on no one's radar until recently. Now, with abundant availability of water from the Mahanadi and commercial production of rice, Bargarh has emerged as a significant rice-producing district of the country. But traditionally, there has been nothing much to speak about in this educationally and industrially backward district. In a place like that, one would normally think that the ITI would be a landmark. Particularly because it has been around since 1994. But like most places, it lived in anonymity.

8

Muni Tigga

The helpless principal at ITI Bargarh kept fumbling with the *ten, six, four, two* question and was completely blank with the number four in the equation. At this point, an old-hand technical instructor who was standing at a respectable distance mumbled something. It was a whisper, almost not wanting to be heard. Years of training as a leader had taught me to always listen to whispers. They carry valuable clues and information. I swung in the direction of the whisper and encouraged the old instructor to speak up.

'Sir, there was a girl in the electronics trade here. Many years back and she was very good at her studies.'
'What did you say she studied?'
'Electronics, sir.'
'Where did she go after finishing her studies?'
'She joined the railways, sir.'
'What does she do in the Indian Railways?'
'She is a loco pilot.'
'What?'

'Sir, Loco pilot. She drives a locomotive engine.'

'I want to speak to her,' I said. 'Right now.'

That day, I realized the power of the government. If the government wants, it can track down any individual under ten minutes even in a country of 1.4 billion people. It takes just four or five phone calls, a couple of them involving the district administration and perhaps the local police and you can track down almost anyone.

That day, Muni Tigga was on the phone with me in less than ten minutes from the time I first heard her name. She had no clue who I was except that I was some big guy visiting her old ITI. She was at quite a loss that her alma mater was suddenly getting in touch because in all the years since she had left Bargarh, no one ever had tried to reach her.

I asked her what she did at the Indian Railways. Like some tribal folks from the western part of Odisha, particularly from Sundargarh district, she was more comfortable speaking in Hindi.

'Mai Muni Tigga hoon. Indian Railways me loco pilot hoon. Mai Bhubaneswar station me posted hoon. Har din, Inter-City Express ko Khordha se Palasa khinch kar leke jati hoon aur wapas leke ati hoon.

I am Muni Tigga. I am a loco pilot with the Indian Railways. I am posted in Bhubaneswar station. Every day, I *drag* the Inter-City Express from Khordha to Palasa and bring it back.'

I stood up from my chair, phone in hand. My mind was exploding with the discovery. It was already too much for a day's work for me.

'Would you give me a ride in your locomotive engine if I came?' I asked. 'Why not?' she said.

Muni Tigga became my star among stars for the rest of my time with the government. In time, she became an icon for the state. She was the lens through which I was to begin understanding the difference between skill development and human transformation.

Muni Tigga was born to Lundru and Fulkari Tigga in a village called Mahulchhapal in Nuagan Tehsil. Mahulchhapal is at a distance of 130 kilometres from the district headquarters of Sundargarh, which is a long way in that part of the world. The tribal village is small. Even today, there are less than 500 inhabitants. Muni Tigga's is pretty much the usual story. Six sisters and one brother. Small piece of land, a few cows and goats. As a girl, she was not required to go to school. But she did. Whenever she had to take the animals to graze, she always carried her books with her. People used to ask her why she needed to do that. As she grew up, she was ready to go to high school. But her village was not ready for a girl to go to a high school and that too, one far away from the village. She needed to get up early in the morning, cycle down a dirt road and by the time she came back, it was dark. The villagers taunted her. It was her mother who persisted, cooking her a meal when it was still dark outside and taking care of her so she could study. When she passed high school, her father said, 'I have got you this far, now you have to be on your own.'

A young Muni Tigga started working as a daily-wage worker in a plant located thirty-seven kilometres from her village. She distinctly remembers her wage at that plant. Fifty rupees and fifty-two paisa per day. During this time, by sheer happenstance, someone she knew spoke to her about this thing called an ITI. That is how Muni Tigga came to ITI Bargarh and enrolled herself in the electronics trade. It is there that she dreamt of becoming a locomotive pilot. After finishing her training, she sat for a competitive entrance examination of the Indian Railways and cracked the test. I met her when I returned to Bhubaneswar.

She was a frail young woman. You could not imagine her hauling a locomotive engine and running an eight-hour shift up and down every day, in good weather and bad. She was responsible for the safety and convenience of hundreds of thousands of passengers every year, who would never know she was in the driver's compartment, eyes on the tracks and signal, while they were sleeping in their berth or looking out of the window, feeling perfectly safe.

To put things in perspective, one of the most abiding images of machismo in our society is the Bullet motorcycle. It's engine generates anything between 20 and 47 horse power (HP). In contrast, Muni Tigga tames the WAP-7 locomotive engine with its 6125 HP engine. At top speed, a WAP-7 can hit 140 kilometres to 160 kilometres an hour depending on railway infrastructure and pull two dozen compartments with anywhere between 1200 to 1500 passengers each.

After I got to know her, the moment of epiphany arrived for me. We obsess about skill development. We aggregate, we approximate and we intellectualize the phrase. We speak about impressive sounding stuff like skilling, upskilling, reskilling, assessments, certification, lateral movements and lifelong learning, etcetera. In the process, all of us miss out a very important thing and that is *identity*. The two years at the ITI had not just given Muni Tigga an employable skill, they had given her an identity that no one could ever take away.

A girl skilled is power delivered to the universe.

9

Where Is the 'Two' in the Equation?

Remember the saying 'The jungle has ears'? This famous line from the legendary American cartoonist Lee Falk's comic series, *Phantom*, which I used to read as a child, repeatedly came to mind as I pressed on with my thirty-day, thirty-district, 3000-kilometre discovery of Odisha. After Pinaki beat the first drum, all the drums in the jungle started repeating the *ten, six, four, two* message. Even before I would arrive at an ITI, the scramble was on to find the role models. But as I went along, I started fine-tuning the idea to constantly raise the bar. Once a principal threw a few names at me, I took out my notebook, diligently wrote the names down and then asked the principal to tell me more about each one of the students. Silence. I urged them on. I wanted to know their full story. Tell me the village the student came from. Who all were there in the family, what the family did, how did the individual come to your ITI, how did they get the job, why should the person be considered a role model and finally, when did the star last visit the institute and what did you do to hold them up for other students to see them as exemplars? When the principal evidently failed the test, I did not rebuke them. I did not make them look bad in front of their colleagues. I did something simple that teachers know well: homework. They were told to do the research and send me the entire narrative and with that, I moved on to the next ITI.

By the time I reached Berhampur, the only city in the district of Ganjam, Dr Rajat Panigrahi, principal of the largest ITI in the state was ready for me. He had lined up Anima Sahoo for me. Anima, like many girls in India, was married off as soon as she reached the legally acceptable age of marriage, which happens to be eighteen. Soon, she became a mother and that was when misfortune struck. She lost her husband. When a young girl becomes a widow, she becomes a burden to her matrimonial home and invariably returns to her parents. There too she remains a liability. Things get worse for her if there is a child, of course. Anima came back to her parents' home with her baby.

Then Dr Rajat Panigrahi somehow discovered her. He asked the parents to send her to the ITI, where he ran a one-year course in tailoring. After completing her course, Anima started a tailoring shop where she now employed six people. It was a remarkable story no doubt, but the question that came to my mind was, why wasn't Anima's story catching fire? Why wasn't this inspiring others like her who did not even think about starting something on their own after they received their skill education? Before engaging with that question, I needed more examples like her.

When you gaze at the sky just after the sun has gone down and night is tiptoeing into the twilight, it takes a while to locate the first twinkle of a star. Your first star. But once you have been able to persist and focus, it is remarkable how quickly you see another one and then another. That is what happened to me. The entrepreneurs were all there but no one had treated them as exemplars, far less as celebrities in their own towns.

When I came to ITI Takatpur in Baripada, Mayurbhanj, I met Buddhadeb Bhanja. He was a middle-aged man who had studied at the ITI a long time ago and until I had asked for the *ten, six, four, two* list, no one had bothered to dig him up. Buddhadeb Bhanja's father had been a renowned music director of Odisha decades ago, who, despite great talent, did not make money. That is how, when Buddhadeb passed his matriculation, he ended up at the ITI where serendipitously, he opted to learn welding. After finishing his training, he decided to do something on his own and bought a welding kit worth one lakh rupees without knowing the ABCs of entrepreneurship. That included understanding something called working capital. Without the working capital, how was he going to use the welding kit? Now, he turned to his father who quite understandably regretted his inability. It was simply beyond his means. Buddhadeb was dismayed. He had the knowledge, the skill and now the equipment but could not start a business because he did not have money to pay for consumables and meet his other expenses until the business picked up with a steady cashflow. It was then that a friend told him that a government office nearby needed some furniture through a bidding process, and if he could perhaps manage it somehow, buy the furniture from Kolkata and supply it to them, he would at least make some money to survive.

Buddhadeb had no option. He did as the friend had suggested and made some money and then some more. But he was not going to be an 'order supplier' living off government contracts. With the money in hand, he was now ready to bring out his welding kit and start his business.

His prospective buyers were typically people who were building a small house in Baripada Town, needing a window frame and grille or sometimes an iron gate. But no one would entrust him with any work because he was so young and inexperienced. They would all want to know, have you done this before?

Buddhadeb decided to change the equation. Every morning, after breakfast, he took out his cycle and went to the outskirts of Baripada Town to sites where folks were just about digging ground to put the plinth of a small dwelling. People who did not have bigger budgets like the ones who lived in the heart of the town.

The young Buddhadeb met them and left his contact details. 'Give me a call after your roof is cast, sir. When it is time to weld the window and the door for your house, I will do it for you.' That strategy to go upstream, to locate customers who had a smaller budget and hence open to a young person seeking their business worked. And calls started coming. Sparks started flying off the welding rods and Buddhadeb Bhanja soon became the go-to person for Baripada's welding needs, in the process and over the years, employing more young people like him.

What the young Buddhadeb did is material fit enough for a case study in business schools. The essence of a start-up is three-fold. First of all, persist. Second, seek out customers in new, underserved markets. Third, catch them before their needs have arrived. Catch them early. Speak about the window frame and the grille and the gate when people are digging for the plinth.

But the biggest discovery I made was when I visited the ITI in Puri, a decrepit place on the outskirts of the famed temple city. It was in as bad a shape as many of the other ITIs I had visited elsewhere, even though it was soon to complete fifty years—something to be proud about anywhere in the world, but that time has a different meaning in India and does not always invoke a sense of history for any institution.

Once upon a time, there was a small boy who had lost his father in an untimely manner. The father was a *sevayat*, a servitor, in the Jagannath Temple. There were many mouths to feed at home. Because the man was a temple servitor, upon his death, one meal a day came from the temple kitchen. That is how the family was saved and the children grew up. The small boy,

Soumendra Das, grew up to finish his so-called BA at a local college. But he soon realized that it was not going to land him any decent enough job.

In what was a truly rare choice for a college graduate, he signed up at the ITI for an electrician course. After he completed it, he got a job at Tata Motors. It taught him a lot. One day, he decided to quit and to start a car body repair business near Bhubaneswar. As he got going, local hooligans started extorting him and, one day, vandalized his garage. He was despondent but for his elder brother who told him to rise from the ashes.

That he did. When I met Soumendra, he had a full-fledged authorized body repair shop for Hyundai. He employed seventy people and had a sales turnover of, hold your breath, Rs 8 crore a year. Except that no one knew about him. Neither ITI teachers, nor the government departments responsible for skill development and technical education and certainly not the thousands of kids who sign up to join an ITI or a polytechnic with the foreboding thought that they were already failures in life.

10

Balasore to Bahadurgarh

Chances are very slim that you know who Deen Dayal Upadhyaya was. He was an Indian politician and ideologue who belonged to the Bharatiya Jana Sangh and is famous for drafting the official political doctrine of the Jana Sangh known as ideal humanism. He became the tenth president of the Bharatiya Jana Sangh and preceded Atal Bihari Bajpayee.

A very well-thought-through, short-term skill training programme of the Ministry of Rural Development (MoRD) of Government of India was named after him. As must happen, the name was quickly reduced to an abbreviation and the programme came to be known as DDU-GKY. It ensured the great man's name was no longer needed.

Unlike the ITI, DDU-GKY skill training courses in various disciplines were designed for school dropouts. It was, in particular, designed for youth who were below the poverty line (BPL) and belonged to rural areas. Later, it was extended to urban areas as well. Unlike

ITIs that ran one- or two-year, vocational training courses, the DDU-GKY programme ran intensive, residential, two-and-a-half-month training that gave a rural youth semi-skilled status and landed them jobs in a textile manufacturing company as a high-speed machine operator, at a retail chain store in a mall as a salesperson and in a hospital as a bedside attendant.

In the first thirty days of my joining, I realized the vast majority of youth that needed to receive employable skill training were not the ITI types. The ITI was way up there in the skill development pyramid. The vast majority of the school dropouts were ideal candidates for training programmes like the DDU-GKY or its cousin, a markedly ill-thought-through, poorly executed variant by the Ministry of Skill Development of the Government of India, called the Pradhan Mantri Kaushalya Vikas Yojana (PMKVY). Neither ministries, of course, ran the programmes themselves. They engaged private agencies that did the actual training. A big difference between the DDU-GKY and PMKVY was that the former was fully residential. It led to higher 'touch-time' with the trainees and helped them develop social skills, which would be very important as they made the transition to work life.

The training provider, officially called a programme implementation agency (PIA), was paid roughly Rs 40,000–50,000 depending on the location for mobilizing trainees, providing them with uniforms, lodging and boarding, training them and then arranging placement with employers. They had to ensure that at least 70 per cent of those trained got a job *and* stayed on the job for at least three months to be able to get the last instalment of the payment. The math was bizarre. The process to get paid was super complex, which gave great joy to the government minions who pored over and scrutinized bills and rejoiced in rejecting claims. Many of the PIAs themselves loved to cheat the government, and the government too loved to be cheated. But despite all this, the DDU-GKY worked well in Odisha, compared to other states. It worked very well in fact.

My real initiation into the DDU-GKY programme happened at a centre for training in 'leather technology'. It was set up in a rented private building on the outskirts of Bhubaneswar, run by a PIA that had a rather unusual name: Black Panther. Started by G.P. Singh, a former central security force employee as a security guard training and deployment agency, the company became a PIA with the MoRD and diversified into whatever skill the ministry was providing a training quota in. Leather technology was one such area.

At the Black Panther training centre, I saw that there were several workstations with various accessories like cutting boards, measuring tapes, patterns and scissors. Trainees bent over them were learning how to cut leather. In the same hall, there were also rows of industrial sewing machines where another set of trainees, most of them young women, were busy stitching leather. It looked like a good operation overall. One thing, however, struck me as odd. There were no leather industries in Odisha or even in nearby states. Where would the trainees get employed after the training was over? Where would the PIA place them? Bahadurgarh, I was told, in Haryana. It has a leather park. That made sense. Big footwear companies ran multi-crore businesses over there and they needed hands.

Most of the trainees were in their late teens or early twenties. In that group, I noticed a woman who wore red bangles that are typically worn by married women. I was surprised. It was not usual to see married women in skill training programmes such as this one. I went over to her. She said her name was Shantilata Patra. She came from Balasore; she had two kids at home.

Then she lowered her gaze and became quiet. 'What happened?' I asked her, lowering my voice so that others did not hear the conversation.

Her husband had left her for another woman. She lived with her in-laws who were old and did not work. She had left her two kids in their care and came here for the training. After the training, she would get a job in a footwear company in Bahadurgarh that perhaps paid her Rs 15,000. She needed to earn money and send it home for the kids to be taken care of. She did not know anything else. Shantilata had no idea where Bahadurgarh was.

This was the first time in her entire life that she was with strangers. She was afraid of everything but she had to make it work. The babies were back home. They needed to be secure even though she had been abandoned. I returned to my office and asked Pinaki to book me a ticket to Delhi. I needed to see the place where Shantilata would eventually land.

The Vistara flight from Bhubaneswar to Delhi was uneventful except for the chance meeting with an Odia gentleman who worked in Delhi. After he knew who I was, he had many nice things to say about my decision to return to serve the motherland. But he also lamented how spoilt people had become, receiving endless government subsidies, and now having lost the motivation to do any work. 'Look,' he said, 'I have been so desperate to get a driver from Odisha for my home in Delhi. It has been so difficult. After a lot of effort, I got this one guy and just before he was to join, the fellow had the cheek to ask me for an advance! These people are so unreliable.' The gentleman was essentially notifying me of the futility of skill training for a lazy bunch of guys who had been spoilt silly by the government. When the flight touched down, he asked me where I was headed that day. When I told him I was headed to Bahadurgarh in Haryana, he was quite askance. Why on earth was I going there? I told him that thousands of skill-trained workers come from Odisha to work in the apparel industry in and around the New Capital Region (NCR) of Delhi as well as the Leather Park in Haryana. He was quite taken aback. He had no idea that people from Odisha worked in these places for a living. The aerobridge docked, we promised to stay in touch, both knowing it was unlikely to be so, and went our ways.

Outside the airport, I was received by B.N. Das, the man who ran the DDU-GKY programme in Odisha as executive director of Odisha Rural Development and Marketing Society (ORMAS), a government agency under the Panchayati Raj Department. B.N. Das and I got into a hired Innova and headed out. It was going to be a two-hour ride to the Leather Park in Bahadurgarh, he told me. The ride was dreary. The scorching summer noon spread on the road to Bahadurgarh like an angry beast. The sights and sounds were a far cry from a drive through Lutyens' Delhi. There were overhead metro lines, listless people by the roadside and, as we crossed the last metro station on the green line at Tikri Border, the flies, mangy dogs, dust and desolation hit me. But I was on a mission, I was going to visit the factory of a leading footwear company of India where Shantilata would soon go to work.

I had read up all about this great company that was going to be her new employer. The founder of the company, a refugee from Pakistan, had started his enterprise six decades ago, making just four pairs of rubber slippers a day with his own hands. Today, it was one of the top five footwear companies in the world. I wanted to meet their top management. I wanted to thank them. I wanted to discuss how we could do an even better job of training our youth for Odisha to be a strategic partner. I wanted to forge a long-term bond with the company. And who knows, the bosses out there may even know me from my days at Mindtree or with a bit of luck, might even have read my books! However, on our arrival at one of the several factory gates, disappointment awaited me.

The burly security guards had no idea who I was and why I was there. Momentarily, a couple of frenzied guys arrived, presumably from Black Panther, and persuaded the security guards to let us in. The guards eyed us with suspicion until an official-looking fellow appeared and let us through. Soon, I was handed over to a middle-aged man who wasn't particularly enamoured with my visit. He was from the HR department. By now, I was beginning to realize that the lofty, big picture, shared vision, ministerial conversation wasn't happening. My host was perplexed with me and somewhat edgy. Who knows if this government guy from Odisha is some kind of a factory inspector who can lead to avoidable nuisance? I did my best to explain the purpose of my visit. That I was a friend. That I wanted to build a strategic partnership and position Odisha as a preferred destination for his company to hire high-quality talent.

After some effort at making conversation, I realized that something wasn't falling into place. Then, I asked if he could show me around the production area. It made him very uncomfortable because people like him were trained to be wary of government visitors and for good reason. After some time, he relented, took me around and what I saw started to dispirit me further. I had thought we had trained our people in 'leather technology' at the Black Panther centre, but the work here did not resemble that.

Out here, workers were bent over stamping machines, were making rubber slippers by the thousands. Some were sorting bins to check defects. There was no joy, no enthusiasm, it looked dreary. At the end of the visit, I persisted with the middle-aged

HR man, 'What could we do together to better engage in skill training in the future?' I asked in a statesman-like voice I tried to muster. Now the man was simply lost. What was I trying to do? He seemed to be saying. Didn't I get it that these people were not workers on the company's payroll? Why would the company care for anything more if the labour contractor could herd them every day at the beginning of the shift and they did what was told to them and the company was within the boundaries of the applicable laws that allowed use of contract workers? Truth can sometimes provide a hard landing. Shantilata wasn't going to work on leather technology, she would cut rubber and make Hawaii slippers. She wasn't going to work for this company. She would be supplied as contract labour by some local guy, on whose payroll she would get her minimum wages.

I had known through my previous readings that more than 90 per cent of India's workforce was in the unorganized sector. Of this workforce, agriculture remained the largest employer. But consider this: in 2023–24, as per the 'Periodic Labour Force Survey (PLFS)' of the Government of India, 62.9 per cent male and 54.6 per cent female workers in the non-agriculture sector had no written contract, mostly no paid leave, no health benefits or insurance and no social security.[*]

---

[*] Ministry of Statistics and Programme Implementation. 'Periodic Labour Force Survey (PLFS) – Annual Report [July, 2023 – June, 2024].' 23 September 2024. Available at https://pib.gov.in/PressReleasePage.aspx?PRID=2057970.

As we stepped out of the place, I asked B.N. Das to show me where people like Shantilata lived when they came to work in Bahadurgarh. The place wasn't difficult to find. At a distance of half an hour away, responding to rapid industrialization of Bahadurgarh and the arrival of droves of migrant workers, the local villagers with some land had seen a new opportunity. They had constructed buildings and rented them to house the hordes of migrant workers.

I was taken to a two-storey building that must have been less than 12,000 square feet in size where perhaps a 100 workers ate and slept. I crossed a row of toilets at the entrance to the ground floor and saw two separate sections for men and women.

There, they slept on the floor with their small belongings on a rack, clothes hanging on a string. I met the off-shift workers. When the factory shift changed, they would go to work; the ones I saw on the shop floor would come and occupy their space. They got under Rs 10,000 a month in hand after all the statutory deductions and after meeting all expenses, managed to send home anywhere between Rs 5000 to 7000.

I sat down with a group of women like Shantilata and asked them the biggest challenge they faced in coming from faraway villages of Odisha to an alien place like this. I expected to hear answers like food, culture, language and safety. No, none of that was an issue here. It is water, they said, water to drink. Bahadurgarh has no groundwater left. There is a hand pump a distance away that spews out contaminated water. It looks like petrol in colour. They cannot drink it. They have food to eat, but it is difficult to swallow if there is no water. Back in their villages, there was little food but the water was nice and the air was clean.

For people like us who take safe, potable drinking water at home as a given, for whom packaged water at their workplace just appears every time they want it, Bahadurgarh is difficult to conjure.

To the politicians, the policymakers, the programme implementation agencies, the factory owners and the labour contractors, it is a non-issue. To them, the living condition of the workers I met, represents real progress. They are better off from where they were before, weren't they? Why were we complaining?

The truth is, we become self-congratulatory when we have simply moved people from poverty to respectable poverty.

11

Knitting the Pieces Together

After my very first visit to the DDU-GKY training centre run by the Bansidhar and Ila Panda Foundation near Cuttack, I had asked Pinaki to get me some data. What were the top three skills we were training for under DDU-GKY? Contrary to popular belief, reasonably good quality data is not difficult to find in the government. It turned out that the previous year, the state's top trade had been that of sewing machine operators (SMOs), the second was bedside attendants and the third was retail salespersons. The Bansidhar and Ila Panda Foundation was training young, mostly tribal girls as SMOs because the demand for SMOs was high and continuous. Odia SMOs were in great demand in Tiruppur, the knitwear capital of India, and Bengaluru, with its many garment factories that hide under the information technology sprawl. Only when shifts change and thousands of young women come out of nowhere and rush to the nearest bus stop that do you realize that there is more to Bengaluru than software. The SMOs are also hired by companies in Kerala and Delhi NCR. After the depressing trip to Bahadurgarh, I had made a mental note to go and check out Tiruppur.

To get to Tiruppur, I flew to Bengaluru and drove down to Coimbatore. From there, I proceeded to Tiruppur which was a little more than an hour away. We arrived around lunch. It is a small municipal town, not even a city, but has the reputation of being the knitwear capital of India that has, since inception, exported a mind-boggling USD 6 billion worth of knitwear. The town, until it became a knitwear park, was a sleepy place and its inhabitants were small farmers. Tiruppur is a fascinating story, as interesting as that of the Indian IT industry. Most of the business, contract manufacturing for global brands like Adidas, H&M, Nike, Reebok and you name it, is run by first generation, local entrepreneurs. It is the ultimate example of what small- and medium-scale industries, organized well, can do to the economy of a state, emerging as a globally recognized force. In Tiruppur, you can count the number of companies with turnover exceeding Rs 500 crores on your fingertips. The typical entrepreneur here has a turnover of Rs 20, 30 or maybe 40 crore and together they employ an estimated 6,00,000 workers. I was told that only half of them are local. Of the other half, half are from Odisha. Tiruppur is powered by Odia workers.

They are hired in masses by the Tiruppur employers, brought by train, kept in residential accommodation with food provided by the employers. They work on assembly lines that drape the world with leading brands sold in Europe and the United States of America. It is hard work. The silver lining in the cloud is that unlike what I saw in Bahadurgarh, here the employers take the workers directly on their payroll and the working as well as the living condition of workers are under international oversight, thanks to the increasing awareness among textiles buyers for 'ethically sourced' clothing. Yet, it is hard work for those who come here.

What makes Tiruppur's work hard, at least in the beginning, for the girls of Odisha? The answer is multi-layered. The girls belong to rural Odisha. They are typically school dropouts who did not make it beyond the fifth, eighth or at the very best, the tenth grade. They are from very poor families. This translates to childhood malnutrition. They come with pronounced iron deficiency, many of them underweight for their age. The assembly line work requires physical fitness of a high order.

Then, there is the idea of work itself. Back home, many of them, being girls, have done a lot of physical work at home, sometimes on their father's land. But work in villages has a very different rhythm. You are in the middle of milking the cow and giving her fodder. Now your friend comes unannounced. You drop the milking. Give the friend some water. She sits down. You chat. As you chat, you go back to milking. Then your mother calls you and asks you to take the leaves off the moringa fronds and your friend lends a hand. That task delivered, the two of you now carry a bag of ragi to give to the trader two houses away and then you see off your friend and return to do more work at home. Work is fluid, organic and very humane. Work may be physical and often demanding but is not a chore, it is woven into your life.

In Tiruppur, you work at an industrial assembly line. This means, you get up at exactly the same time every day, get ready, reach the factory punctually, punch your card, go to your assigned station, work an eight-hour shift that has three pre-determined breaks, two for tea and the restroom and one for lunch. You cannot take your eyes off the garment you are handling. You cannot talk to anyone except for work. You are not allowed to be distracted in any which way.

The global buyer pays for quality and most Tiruppur manufacturing units run an almost Six-Sigma-like operation that leaves no room for error. Secondly, in Tiruppur, time is everything. They say, the garment export industry runs with twelve and not four seasons.

The mannequins in departmental stores all over the world have a rhythm of twelve planned changes of wardrobe in a year, which translates to a twelve-time refresh of corresponding fresh stock on the floor. Worked backwards, you need predictable shipment and that needs to be further backward integrated with the entire process of the sourcing and manufacturing.

One miss in this complex chain and your goods will return at your cost from New York, London and Milan because the mannequin was not draped by the merchandiser at the exact time and day it was supposed to be. The girls of the DDU-GKY programme have to become a part of this intertwined clock, which changes the meaning of work in a gigantic, bustling global economy.

Typically, the girls arrive in Tiruppur with some familiarity with each other because many are from the same or nearby villages and if not, they became friends during the two and a half months of their residential training. But that does not take away their homesickness. Odia girls are very attached to their families. They miss home even as they may eat better, earn money and sleep in a much better place here than the girls of Bahadurgarh. That is why some run away after a few months; many stay at least for a year. What happens in that one year? Why do they fight the monotony of the assembly line and its isolation? For a very predictable pattern of reasons. There is a family loan to be repaid. There is someone sick at home. There is no income back in the village any longer after the father has turned fifty; he is old and does not want to work any more. And then, there is a really big reason: all of them need to marry and no one at home can pay for it. They have to earn to save for the cost of the marriage. In India, at the bottom of the pyramid, a girl cannot stay unmarried for a long time. It is not acceptable and it is not safe. A couple of years in Tiruppur means a savings of a lakh rupees, with which she can perhaps fund her own wedding. But only if the money has survived her father's drinking, mother's sickness, brother's demand for a new mobile phone and perhaps even a two-wheeler and the temptation her friend has shown, that of putting her money in a chit fund back home that promises to double it in six, but inevitably proves to be a scam.

12

Basanti Pradhan

After lunch that day in Tiruppur, accompanied by Chithra Arumugam, an IAS officer from Odisha who was in charge of the textile department, B.N. Das of ORMAS and a few other officers from Odisha, we went to Cotton Blossoms, a mid-size and very typical Tiruppur entrepreneurial story. This company, I was told, treats their workers very well. It was very evident to me on my arrival. A dozen girls, dressed in their very best, were waiting for me because they had been told someone big from their state was coming and that he wanted to chat with them. They were beaming. It was amazing to see them, dressed up in their finest clothes and jewellery; they did not show the strains you would normally see on displaced, migrant workers. Inside the conference room, we chatted over tea and biscuits. It felt very different from the cold reception at the Bahadurgarh footwear company where the HR guy had received me, with part concern and in part a feeling that I was a waste of his time. At Cotton Blossoms, the atmosphere was very different. I was warmly received by the owners, Milton Abraham John and Philomena John who I was told were one of the most progressive employers. It was quite evident from the walk-through and conversation with the management as well as groups of workers that the company valued its human capital and saw the linkage between employee satisfaction and global competitiveness.

After the conversation at Cotton Blossoms, I was taken to Anugraha Fashions. I had heard about this company before. Its website opens with the line, 'You can have anything you want in life, if you are dressed for it.' It was a quote from Edith Head, the most awarded woman at the Academy Awards who had designed costumes for many old Hollywood movies. Rows upon rows of sophisticated machines, all kinds of clothing in many different stages of production. Every worker at her station, quietly focused on her assigned task. Things moving like a clock's hands. As we were walking around, I turned to my host and asked if I could meet someone who came here as an SMO but had worked her way up. He gestured at a young woman overseeing a bank of workers. 'That one there,' he said, 'is a line supervisor. Her name is Basanti Pradhan.' 'Could I spend some time with her?' I asked. 'Why of course, you could do that, sir,' he told me.

Basanti Pradhan and I met in a small conference room. I asked her to tell me about herself from the very beginning. She told me that she came from a village near a place called Patnagarh. It instantly endeared her to me. I was born in Patnagarh, a subdivision of the Balangir district in western Odisha. There, my father was a junior-level government servant. It was almost seven decades ago. And this was the first time I had met somebody who was born around the same place. I felt a special kind of bond with her.

Basanti Pradhan's father was a goatherd. She was the third child in a family of seven daughters. It was obvious that her parents were trying hard for a son. And that was never to be. When her mother was pregnant for the third time, sympathetic villagers told her that this time around it was going to be a boy. But no. It was a girl. When Basanti grew up to hear that story, she told her father that she would be both a son and a daughter to him. It meant that she would tend the goats, take them to graze like boys her age did, but she would also climb trees to cut branches. She would then carry them on her shoulder on the way back home. Goats eat all night. While a girl could herd the goats, not every girl could climb trees to cut the branches like only boys could.

The family managed life one day at a time. When the time came for the oldest daughter to get married, they found a suitable groom. With whatever money the family had, the girl was married off. This was around the time Basanti Pradhan was studying in Class 8. Very soon, it was the second daughter's turn to be married. But this time around, the family did not have much money left. Meanwhile, Basanti had gone up to her Class 10, but she failed in her examinations. I asked her what subject she had failed in. She said she couldn't understand English and failed. This is when she heard about the DDU-GKY training programme. A PIA called ILFS was mobilizing girls for SMO training in Balangir. She asked her parents' permission to go there. Her parents would not agree. After all, sending a young girl from a village all the way to Balangir and then God knows where, was simply impossible.

Basanti asked her father a defining question. She said, 'You got your first daughter married. Now it is your second daughter's turn. How will you marry her until and unless I go and earn some money?' The reality sank in. Her parents agreed to send her to Balangir.

And that is how Basanti Pradhan started her training and eventually reached Tiruppur. Once she arrived in Tiruppur, she worked very hard. She diligently sent money home and got her sister married. But beyond it all, in Tiruppur, Basanti Pradhan was determined to chart her own life. She learnt the local language and impressed her supervisors with her work ethic. She was here to stay.

Soon, her parents wanted to get her married because word was getting around in the village that the daughter has gone off to some place far away and was not getting married; who knew what indignity she would bring. Hence, it was more important for her to come back, get married and get 'settled'. Money brought food, but marriage brought honor.

Basanti Pradhan said no to her parents.

She said she would get married, but she would get married only when *she* decided. And only after she had saved enough money for her trousseau. Eventually, she found someone who was also working in Tiruppur who happened to be a boy from the vicinity of her village. There was great joy in the family, but no sooner was the wedding over than both her parents and her in-laws wanted her to get pregnant. They wanted a child. In a village, if a young girl did not get pregnant, tongues wagged. It was a matter of disgrace for the husband. To prove a point about his manhood, the woman had to bear a child as soon as possible. Preferably a son. This time around, Basanti Pradhan again said no to both her own parents and her in-laws. Yes, she would give them a grandchild, but it would happen only when she decided. Right now, it wasn't a priority for her.

After she narrated her life story, she told me that over the last two years, she and her husband had saved enough money to have a television at home; they had recently bought a two-wheeler. I was fascinated. I asked Basanti how she managed to go up several rungs, from being an entry-level sewing machine operator just a few years ago to becoming a line supervisor. What I got from her was a short lecture that needs to be read out to every IIM or ISB student. An animated Basanti listed out all the qualities needed to forge ahead in life.

'First, you need to learn your own job very well,' she said. She sounded like she was instructing the intern. 'You need to be excellent in what you do so that your supervisors notice you and know that you are dependable. Then, you should be good at teamwork. Beyond that you need to understand what happens in the overall production process. After all, you depend on someone else for your input, and someone else depends on your output for the work to move.' Here, she paused and asked me, 'You do understand what is input and output, right?' I assured her I did. She then went on to tell me that a time comes when you are ready to oversee a line. 'Now, you must take the initiative, you need to show enthusiasm. After you become a supervisor, you must train and motivate your line workers in your charge. Their work determines your success. You must know them individually and not just deal with them as workers on the shop floor. You must help them settle down when they arrive in Tiruppur. You must take care of their emotional needs. And that is not all. A good line supervisor doesn't just focus on her own line. True, it is very competitive. But you must help other line supervisors if they need help. After all, your line can succeed only when the entire plant succeeds. Right?'

Like an awestruck student in class, I nodded meekly. We said goodbye to each other. She did not know that she would meet me again soon.

On our way back, I told Chithra Arumugam that we needed to get her to meet the chief minister someday. She smiled. 'I have thought about that, sir,' she said. When I returned to Bhubaneswar, I told her story to the chief minister; he asked for her to be flown down so he could shake hands. And that, of course, was duly arranged.

Edith Head, I am sure, would have been immensely proud of Basanti Pradhan if she was alive today. She would have perhaps written her quotable quote a little differently.

You can be anything you want in life, if you dress up the world for it.

Part III

Living in a Bubble and the Enemy Within

13

They Cannot Even Read or Write!

One of the three things the chief minister and I had agreed in the beginning was that we would keep the agenda of skill development above politics. It would be a non-partisan agenda, free from controversy of any kind. That is why I had requested him to let me have a meeting with the leader of the Opposition in the Assembly soon after my thirty-day, thirty-districts and 3000-kilometre tour, so that I could take him into confidence on who I was, why I was here and what I planned to do.

The meeting was coordinated personally by Chief Secretary Aditya Padhi. We chose the official residence of Narasingha Mishra, leader of the Opposition. Mishra, a lawyer before he became a politician and belonged to the Indian National Congress, was a man respected by everyone across party lines for his long standing in active politics and his civility. It was a sparse room where he met me. Politicians keep their residences as ordinary-looking as possible so that their visitors, people mostly from their constituency, can relate to them.

Narasingha Mishra shook hands, asked me to sit down and looked at me with curiosity. Obviously, the news of my arrival in Odisha was no longer news. The announcement had been made in the Assembly at the end of April when the position of chairman, OSDA was created and the chief minister had informed the House that I would be taking over the role in the rank and status of a cabinet minister, reporting to him, for a salary of Re 1 per year. No such animal had ever been seen in the forest before, and that I had sought a meeting with the leader of the Opposition and showed up voluntarily at his door was reason enough for his curiosity. I introduced myself, told him about my past life, my early impressions about skill development in the state and how I intended to go about my work. I was here to seek his blessings, advice and cooperation.

He listened to me without any interruption and then, playing the part of the Opposition leader, told me of the futility of it all. It was a good intention on my part all right but as far as the government goes, it was perhaps too little, too late. 'What will you be able to do when the education system itself is broken?' he asked. 'What can happen when a Class 5 student could not read and write, and a Class 9 student could not do simple arithmetic at the level of the Class 5? What skill development can be done when these kids do not even go to school?

But this was a match I wasn't going to play with him. I was there to discuss avenues for employable skill development for the youth but he was opening a Pandora's box that was beyond my charter and my capabilities. I listened to him quietly. Then I told him, 'Sir, now that I am here, I do not have a choice. Whether the kid knows how to read and write or to do the math or not, that kid is a reality. It does not matter whose fault it is. From now on, that kid is my kid. I have to start by accepting the kid *as-is*.'

Mishra wasn't quite expecting that from me. It touched a chord somewhere. Politicians like ownership and definitive statements. He lowered his guard. The tea and snacks arrived. The conversation shifted to the fact that he knew my family well, particularly my elder brothers. I added to that. I told him, I was born in Balangir; it was his district. He noted that piece of data with satisfaction. At this time, his grandchildren came running from inside and his mood changed quite visibly.

Narasingha Mishra is from Loisingha constituency in Balangir. Loisingha is about two hours from Patnagarh where I was born and is a little farther away from Basanti Pradhan's village. It is now a *tehsil* but until recently, it was a village. People like Mishra have an angry and valid view about the breakdown of the education system, meaning government schools, everywhere in India.

The associated failure of driving down the education system to the ground is ascribed to the government of the day. The larger society and the children's parents are generally exonerated. Most break down the failure to teachers who are not in place, or are incompetent and unmotivated. And there is no such thing as accountability. The accusation is true but it is not the whole truth.

When a child cannot comprehend what is taught in class, we seldom link it to a physiological deficiency caused by chronic malnutrition. Before coming to Odisha, I wasn't even aware of the fact. Chances are that most readers have never heard that before or have a very vague notion about it.

Maternal malnutrition directly impacts the mother's lactation and her ability to breastfeed the baby. When the baby cannot get enough milk from the mother, malnutrition starts setting in. Beyond the mother's milk, as the baby starts eating other foods, a poor diet and hunger lead to further malnourishment.

There are two clearly visible indicators of malnutrition. These are called stunting and wasting—two words I had never heard before even as I had considered myself to be a concerned and involved citizen all my life. Stunting is a visible physical condition where the child's height is not right for the age. Wasting refers to low weight for height ratio. Both severely impact the development of a child's brain after birth, because a baby is 'factory-fitted' with a tiny brain with only basic functions that equip it with the ability to breathe, eat and after a few months, sense danger. Much of the brain physically develops from birth until the age of eight. That brain has the frontal lobes that control language skills and math-logical capabilities.

When stunting and wasting set in, the brain does not develop as it should. What happens when the brain does not develop as it should? The child clearly cannot do five things:

Pay attention and follow instructions.

Remember things.

Build language proficiency through reading and writing.

Do math and develop logical thinking.

Finally, growing up as teens, build the ability to judge situations, and make decisions based on thinking through what is good and what may be harmful.

Let me now shift to a routine many of us have enacted before. We tell the driver or the maid to bring their child with the good intent of teaching the kid during our free time. After the initial enthusiasm for a few days, we get frustrated. We do not understand why the child cannot 'pick up'. The child has difficulty remembering dates and events while learning history, cannot spell words or follow grammar, cannot count and multiply and divide. Soon, the child is declared 'not interested in studies' or perhaps 'not intelligent, not smart'. It is often seen as an attitude or interest problem. We do not relate the inability to a poorly developed brain due to malnutrition in early childhood.

A child with stunting or wasting does not do well academically and eventually drops out of school, never to go back again. How large is the size of the problem? According to the 2024 Global Hunger Index, 35.5 per cent Indian children are stunted and 18.7 per cent are wasted. Among 127 countries in the World Hunger Index, India stands all the way down at 105!* Where do these children study? Government schools, where else?

It is true that the government school system is broken. There aren't enough teachers, teachers are not paid well, they are not motivated, teaching methodology is archaic, parents are not interested and a plethora of other reasons. But the underlying narrative as to why kids drop out of school after Class 5, 8 or 10, often never to return, has also to do with the irreversible mother–child malnutrition problem. And who gets short-changed in all this? The girl child, of course, who must eat only after her brother has eaten. She starts off at a disadvantage in her own home. Then, she is sent off as a bride as early as seventeen or eighteen, to get pregnant in a year perhaps and then she does not lactate enough. It is a vicious cycle.

Until I arrived in Odisha, I had no idea what stunting and wasting were. I did not know where India stood in the world index and I had always considered myself very well informed about the country, that I understood her development issues and perhaps had solutions to her many problems. I was as frustrated with the system as the leader of the Opposition.

After my arrival in Odisha, I realized that most white-collar folks live in a bubble. And many people who come from the private sector, quick to make

---

* Concern Worldwide, Welthungerhilfe and the Institute for International Law of Peace and Armed Conflict. '2024 Global Hunger Index.' Available at https://www.globalhungerindex.org/pdf/en/2024.pdf.

judgement about the government, live in a bubble within that bubble. And many people like me from the IT sector, live in a bubble within a bubble within a bubble.

As I slowly began emerging from one bubble into the other, I started to realize the deeper truths about everything; I was beginning to recast my brief on skill development. This is when I saw enemies within who make the efforts at skill development frustrating and sub-optimal. These had to do with a social system that had scant respect for the skilled worker, the consequent low self-esteem in them and the pervasive information asymmetry that closes the door further for the kid who cannot read or write properly in Class 5 and the one in Class 9 who cannot solve a Class 5 math paper.

14

The Non-Performing Asset

When the police pilot vehicle ahead of me blared into the district town of Deogarh, I saw scores of startled people, two-wheelers, a few buses and trucks had been held at the intersections by traffic constables for our vehicles to pass. The extraordinary arrangement told me that no one of significance ever came here because the local authorities had clearly gone overboard with what is called *bandobast*. It made me somewhat sad. But upon my arrival at the venue of the review meeting, when I met Collector Poonam Guha Tapas and the superintendent of police, Sarah Sharma, my sadness lifted. In a place like Deogarh, seeing two women officers in two top-most positions of the district was inspiring. It kindled hope. We sat down for the formal review with assembled district officials and afterwards, the collector took me to see a training programme being run by the Rural Self-Employment Training Institute (RSETI) run by a nationalized bank. Every district had one of those. I was told that today was the last day of a training programme. The participants were from the BPL category who were given training in rearing goats. At the end, the bank would lend them Rs 30,000 to buy a few female goats. Goats deliver kids twice a year and if tended well, they can fetch a steady income. Here I was to make a speech to the assembled people before they got their loan. When I entered the hall where they had been made to wait, my heart sank. All of them were seated on the floor. There were a few plastic chairs with the mandatory white towels for me and the collector and other senior officials. On the floor, in the front of the assembled group, sat a few women and then behind them the rows of menfolk. These people had no idea who I was and why they had been herded there, but the poor always cooperate and there they were. I looked around and asked the plastic chairs to be removed and sat down on the floor with the assembled folks. The hosts followed suit. Then, the RSETI banker spoke about the programme and a few speeches followed. But through it all, even as I was paying attention, I was constantly distracted by the sight of a beautiful baby, calmly sleeping on her mother's lap in the front row.

He must have been two years old, the mother looked no more than perhaps thirty. Toddlers, like puppies, always distract me. As soon as the programme got over and the assembly got up, I instinctively walked up to the young mother and asked for the baby. She gave me the baby and I held him in my arms while chatting with the mother. Then to my surprise, another woman came forward. She seemed to want to say something.

Baby in arm, I turned my attention to her. 'Babu,' she said imploringly, 'please take the baby with you.' I was taken aback. 'Yes, please take him,' she repeated. 'What do you mean?' I asked her.

'The mother of the baby is a young widow. She already has three kids. This is the fourth one. How will she ever be able to raise all of them?' the woman said in one flow. 'If you take the baby with you, at least the little one will eat well and his mother may get some relief.' Now, I realized, she was quite serious. Not knowing how to react, I gave the baby back to her mother and turned to leave. As I returned, from Deogarh that evening, the ashen face of the mother, her beautiful baby and the words of her well-wisher kept hitting me hard. The next morning, I called Poonam Guha Tapas and asked her about the young mother, wondering if there was a way to give her a grant under some scheme and not a loan. She said, she would certainly look into it. Then I asked her what the woman's name was. The collector told me, 'Her name is Sahebani.'

A sahebani is the female version of a saheb. A person of power and authority, living a life of opulence. In the hamlet she was born, this is how aspirational it got when her parents had dotingly given her this name. And here she was, with loss in her life and a baby on her lap, hoping for a RSETI loan of Rs 30,000 to rise from the ashes. I wondered what she had named her child.

* * *

A few days later, I was in Bhawanipatna, the district headquarters town of Kalahandi. There, I was taken to another RSETI-run skill training centre where a group of women were being trained in tailoring. All of them sat on the ground, each with a hand-sewing machine. They had been put through a drill to start their sewing machines in unison upon seeing me enter, making a harmonized sound that suggested a mistaken sense of purpose and progress. But in public life, you cannot be cynical. I smiled at them, spoke encouraging words, wished them the very best and went on to have a formal review with the banker who was in charge of the centre.

He sat in an adjoining, well-appointed, air-conditioned room. Having been through a few other RSETI centres by now, I asked him to tell me what would happen to the women I had just interacted with after their training. He looked blank. I changed the subject and asked him to tell me how many loans had been disbursed since he took charge of this RSETI. He was reluctant to give me the number. This was his pre-retirement posting. He had been here since the last year and had one more year to go. He had not given any loans so far and for a very valid reason. 'They become NPA sir,' he said uncomfortably.' NPA in banker-speak is non-performing asset. The term is usually used in connection with big businessmen like Nirav Modi and Vijay Mallya, defaulters of scale, fleeing the country after failing to repay thousands of crores in loans.

But the about-to-retire banker had an understandable reason to avoid potential NPAs among his trainees. A person assigned to head an RSETI, like our man here, is usually an about-to-retire banker or someone the bank does not know what to do with.

The last thing that person wants to do is to get embroiled in issues with, questions about and inquiries related to loans that can become NPA. And certainly not invite the nightmare of a vigilance case that could dent a lifetime of peaceful non-performance.

The RSETI training centre had been built with state government money. I looked at the *tahsildar* who was present at the meeting. I asked him the current value of the land the centre stood upon and the possible cost of the building. Tahsildars are tax collectors for the state and adept at valuation. He said that the land would at least be valued at Rs 2 crore and the building a quarter of that. It added up to Rs 2.5 crore. Now, I turned to the banker. I asked him, if the state government had put that money in a fixed deposit, how much would it have earned? That much, at least, should have been loaned out. He was nonplussed. Silence followed. Then I told him, it was *he* who was the non-performing asset.

It was a dramatic statement borne out of my frustration. In reality, the banker's predicament arose from a variety of systemic reasons. He was neither trained for his job, nor was he empowered to do it. The training he truly lacked was talent scouting, and the empowerment he needed could only come from impact investing, not bank loans.

Talent scouting would teach him to get to know each of his twenty-odd trainees toiling in the adjacent, non-air-conditioned room personally. Among them, all he needed to do was to identify four women. One who stitched fabulously well and had great skills. Another who knew how to count money, had financial literacy and could perhaps keep tab of the income and expenses of a business. Then, he needed to find a woman who knew where to source cloth from and which weekly market in which town had the best deals. And finally, he needed to pick one who was extroverted and seemed to have the aptitude to go out and get customers.

Following this, the banker needed to get these four women to his room and tell them that if they came together to start a business, he would give them a loan. He would try and get them a few business linkages and connect them to a mentor perhaps.

Whether it is a venture capitalist on Sandhill Road in Palo Alto, a private-equity guy in Bengaluru or an RSETI banker, the foremost capability needed is talent scouting and then backing them with risk capital. Talent scouting is part science, part art and part witchcraft.

Then, of course, is putting the money on the table. It is inherently a high risk. The venture capitalist and the private equity guy are rewarded for two successes in twenty deals they make, they are not penalized for their eighteen failures. But with that ratio, the banker of Bhawanipatna could go to jail.

15

Manjulata Bhukta and the Nursing Skill Gap

Subarnapur is like any other dusty little district headquarter. Once a kingdom ruled by the vassals of the Bhaumakaras of Toshali and then the Somavamsis, the town's recorded history goes back to the eighth century, when it was called Swarnapur, the Golden City. When I was growing up in Odisha, this was just a subdivision of Sambalpur; now, it is one of India's 766 districts. Per the 2011 census, Subarnapur's population is around 6,00,000 people. Despite its hoary past, rich history of textile, terracotta and other handicrafts and more than 100 temples around town, the place is, at best, a work in progress from a developmental point of view.

The district has a few good schools, an ITI, a polytechnic and a few colleges. But what had drawn me to this sleepy little place was the government's newly built ANM Training School. It is located by the Mahanadi River which does not show her ferocity here as she lies languid for much part of the year. She induces lethargy here.

Wherever I went to districts like Subarnapur, I was always impressed by two things: the quality of roads and bridges and newly constructed government buildings that housed various government institutions like this 40,000-square-feet, brand-new building of the ANM Training School. For that huge, impressive structure, it had only forty students. All of them girls. This was the very first batch to be admitted. They were here after an online selection, based purely on their academic record. The students spent their mornings learning nursing theory and then shadowed real nurses at work at the district hospital. But why were there only forty students in a 40,000-square-feet training school?

Well, nursing training in the country is regulated by something called the Nursing Council of India, and it mandates a ratio of the number of nursing students based on the number of hospital beds in the vicinity. Illustratively, you can only train 100 ANM nurses against 300 hospital beds. This did not make sense to me because whenever I have visited a government hospital, I have seen patients lying all over the place and in any case, one bed does not mean one patient. The same bed may have three patients on any given day, not counting the ones in the corridors outside.

The rationale behind the trainee-to-bed ratio is obvious. Nursing is a hands-on skill. The number of hospital beds limits practical learning on real patients. However, should we not be looking at the number of in-patients and not the number of hospital beds? But I was not in Subarnapur to labour that big question.

There are two kinds of nurses at the entry level. One group is called the GNM nurses. These are ones who do a three-year course in general nursing and midwifery. They commence nursing studies after their 10+2 course that must have physics, chemistry and biology as subjects.

One step below the GNM nurse is the ANM nurse. ANM nurses do a two-year diploma. ANM stands for auxiliary nursing and midwifery. The ANM nurse's focus is on maternal and child health. They too start the course after senior secondary school, but it is not necessary that they come from the science stream. From a community health perspective, the ANM nurse plays a huge role in a country like India. She is the last mile in delivering child and maternal health. She is the one who goes to the remotest places and locates a pregnant woman even before the family may be aware of the pregnancy. And from that point onwards, she tracks the trimesters, follows through with supplements and then brings the expecting mother into institutional delivery. Even now, 10 per cent of babies in India are delivered at home at great risk to the mother and the baby. That is about 6738 babies born at home every day!

That day, I was meeting students of the very first batch of ANM trainees. They were my joy, my first swallows of the summer for a hope that Odisha someday could become a major global provider of nurses. As soon as I arrived there, after the customary greetings with bouquets from the principal and her staff, I was shown around the huge building with its many rooms and lecture halls. For a government building, it was very well designed and well constructed. After that grand tour, we came to the room where the forty trainees were waiting for me. I was given a brief welcome introduction and then the principal requested me to address the student nurses. I launched into my inspiring best, congratulating them for choosing the noblest of all professions and assuring them of the brilliant future that awaited them. I spoke to them about Florence Nightingale. I told them about how I have come to learn about the critical role a nurse plays from great doctors like Govindappa Venkataswamy, founder of the world's largest eye hospital, Aravind in Madurai, and Devi Shetty, one of India's greatest cardiac surgeon, medical entrepreneur and an authority on public health.

I was quite impressed with myself. I told them the great global opportunities that awaited them if they focused on building expertise and empathy right from the beginning. Before wrapping up, I asked them if they had any questions. There was an awkward silence for a few moments and then a hand meekly went up.

A student nurse, a girl in a small frame seated in the front row, stood up awkwardly. Her name was Manjulata Bhukta. Manjulata, like the rest of her cohort, was new to Subarnapur. They had all cleared the state-level selection and then allocated to this ANM training centre. They had come from all over

Odisha. Though she had raised her hand to ask me a question, she seemed very hesitant, as if she should not have done it. I prodded her. 'Go on, ask me,' I said. Haltingly, she started.

'Please tell me one thing. Why do the local people taunt us every day when we are on our way to the hospital for the afternoon practical classes? Why do they say, we have loose character and that is the reason we have chosen to be nurses?' At this moment, she started sobbing. And suddenly, all the girls started sobbing.

It was the most awkward moment of my life. I felt as if I was dismantling in full view, crashing down like a building in the middle of an earthquake. I was dumbfounded. I felt stupid and angry with myself for the rhetoric I had just delivered. I felt like a self-absorbed superfluous jerk. I had no words for Manjulata.

I just held her hands in mine and apologized to her for the ignominy caused by an insensitive, ignorant, ungrateful and abominable society.

That one incident wasn't random for me.

Once, I had gone to the farthest district of Nuapada, bordering Chattisgarh. When the tour programme went for approval to the chief minister's office, Pinaki Patnaik said, 'Sir, the chief secretary wants to talk to you. He does not want you to travel by road. Nuapada is high on left-wing extremist activity.' But I was not going to give in to that. If anything, Maoists were waging a war because they were angry with the historic neglect of their regions and exploitation of their people, and perhaps they should see an ally in me. The inspired logic, Chief Secretary Aditya Padhi later told me, was misplaced.

One of the things you learn in the government is not to trouble trouble until trouble troubles you. He had to run the state and did not want to deal with the one-in-a-million chances of my martyrdom. He said, 'You cannot go by road, sir. Please use the state helicopter.' I relented.

The district, home to some of the most stunningly beautiful, dense forests and hills, with no institutions of higher learning, certainly no engineering colleges, had only one government ITI in Nuapada, the district headquarter town. And it wasn't among our best-performing ITIs. Yet, I had assumed, being the only technical institute in the district, there would be a lot of attention on it. Everyone would know about it in Nuapada and have some pride associated with it. I was mistaken.

At the end of my tour to Nuapada, as I was bidding goodbye to the district officials at the helipad where my ride was waiting to whisk me to the state capital, I shook hands with Md Sadiq Alam, the young collector who was comfortable enough with me by now. He said, 'Sir, before you go, I want to tell you something. There is a saying in Nuapada. It goes somewhat like this: "*Pua bigidi gale ITI jiba. Jhia bigdigale nurse haba.* If a boy becomes wayward, he must be sent to the ITI and if a girl becomes wayward, she becomes a nurse."'

* * *

Between the time I got my first call from Chief Minister Naveen Patnaik and the day I had said yes to him, I read anything and everything on the subject of skill development that I could lay my hands on. One such document was a skill-gap analysis report published by NSDC under the Ministry of Skill Development and Entrepreneurship. The report had one message: Given the economic growth rate of India, India's demographic dividend vis-à-vis the world demand for skilled manpower, there was a huge gap in every sector. One such sector was nursing.

I knew that already. Dr Devi Shetty, globally known as the Henry Ford of heart surgery, reminded me of that whenever we met. He was always vocal about the critical role a nurse plays in determining the patient outcome in a hospital. In his first hospital in Bengaluru, he had once granted my request to watch while he performed a heart surgery on a two-month-old baby. The girl had cheese holes in her heart. Tiny holes in a tiny heart which make pumping blood laborious and fatal.

Detected in time and given medical access, it can be repaired. Surgeons embroider the heart with almost invisible stitches closing the holes. After the surgery, the baby girl was taken to the paediatric intensive care unit. There, Dr Shetty showed me how each baby had a dedicated, 24/7 nurse until the child fully recovered.

Dr Shetty told me that Narayana Hrudayalaya had a 94 per cent rate of success in paediatric heart surgery. It did not mean 94 per cent of the children would survive. It meant that 94 per cent of children operated upon at Narayana Hrudayalaya would never have to come back to a heart hospital. A big part of that success equation had to do with the trained nurses of Narayana Hrudayalaya. However, Dr Shetty simply could not get enough competent nurses and finally started his own nursing school.

I had also learnt from another doctor friend, Dr Sharan Patil, founder of Sparsh Hospital in Bengaluru, what critical role nurses play and how difficult it is to get trained scrub nurses for operation theatres. In the United Kingdom, where he did his training, a scrub nurse had every doctor's respect. I had also read a lot about how Aravind Eye Hospital had found the lack of trained nurses to be the single largest bottleneck in scaling up eye care in India and how a special breed of Aravind nurses was created. Apart from all these, I had also read numerous media reports on the nursing brain drain from India. There were reports of countries like Canada and Australia offering green cards for permanent residency to trained Indian nurses even as getting work permit for software engineers was becoming increasingly difficult. I had come across newspaper reports that highlighted nursing shortages in Maharashtra, which was apparently losing nurses from its government hospitals to hospitals in the Middle East that paid way more.

The NSDC report that I was pursuing in preparation of crossing over to the government highlighted that in India alone, the nursing skill gap was more than 2.2

million. It is in this context that, upon my arrival in Odisha, I first looked at how many nurses Odisha produced every year. For a state the size of Odisha, with a population exceeding 40 million in 2016, the number of trained nurses graduating every year was less than 7000 a year. Of these, half came from private 'nursing schools', most of which were educational rackets and did not merit conversation.

To me, all of this pointed towards phenomenal possibilities. But there are societal challenges that come in the way of what may seem to be obvious and common sense to people like us. Manjulata Bhukta's tears were a sad commentary on how Indian society looks at a skilled worker.

16

The Plumber of Santa Clara and the Barber of Bhubaneswar

Where El Camino Real, 'The Royal Road' in Spanish, crosses Lawrence Expressway in Santa Clara, California, there used to be an $18 a night, EZ-8 Motel. Back in 1990, the Indian economy was at a brink, the country had very little foreign exchange and for people like me who used to travel to the Silicon Valley to solicit software projects, EZ-8 was a godsend. Back then, I did not know the difference between a motel and a hotel. A motel is a cheap place for a motorist to just spend a night along the highway before moving on the next morning. You got a no-frills room with a clean toilet, free coffee at the reception and nothing else. But motels are always near eateries, sometimes the typical American 'diner' where you could get a sumptuous breakfast that held you up until dinner.

During my maiden stay there, I found the bathroom's faucet leaking, with water all over the floor. I called the front desk and a man told me not to worry, someone will be up there soon. In a few minutes, the doorbell rang and as I opened the door, I saw this big man, better clothed and perhaps even better fed than me, standing there with a big smile on his face. 'Good morning, buddy,' he bellowed, 'I am here to fix your faucet.' I greeted him and gratefully let him in. He was whistling a tune I couldn't place as he came in. He had his entire gadgetry, tools of all kind, perhaps two dozen of them, neatly hanging from his belt. He had everything from a screwdriver to a flashlight. I had never seen such accessories, so systematically arranged, ever before. He went into the bathroom, called and asked me to explain how the problem occurred. As I explained, he listened with the air of a surgeon about to get into the operation theatre to perform a brain surgery. When he had understood the issue, he told me that he would fix it and I stepped out. After perhaps half an hour, he called me back and showed me all was good. He asked me to try things out while he stood overlooking so that I was truly satisfied. Then, waving his hand, he said, 'Have a nice day!' and was gone. I was amazed at his professional approach, his upkeep, but most importantly his body language. He was a plumber; I was a hotel guest. But the equation was between equals. I had a problem. He knew how to fix it. He was led by expertise, with no air of subservience. I was his buddy.

Years later, we lived for some time in the East Coast of the United States, this time in New Jersey. Our two daughters were in college, and it wasn't easy to support that as a single-income household. Susmita decided to work in the local PNC Bank as a teller. It was an entry-level position that did not pay a whole lot but it helped. She liked her work. But now, she had to go to work six days a week. Along the way, she became very good at her work and the bank started sending her to other branches, often an hour or two away, to train staff there or fill in when someone was on long leave. All this meant, we now needed help for the upkeep of the home that, despite the weekend vacuuming I was good at, wasn't quite working out.

That is when we decided to try out the services of a house cleaning agency called Molly Maid. We called them and set up the appointment. On the promised day and time, a Toyota car pulled up with the Molly Maid sign on it, two young women got off, smartly dressed, pulled out all their professional equipment including a heavy-duty vacuum, their cleaning supplies et al., took over the house and went about their work. After they were done, we offered them coffee and cookies and sat chatting. As we conversed, we learnt one of them was a college student. She, like our two daughters, was studying at the Rutgers University. Coffee over, they reloaded their stuff and off they went in their Molly Maid car to their next appointment.

Back now in Bhubaneswar, Susmita and I had moved in with our in-laws for a few weeks in their Sahid Nagar home until the government quarters allocated to me was ready. During this time, I met Upendra, the local barber who made a home visit for his regular customers. I needed a haircut. So, on a particular Sunday morning, he appeared with a scissor and a comb wrapped in a cloth towel and asked for a mirror, a wooden chair and a mug of water. The chair was duly installed on the small veranda, he wrapped me in the cloth and got to his work. The difficulty of giving me a haircut is in finding the hair on my head to begin with. I am quite hair disadvantaged and contrary to it being a short job for a good barber, they actually take longer, going after each hair with excessive care just to make me feel good. This stretches the time, but I generally make use of the occasion to have a conversation. Barbers quite like that. Now that I was in the skill development business, all conversation veered around that subject. This once, I wanted to understand how he learnt his trade and how his capabilities could be replicated. After all, everyone needs grooming.

Upendra was a man in his late fifties, he could even be in his mid-sixties, there was no knowing for sure. He had three daughters, all of them married. That was really nice to know because that was a huge financial burden for a man like him. 'What were they doing?' I asked him. They were all home makers, tending to the husband and the children, of course. 'Why didn't he teach them his skills?' Upendra's snippers stopped in mid-air and he didn't know how to answer that question. He thought for a second and then said that wouldn't have been nice. It was a stupid question at two levels. First, if a barber has to teach his children his skill and induct them into his trade, it means he has failed to raise them right. Success is in vacating your parent's vocation and doing something that is socially more aspirational. It is okay for them to go to high school, maybe even the so-called local college, and do nothing afterwards, to buy a bike and a mobile phone with their father's money and roam around unproductively. But to be seen as a barber like the father was a demotion. At the second level, it was a stupid question because I was asking about the man's daughters. They were meant to be married off by the time they were seventeen or eighteen with whatever small dowry was possible. They could not cut other people's hair.

But Upendra's skill was hugely valuable even in a place like Bhubaneswar. Each time Susmita needed her hair done, she sought an appointment with Kelsang Chonzom Bhuita, a young lady from the North-east at the Mayfair Hotel. There are other hair stylists there but for Susmita, it had to be Kelsang each time because *she* understood her, before she understood her hair. If Kelsang was busy that weekend, Susmita would wait for her next free slot.

Kelsang was an important part of the very upmarket Mayfair Hotel. Her clients respected her for her expertise. Between the salary and the tips, she made more money than many so-called white-collar workers in the city. Just the same way, in Bengaluru's posh hair salon, *Blown* on the Vittal Mallya Road, a sophisticated young man named Yogesh worked as a hair designer. Whenever our daughters came to India, visiting him to get their hair done was on top of their to-do list. And for that, they usually took an appointment even before leaving the United States. Yogesh did not *cut* hair. He *knew* hair.

But Upendra would not entertain the idea that his three daughters could be like Kelsang and Yogesh. Unlike Kelsang and Yogesh who probably went to a training school to learn hair styling by paying good money, Upendra could have personally given his daughters the head start. But cutting hair and that too in a 'beauty parlour' wasn't a welcome idea to him; it simply wasn't socially acceptable.

After the haircut was done and I was dusted, my father-in-law appeared with the money in hand. At this time, Upendra got out of his rubber slippers, kept the comb and the scissor aside, bowed respectfully and took the money in both hands. His palms cupped together, he did his namaskar and went his way.

In the ensuing few weeks, at my in-laws' place, I saw plumbers, carpenters and electricians come and go for fixing this thing or that. So did the maid who had regular timings and tasks. None of these people brought their footwear in. None of them had the confidence and the body language of the plumber of Santa Clara or the Molly Maids of New Jersey. In my in-law's home, these people were treated affectionately but not respectfully. Sometimes, they were offered a cup of tea or a snack but these were in separate utensils kept separately for 'such' people. In most other households, they would be treated with disdain, forget about being offered a cup of tea.

In India, a maid is a maid *servant*. A construction worker is a *site labour*. They are not respected by society and hence, lacked agency. Marry the skill they have with a caste system that is still doing well after eight decades of independence, and you get a dreadful combination that tells every Upendra to look at their vocation as a burden, sometimes a curse. Not a source of professional pride.

17

Information Asymmetry

I met Sumati Nayak at the Westside store that towers over the point where Bengaluru's Commercial Street branches off from Kamaraj Road. It is a flagship store of Trent, the retail company owned by the Tata Group. I had gone there to meet a batch of trainees from Odisha, freshly minted by the DDU-GKY programme in retail selling. Trainees like them also get absorbed by companies like Teamlease who in turn place them in the cloth, cosmetics, jewellery or other stores that you go to in a mall or an airport shopping arcade. Trent is one of the few high-end companies that directly employ these people on their payroll. The two-and-a-half-month training equips them with the basics of retail selling, merchandising, using cash registers and customer interaction skills. Most companies take these young people with a use-and-dispose-of mindset. In contrast, Trent pays great attention to their assimilation, welfare and career progression.

On reaching the impressive Westside store with its large footprint, I met dozens of smartly dressed, confident young people from Odisha working in different sections of the store. Depending on their performance, sales associates like Sumati are moved up from sections of the store selling low-priced, low-margin products to sections that stock higher value, higher margin products. The skills and sophistication needed between selling trousers and wrist watches are very different.

After going around the shop floor, my hosts took me to the training room at the back of the store. I wanted to interact with some of the sales associates to understand how they were transitioning from the initial training in Odisha to their eventual deployment.

There, the general manager of the store told me, pointing towards Sumati Nayak, 'Sir, look out for this girl. One of these days, she will take my job.' I was surprised by that statement. It sounded nice but exaggerated and I asked him to explain.

Sumati Nayak came from a small village near Bhadrak. She was a tenth-fail. After the academic disaster, she lost all interest in her studies. While generally wasting her time for a few months, a friend told her about the DDU-GKY centre nearby. She signed up for it. After her training, she got selected by Trent. When she arrived in Bengaluru, she could speak only Odia and a smattering of Hindi. But now, she could speak good English and was fluent in Kannada. How Kannada? She told her local friends to speak to her only in Kannada and in the course, picked up the language and became fluent in it.

Take any profession or skill and give it to a multilingual person, it changes everything. During one of our meetings, Manish Sabharwal had driven the point home to me. He had said, 'I pick up a school dropout from a state like say, Chattisgarh or Odisha and another one from the North-east. The kid from the North-east can manage some spoken English. The other kid cannot. The kid from the North-east gets a front-office job as a receptionist or serves guests in an upscale restaurant and the other kid loads stuff at an Amazon warehouse. The former gets paid upwards of Rs 15,000 a month and the latter, ten or twelve. English,' Manish explained to me, 'is the new language of skills.'

Sumati knew her basic job well like any other member of her cohort but she could switch languages based on who her customer was. It made her a very valuable resource for Trent.

Her manager's prophecy was no casual embellishment. A couple of years later, when I wanted to track her down to see where she was, it turned out Westside had opened a brand-new store in Coimbatore, and she had been sent there. Sumati took a picture of her newly acquired name tag and sent it to me. It read: Sumati Nayak, Department Manager.

How many people in Bhadrak knew about the success story of Sumati Nayak? Not the district employment officer, nor her teachers at school, nor the thousands of girls and boys at the local high schools who would either drop off from school some day or aimlessly sign up for a local +2 college which would not take them anywhere in life.

A few years after meeting Sumati, I met Hemant Tudu. Hemant, unlike Sumati, had passed his high school. Things were not easy for him. His father had died of tuberculosis. He had lived all his life in a tribal village deep inside Mayurbhanj. When his father died, he was despondent. He did not know what to do next. One day, his friend came home and asked him to come along to the Integrated Tribal Development Agency (ITDA) office where the former had some work. In small places, particularly among young people, errands are always run with a friend in tow. It was the normal thing to do. That is how a listless Hemant came to the ITDA office where, waiting for the friend to get his work done, he randomly came across a notice pasted on the bulletin board.

It said, Central Toolroom Training Centre (CTTC) in Bhubaneswar was offering a course in CNC turning and it was free for tribal youth. Not knowing what it was all about but trusting the ad because it was pasted in a government office, Hemant decided to give it a try and came to Bhubaneswar. At CTTC, his instructor found a fascinating capability he had. If you showed him any 2-D engineering drawing, he instantly could see a 3-D rendition in his mind's eye.

He was taken out of the short-term training and placed in a higher category. In time, he became a trainer. But more importantly, one day, he made it to the IndiaSkills Competition in the CNC turning category after winning a silver medal at the regional level.

Like in Sumati's story, what are the chances that anyone in Mayurbhanj knows about CTTC? And what are the chances that people in Bhubaneswar know that the trainees of CTTC make components that go into ISRO's satellites and spacecrafts like the Mangalayan.

Then there is the Central Institute of Petrochemicals and Engineering and Technology (CIPET) with two training centres, one in Bhubaneswar and a bigger one in Balasore. In the same trip that had taken me to Bahadurgarh, I had visited the Japanese auto-component maker Takahata in Nimrana, Rajasthan. There, I had met dozens of young women and men who had trained at CIPET and were earning respectable salaries with safe housing and transport.

In Bhubaneswar, most people have no idea where CIPET is or what they do. In Balangir town, not far from Narasingha Mishra's Loisingha, there is a state-of-the-art, fully residential hotel and hospitality training institute run by the government. Students who have done well there work at Hilton and in cruise liners. But no one knows about it, not even the local MPs and MLAs.

Every district, under the overall leadership of the collector, has district-level officers who manage different verticals. Among several, there are four who could directly impact counselling, mobilization, skill training and employment of young people. These are the district education officer, the district welfare officer, the district employment officer and finally, the project director, District Rural Development Authority under the Panchayati Raj Department. The district education officer has direct oversight on schools. There are more than 50,000 government schools in a state like Odisha.

The district welfare officer is charged with the development of people belonging to the Scheduled Castes, Scheduled Tribes and other backward classes and well as minorities.

The State, under the direct purview of the district welfare officers, has hostels for Scheduled Tribe students that have more than 6,00,000 students. Of these, at least 20 per cent should be in Class 8 and above, the age where they need exposure on career options. The district employment officer is the nodal officer in charge of skill development and has linkages to ITIs and polytechnics and is expected to know about potential employers. Finally, the project director for District Rural Development Authority is the one who oversees the DDU-GKY implementation.

The problem is that none of these people talk to each other. They do not think they could collaborate and create tidal waves of opportunities for the youth. They have asymmetric information on avenues and opportunities and that asymmetry cascades to the schoolteachers.

In Jajpur, I was taken to the District High School. It has the proud distinction of producing four chief secretaries of the state, apart from the fact that the legendary Biju Patnaik was a student here for some time. While speaking to about 200 students from the higher classes, I asked them how many knew what an ITI was. No one did. A brand-new ITI had opened in the district. Then, I asked the teachers how many had ever visited the local polytechnic? No one had ever gone there. And no one knew what was taught there. And it goes without saying that the principals of the ITIs and the polytechnics had also never taken the time to visit the high school to talk to the teachers and the students. After all, these students who could be their future intake.

And just for the record, Jajpur's polytechnic was one of the best the state had with a 100 per cent placement track record. Students who graduated from there with a three-year diploma started life at an entry-level package of nearly two and a half lakhs.

There was training infrastructure. There were avenues of employment. But those who needed to know, did not because government officials worked in their own silos. Opportunities became irrelevant because of information asymmetry everywhere.

18

But They Are Not Our Children

Arati was a part-time domestic help at my in-laws' home in Bhubaneswar. She, her husband Pulin and their two sons would come to Bhubaneswar seasonally from their village in Midnapore of West Bengal that lay on the border with Odisha. They had a small holding of agricultural land there. Between the intervals of sowing and harvesting, they came to Bhubaneswar. Arati picked up work as a maid for a few months and Pulin mostly did odd jobs. When their older son finished his Class 10, Arati and Pulin brought the boy to me and asked me to get him a job. I suggested that they send him to a vocational training institute instead, and they, as expected, had no idea. That is when I called a private university in town that had a large vocational training centre. They told me that they were about to commence training in automotive engine maintenance and repair in collaboration with a leading Japanese company that was rapidly gaining market share in India. The company had given them the vehicle engines and curriculum free of cost to train mechanics. After the successful completion of training, I was told, the company would pick up the trainees for their expanding two-wheeler business in India. The course lasted six months and the cost was Rs 60,000.

I told Pulin and his wife about the programme and they said they did not have that kind of money to spend. Because of the family's connection with my in-laws, Susmita and I said we would pick up the cost if the boy was willing to take the training seriously. And that he did. At the end of six months, I happened to be at the same university as they were hosting an event for the Government of India and the Union Minister for Skill Development and Entrepreneurship, Dharmendra Pradhan, was the chief guest. The event coincided with the completion of training for Pulin's son, and the university thought it appropriate to have the best three trainees receive their award from the minister.

I was delighted that Pulin's son was one of the chosen three. I was told the boy would soon have his job offer in hand as well.

A few months later, I asked the boy to come over and tell me all about his new life in his new world. He came dutifully and told me he was now working with a motorcycle service centre, a franchisee of the Japanese company. I had a lump in my throat. The subsequent story runs like this. The Japanese company has collaborated with the university with a straightforward objective. The more the number of trained mechanics on their engines, the better it is for the popularity of their bikes but more importantly, there is the big, lucrative after-market business. It is well known that automotive companies the world over make more money on servicing, repair and spare parts than on the sale of the vehicle itself.

I asked the boy how much the service station was paying him. He replied, Rs 6000. They had told him that he was a trainee and that this was his 'stipend'. After the successful completion of his apprenticeship, his regular salary will be around Rs 8000. I was shocked. How does someone survive in a city with that kind of money? It would barely be enough to spend on his daily commute and food. What about the rental? What about all the other expenses that he must now incur?

After the boy left, I asked Pinaki to pull information on the job offers in hand of our graduating batch of ITI students who had completed their two-year courses. The scenario was pretty much similar. They would get around Rs 8000 a month.

Unlike Pulin's son and his counterparts from ITIs, who got private-sector job offers, the public-sector employers like the railways and naval dockyards paid three times higher with additional benefits and, of course, job security. But how many public-sector companies were hiring? Most, like Pulin's son, would end up with the manufacturing sector of the economy where, depending on the location, they would start life at six, eight, at best ten thousand rupees a month. Many of these jobs would be in the unorganized sector.

Jobs with the unorganized sector have broadly five implications: a very low salary with little or no regard to government-mandated minimum wages, payment in cash, no upskilling and further career prospects, no social security like provident fund and medical insurance and usually no housing.

In India, we look the other way because we rationalize the situation in a fatalistic manner. After all, what are the alternatives? The guy is at least earning something. If he did not get this six, eight or ten thousand rupees, where would he be?

In 1990, when Biju Patnaik became chief minister of Odisha for the second time, in a sweeping move, he raised the minimum wage for unskilled workers from ten rupees a day to twenty-five rupees a day. I was on a short visit to Odisha at the time and remember the hue and cry among educated people. I heard many people I knew angrily saying that those maid servants and rickshaw pullers, the 'labour class', would not now listen to anyone; they will refuse to work and their arrogance will destroy everything. And besides, where would the money come from?

Six years later, Wipro chairman Azim Premji had sent me to Japan to learn how Japanese companies had gone about their total quality management journey. I visited manufacturing plants of some of the leading Japanese companies. Interestingly, even in the 1990s, the entry-level worker in companies like Toyota and Honda was a high school pass out. Wherever I went, I asked them, what is the wage differential between that worker and the head of the plant? The answer was pretty uniform. Around 1:6.

Twenty years on, as chairman, OSDA, I began to realize that nothing much has changed in India. Much of our competitiveness is based on suppressed wages. In 2016, manufacturing jobs in Argentina and Mexico paid about $10 an hour, workers in Mexico made $4 an hour and their Indian counterpart made under $2 an hour. In April of 2018, the *Economic Times* carried an interview with Manny Maceda, worldwide managing partner of Bain & Co. The crux of the interview was how much private equity interest India was attracting because of the wage competitiveness of India. The interview said, at $2 an hour, Indian workers cost less than robots.*

That it is a tragedy, that the so-called competitiveness is at the cost of young people like Pulin's son is lost on most people.

It doesn't quite disturb us because they are not our children.

---

* Bhalla, Mohit. 'Average Cost of Factory Labour at Less Than $2 per Hour Gives India Big Advantage of Wage Arbitrage: Bain and Co. Worldwide Managing Partner, Manny Maceda.' *Economic Times*, 3 April 2018. Available at https://economictimes.indiatimes.com/opinion/interviews/average-cost-of-factory-labour-at-less-than-2-per-hour-gives-india-big-advantage-of-wage-arbitrage-bain-and-co-worldwide-managing-partner-manny-maceda/articleshow/63554253.cms?from=mdr.

Part IV

A Time to Act

19

The Success Managers

Upon joining, I had requested Chief Minister Naveen Patnaik to give me three success managers for the assignment who would be available to me whenever I needed them. Whenever someone is invited to take on a high-stakes organizational assignment, it is important to be tagged to a few people who are already in the system who would ensure that the incumbent succeeds. A success manager is mandated in some sense to help the incumbent. On their part, the success manager does not see the mandate merely as a directive from the top but is emotionally invested to ensure that the newly inducted person succeeds.

The three men given to me were the chief secretary, Aditya Prasad Padhi, the development commissioner Raju Balakrishnan, and the chief minister's private secretary, Karthikeyan Pandiyan. All were officers of the Indian Administrative Service. Aditya Padhi was to align the principal secretaries of various departments to embrace the skill journey as theirs.

Raju Balakrishnan was to remove large boulders on the way and the inevitable, occasional nuisance. Karthikeyan Pandian was to enable me to have clear access to the chief minister whenever I needed and to signal to the larger system that I was here to push the chief minister's agenda.

Aditya Prasad Padhi came from an illustrious family of civil servants with his roots in the district of Ganjam. He had studied physics at the St Stephen's College in Delhi before joining the Indian Institute of Science where he received his engineering degree in electronics and communication engineering, later joining the IAS in 1983. While in service, he went to Yale for a master's degree in business administration. He had held several key positions with the Government of Odisha and the Government of India, which included a long stint as the additional chief secretary in the chief minister's office. Aditya Padhi had a deep understanding of matters of the State. Soft-spoken and somewhat reticent, he was a man every bureaucrat looked up to. He was quiet, efficient and very courteous but could deliver a blow with a feather touch if a situation warranted it. He did not suffer fools lightly.

Raju Balakrishnan was a maverick. He was born in Natham, in the Dindigul district of Tamil Nadu. As a schoolboy in rural Tamil Nadu, he was drawn to politics as an ardent fan of Kamaraj Nadar and started electioneering for his idol. The young boy could deliver passionate speeches and became a novelty in election rallies and the party presented him as something like an

Indian Idol star in various election meetings. One day, Kamaraj Nadar heard about him and sent for him. He asked the boy to ride with him in his car. Balakrishnan was on cloud nine. Except that, in the car, Kamaraj Nadar gave him a thorough dressing down and said, 'Don't waste your time in politics. Go and study hard. You should join the IAS; you should be a collector.' That changed everything.

Balakrishnan studied Tamil literature in Madurai and became a sub-editor at the *Madurai Dinamani* daily newspaper. But Kamraj Nadar had set his compass. His words continuously rang in Balakrishnan's head. In 1984, he wrote the Union Public Service Commission test in Tamil. He was not proficient in English. After cracking the IAS, he was allocated the Odisha cadre. Over the years, he built a strong reputation as an administrator. He was an effusive man who made up for Aditya Padhi's reticence.

Born in Madurai in 1974, Karthikeyan Pandian was almost fourteen years younger than Aditya Padhi and Raju Balakrishnan. He went to study agriculture science at Tamil Nadu Agriculture University and later, did a master's from the Indian Agriculture Research Institute in Pusa, New Delhi. He was a 2000 batch IAS officer who had demonstrated exemplary leadership as a young collector in Ganjam, which was Naveen Patnaik's constituency. It is there that Naveen Patnaik recognized him and made him his most trusted aide.

The three men, my success managers, made sure I delivered sustained, peak performance. In my new assignment, I needed to work *with* and *through* the vast system of bureaucracy of the State. To an outsider, this could have been a self-destructive move. When Nandan had cautioned me about being chewed and spat out, he was referring to this beast. Aditya Padhi, as the senior-most bureaucrat of the state, made sure his senior colleagues paid attention to me. He was my sounding board for new ideas, a voice of reason and, very importantly, if I ever got carried away, it was he who politely said, it was a bad idea.

Raju Balakrishnan's task was to be my cheerleader, my supplier of rocket fuel and when needed, my early warning system. He was the man who would get the mountains moved for all my out-of-the-box ideas and push for changing the system whenever it needed to be altered to accommodate ideas and actions that had no precedents. Government draws comfort in precedence. Raju Balakrishnan had scant respect for such things. He was an outlier in some sense and a man who loved a degree of wildness.

Karthikeyan Pandian was going to be the one who would ensure that nothing came in the way of setting monstrous goals, which were to grow increasingly hairy, large and audacious over time. On behalf of his boss, his job was to send signals to both the bureaucratic and the political system as to who I was, why I was brought in and why it is not a good idea to mess with me.

Between the four of us, we spent hours poring over all the insights that I had collected during the early days. We agreed that we had to come up with a vision that had never been seen before, something that would aim at making a generational shift. We built several strawman ideas and doodled the future. Finally, we began to develop a sense of where we needed to go, what would be the point of departure and the subsequent point of arrival in a decade's time.

When we were ready, I requested Chief Minister Naveen Patnaik to convene a cabinet meeting where I briefed the cabinet on what I saw on the ground and what the imperatives and choices were before us. It was the first time ever in the history of the state that an outsider had been allowed to address the state cabinet. At the end of the meeting, the chief minister asked me a pointed question.

'Mr Bagchi,' he said, 'what would you like us to do for you?' He was clearly giving me space to ask his cabinet colleagues for anything I needed from them and in this meeting, he was not giving anyone any options.

Sometimes, when a person in great authority says, ask for anything, the wise thing to do is not take the offer literally.

In reply, I simply thanked him and his cabinet. I told them what a great opportunity they had given me to pay a small part of my debt to the motherland. That, with the collective blessing of the cabinet, we would now hit the road with the comfort that they will be there and yes, I did have a small ask from them.

Whenever their travel took them to any place and they saw the signboard of a skill development centre they must always stop and drop by even if for a short while. With that, the cabinet meeting ended.

A few days after the cabinet briefing, Aditya Padhi convened a meeting of all the principal secretaries of various departments and a few other senior bureaucrats. Unlike the cabinet meeting, this was a long one and here I made a pictorial presentation of my first thirty days in the field. This was a crucial meeting for me, and I poured my heart into the presentation.

I told them about my impressions without holding anything back. I told them that the biggest thing going for the state was a genuine desire for human development at all levels. The vision at the top had seeped into the entire system. It did not need explaining. I told them about skilled workers like Sumati Nayak and Basanti Pradhan, who were regarded so well by their employers. The perception outside the state was that Odia workers were humble, hardworking, pleasant and religious. These were ad-verbatim words from employers I had met in several states in India across sectors. The infrastructure created by the government had exceeded my expectations. Coming back to the state after four decades, I had no idea how many good roads and new buildings had been built while I was away. I also told them how impressed I was with most individual officers I had met across the hierarchy and of course, there were pockets of satisfactory underperformance that we needed to address. I told them about all the things not going right. I showed the assembled top officials the ghastly pictures of the government ITI in Bhubaneswar that had dark, ugly marks on the walls. I showed them pictures of ITI Subarnapur, brand-new building, impressive equipment but no teachers or students in sight when I had arrived unannounced at 10.30 a.m. I spoke about the challenge of information asymmetry that prevented young people from taking advantage of existing resources on the ground. I showed them pictures of training centres run by private companies and the programme implementation agencies who made our trainees sleep and eat on the floor. At that point, a very senior officer, a well-meaning person, stopped me. He asked what was wrong with them sitting on the floor for their meals.

'Isn't it part of our culture?' he wanted to know. I told him there were two problematic issues with such a position. One, if it was our culture, how come it did not apply to those seated in this room? Their children sit at the table for their meals. They do not eat sitting on the floor. Second, and this was more problematic, when future employers come to recruit these trainees, what message are we giving them? Are we not signalling the baseline and telling them that anything even slightly better is acceptable? This wasn't the way to make skill development aspirational. Far less, world-class.

In the ensuing conversation, several things came to the fore. We discussed the need to look at skill development, not as an end in itself but as a means to human development. The example of Muni Tigga was a classic pointer to what happens to an individual when that person has access to vocational education and acquires a well-defined skill. It changes the track for many subsequent generations to come. We discussed the need for collaborative and fast-paced leadership. We talked about focus on the individual, to build a human face while discussing policy, schemes, allocations and impact assessments. The need for engaging with the outside world, bringing Odisha to the attention of high-quality employers and opinion leaders was urgent because most did not even know where Odisha was. It had surprised me that almost all the employers I had met outside the state who had Odia employees had never visited Odisha. We spoke about the need for empathy ahead of data at every level of the system. I presented them the need to not just do existing things more efficiently, but for us to innovate. Without innovation, Odisha's efforts would be considered marginal in the eyes of the outside world. I brought up the need for government officials to be visible on the ground so that the skill ecosystem saw them as engaged participants. There was of course a lot of conversation around the girl child.

We ended the meeting with agreement across the room that we are indeed staring at a huge, once-in-a-lifetime opportunity for all of us to make a big difference. I came out of the meeting feeling as though I was no longer an outsider. There may have been varied levels at which the leaders in the room were seeing what I was seeing, there may even have been varying levels of confidence in the outcome, but I felt accepted. Now was the opportune time to set the vision.

20

The Day the Chariot Moved

Seven weeks into my joining, on 17 June 2016, the formal launch of the Odisha Skill Development Authority took place. It was a day of symbolism and hope, a statement of bold ambition and publishing of leadership intent. The symbolism started with bringing in 500 ITI students from all thirty districts, dressed up for the occasion in a specially designed outfit with an embroidered logo of the state proudly on their chest. Most of these kids had not seen Bhubaneswar before. They were brought to Bhubaneswar a day prior, housed in good venues and then taken on a walking tour of the city. The state capital had never seen such a thing before. Hundreds of ITI students being shown around, herded by none other than the principal secretary of the Department of Skill Development and Technical Education, L.N. Gupta. The next day, they were brought to the venue where an impressive skill exhibition was showcased. Ahead of the formal launch by the chief minister, the day saw several sessions with skill ambassadors chosen from the *ten, six, four, two* search. There was Muni Tigga herself. We flew Nunaram Hansda from Bengaluru. Popular cine actor Kuna Tripathy interviewed them on stage. At hand also was the acclaimed sand artist, Sudarshan Patnaik, who spoke about his journey from being a servant in someone's house in Puri as a small boy to how he came to be globally renowned. The assembled ITI students were captivated. The media lapped it up. The effect was electric.

The message was clear that henceforth we would do things very differently. We would put a human face to the narrative. We would bring a sense of joy to whatever we did.

We would celebrate skills.

That day, we presented the OSDA's purpose and vison. The overarching purpose was to look at skill development as an instrument of human transformation. Muni Tigga, Nunaram Hansda, Basanti Pradhan and Sumati Nayak were living examples of it. From now on, anyone connected to the skill development efforts of the state had to understand and embrace human transformation as the larger purpose, for their endeavour to go beyond being a government initiative to eventually become a movement.

To make skill development a driver of human transformation, we needed to use the power of a brand to build the concept.

Brands are very powerful; they provide the emotional and rational wrapper around the intrinsic value of an idea, a product or a service. They pull people towards them. They evoke urgency. They trigger a call for action. They create differentiation. That is why 'Made in Japan' is not equal to 'Made in China'. 'Designed in California' has an entirely different connotation. In today's hyper-competitive world, nations, companies, products and even intangible services must get branded so that they convey the purpose, the 'brand-promise', such that they evoke distinctive mental imagery and create a call for action. Ultimately, that call for action is for the world to pick you over comparable choices, to endorse you and recommend you to others.

For this reason, the brand idea of 'Skilled in Odisha' came up. But it did not arise from a flight of fancy. Far less was it a statement of vanity. It stemmed from direct customer feedback. It had basis.

During my visits to Haryana, Uttar Pradesh, Karnataka and Tamil Nadu, I met scores of employers who had many choices in an immigrant economy. All of them uniformly said that the Odia workers stood out with their competence, work ethic and soft demeanour. The foundation of the brand promise was real.

But the intended brand of 'Skilled in Odisha' sought to go a step further. It needed to convey that the best-skilled people come from Odisha. After all, their ancestors made the Sun Temple at Konark that has stood the test of time for 1200 years with its design and sculpture that mesmerizes everyone. And look at the Sambalpuri saree, *dokra* work, appliques and palm leaf inscriptions and, of course, Odissi dance form. Look at the maritime skills, from boat building to navigation on high seas that took our trade, architecture, culture and narratives to Cambodia, Indonesia, Thailand and Sri Lanka.

The DNA of the brand was not an empty claim. It was a credible plank to hoist our youth. But the thing to do was to not gloat over the past but focus on the future such that people would say the best CNC operators, the best undersea welders and the best animation artists came from Odisha.

Now that the essence of the brand was settled, we needed to articulate a set of broad, time-bound goals that would guide us as measures of success. We thought of three.

First of all, in the near-term, which we defined as three years, high-quality employers were to 'lock-in' talent in skill institutions of Odisha. Second, in five years, global employers were to come to Odisha to look for high-quality talent. And finally, Odisha needed to emerge as a sandbox for innovation. Great ideas on skill development should be experimented in Odisha and then replicated elsewhere.

Each of the three success measures had underlying layers of logic.

For the first, we needed to get good-quality employers to know where Odisha is. In all my visits outside the state, in most cases, potential employers had no idea where the state was. We needed to change that.

Then, we went a step further. We told ourselves, just as leading global IT companies come to engineering colleges and make job offers to students in their pre-final years to 'lock-in' talent, why could that not happen to an ITI or a polytechnic? Beyond any other indices, that is the true measure of how good a vocational training institution could be.

But in the longer term, Odisha had to set her eyes beyond the national job market. With several countries facing the issue of an ageing population, our goal had to be to fulfil the need for a global workforce, however unattainable it may seem at the point of departure for leading companies in countries like Singapore and Dubai to hire our talent. At the time of stating this intent, Odisha did not even have international flight connectivity as it does with Singapore and Dubai today.

Finally, perhaps, there was the most uplifting of all the visions: to make Odisha a sandbox of innovation. We needed to innovate with new ideas, new ways of doing things. Because Odisha needed to catch the imagination of the world as the place to go to, it was necessary that new ideas and concepts should be test-bedded here. When you become a sandbox of innovation, people elevate you in their esteem. And that is what we needed: reputational capital in a world where reputation is the new currency.

But, perceived to be a remote and economically backward state, what credibility did Odisha have to set such a goal? We turned to Bangladesh for inspiration. After all, who gave the world the idea of micro-finance? It did not come from Goldman Sachs or Citibank or the International Monetary Fund. It came from a hitherto poor country like Bangladesh. It happened because they test-bedded it there. We told ourselves that we too could try new ideas that had the potential to be replicated elsewhere. It felt audacious. But it was an audacity of hope.

However, hope alone does not deliver change.

Change is a child of great, inspired and relentless execution with a plan that is granular and actionable. For this, I now needed my 'A-team' to be in place.

21

My A-Team

The first one to join the team was Balwant Singh, a young IAS officer who had just been moved from his position as collector and district magistrate of Sambalpur, a large and very significant border district of Odisha. The second one and the leader of the pack was Sanjay Singh, an IAS officer who had recently returned to Odisha after a deputation stint to his home state in Bihar. The third was Rajesh Patil, an IAS officer who had earlier been collector of Mayurbhanj, the district that subsequently gave India her second woman president, Smt. Draupadi Murmu. These three were, in time, succeeded by three other outstanding leaders from the IAS about whom I will write later.

As an entrepreneur, it has always been a matter of great satisfaction to me that Mindtree had a stellar set of co-founders. Each one was individually capable and we were collectively complete. We had a sense of shared vision and a belief that we were there to do something big together. It made us overcome many odds.

It made the collective journey memorable. When I look back at the eight years of service to the state, it was with the spirit of a startup entrepreneur, and these three officers were like co-founders for me.

Co-founders must have something that binds them together, even before they are brought together by the desire to build something worthwhile. Mindtree co-founders came from ordinary, hardworking, middle-class families. It gave us a unique bond with each other and we were able to see issues and opportunities through a similar lens. We got excited with small achievements and big possibilities the same way barefoot village kids respond to a muddy field and a football to kick around.

When I found the three IAS officers, it brought a sense of déjà vu. What did the four of us have in common? Even as they were fifteen to twenty years younger to me, we came from an India that was miles behind urban development. Sanjay Singh, Balwant Singh and Rajesh Patil, like me, were children from hinterland India. We were children of less. And here is an interesting trivia: all four of us were born at home. Institutional delivery had eluded our mothers and perhaps, that was a common bond that made us view the development agenda differently from others.

Balwant Singh was born in Kalewa Panchayat of Patodi Tahasil of Balotra district in Rajasthan, known for salt making in the deserts. As the crow flies, Kalewa is 150 kilometres from the Pakistan border. The landscape is made of sand dunes, arid lands, khejdi, aak and jal trees, camels lounging philosophically when not pulling carts, men in colourful turbans and women in veils.

His family have been farmers for generations. When he finished his high school and then college a few kilometres away from his village, he was breaking a family record. In his extended family, no one had ever gone to a college. Both his school and college education were in the Hindi medium. Balwant's first job was as a revenue inspector (RI). An RI is the smallest unit of the revenue administration of the state, whose job is to know which land belonged to whom and in small-town India, it can be a very powerful position because you have to approach the RI to get a certificate of land ownership. This made the job lucrative to many. On top of that, you stay near your village where everyone knows you.

You are locally important and each time land changed hands, you were paid small and sometimes significant gratification. But Balwant Singh knew this job was a just a stopgap for him. He had his eyes set on the Rajasthan Civil Services. That aspiration had its roots in his childhood.

Once in a blue moon, officers from the district headquarters descended on the Gram Panchayat in their government jeeps. To young Balwant, they were heroes. He wanted to be like them and he was told, the path was to appear for the Rajasthan Civil Services examination.

So Balwant Singh got into the state civil services and while on training, his friend Dilip Singh told him to switch his ambition and got him to write the civil services examination conducted by the Union Public Service Commission instead.

He got selected and, after his training at the Lal Bahadur Shastri Academy of Administration, was assigned the Odisha cadre. Odisha was the farthest he had ever travelled in his life. In his village, the elders in the family simply wondered what was wrong in becoming an RI, staying around and leading a good, decent life. Where was Odisha?

When I first met him on 18 November 2014, was very much at Mindtree, unaware that one day, I would return to Odisha to work with the government. Balwant had already made a name for himself as the driven, egoless and accessible collector of Sambalpur. I had been invited by the alumni association of the local Chandra Sekhar Behera Zilla School to speak to their students as part of their 150th year celebration. When I arrived at Sambalpur, my hosts told me that the collector of the district had heard I was coming and wanted to meet me at my hotel.

As a child growing up in a government household, I was taught the importance of a district collector by my father. The holder of the office was like no other. That person represented the Republic. How could I then receive the collector at my hotel? Instead, I offered to go and see him in his office. That is how, much to Balwant Singh's embarrassment, I arrived at his office the next day.

He looked nowhere near the plenipotentiary, the head of the Republic of Sambalpur. Instead, I saw a shy schoolboy, with a nerdy look, but very much at ease with his role. I liked him in that one instance, not knowing that we would be colleagues one day. He showed me around his newly renovated office. The old building had been redone by him with an open office format, smart cubicles, just like in a software company.

I asked him why he had wanted to see me. It turned out, he had read *Go Kiss the World* even before he had joined the IAS and when he heard that I was coming to Sambalpur, he wanted to shake hands.

Weeks after Balwant came on board, Sanjay Singh joined the team. Sanjay was born in Gulni village in Nalanda district of Bihar, just forty kilometres away from Patna, but in Bihar of 1971 that was a lot of distance in the context of economic development and policy outreach. His grandfather came from a family of four brothers. Three of them did not marry, they did not feel confident that they could feed a family. Only his grandfather, the youngest of the four, married and raised a family. Sanjay's father grew up in a brood of two brothers and four sisters. With some education, he got a job as a clerk in the Bihar state. Sanjay was the first of three children who grew up in a mud house in Gulni with his mother and the extended family while his father worked in faraway Jamshedpur.

When Sanjay was four years old, his father quit his government job and came to Patna, where he opened a small shop and sold paint. The man valued education and put Sanjay in a so-called English medium school.

They lived in a rented house. In time, Sanjay's younger brother and sister arrived.

His father's paint business was often in the red, he defaulted in paying house rent. At one time, the landlady disconnected the electricity line and threw their belongings on the road. When Sanjay finished high school, one of his friends, the son of a bank employee, moved to Delhi and got admission at the prestigious Delhi Public School at R.K. Puram.

This had a magic effect on a whole bunch of fifteen-year-old kids, Sanjay included, who arrived in Delhi. DPS sent them all back because their final marks were still not published. Disappointed, they went back to Patna. But Sanjay persisted. He returned to Delhi as soon as the mark sheet arrived. His heart was set on DPS. But he had no place to stay in Delhi. Karu Ram, a kind-hearted man in charge of Bihar Bhavan, used to refugees like Sanjay, let him in, allowing him to sleep in the office room at night while Sanjay persisted for a seat at DPS. But DPS wasn't ready for him yet. It took one whole semester of running from pillar to post before he got his admission. After passing his +2 there, Sanjay studied economics at the Hansraj College, went on to the Delhi School of Economics and started his work life at Small Industries Development Bank of India (SIDBI) before joining the IAS in 1977.

I met Sanjay for the first time when I was still at Mindtree. Sanjay had just returned from his deputation in Bihar and taken over as managing director of the Industrial Development Corporation

(IDCO) of Odisha. IDCO had leased the twenty-acre land on which Mindtree's campus was built. Despite a one-time lease amount, every year, we had to pay a rent to IDCO that was based on the original price of the land. All of a sudden, because someone lower down had made a perverse interpretation of the statute, we were served a demand notice that calculated rent based on the current land prices. This was absurd.

That is when I had met Sanjay and presented Mindtree's case. I showed him counter evidences from other states like Karnataka and Maharashtra where the government either did not have a rent or fixed it on a one-time basis. He was receptive but said he wouldn't give any immediate relief to Mindtree. It couldn't be a one-off remedy, however deserving, he said. He would get data of all the similarly affected companies, go back to the government, move the files to seek necessary changes at the policy level and then fix the problem once and for all.

I was quite disheartened. What if he was transferred tomorrow? What if some minion put some other spanner in the wheel? But a few months later, I was pleasantly surprised to receive a call from him. He said that the rules had been clarified, government approval received and the problem was systemically fixed. We need to do what is right, but in the right way, he said to me. I was to experience his style again and again in the many things we worked on together in the days ahead.

The third member of the team to arrive was Rajesh Patil. I had first met him during my thirty districts in thirty days journey. He was the collector of Mayurbhanj at that time. When I arrived in Baripada, the district headquarters town, I had an uninspiring meeting with his officers. The district employment officer had come unprepared to the meeting and could not tell me what the population of the district was. If the man could not say that and did not know the demographic profile of the district, how would he ever plan anything meaningful to steer employment? My first impression of the district was this man. After the review was over, Rajesh Patil patiently took me to see ITI Takatpur.

The ITI had invited a few past students like Buddhadeb Bhanja to meet me and share their success stories. Among the past students was Sudarsan, a young man with a severely hunched back. When his turn came, he told me that as a child his parents sent him to beg everyday, which he deeply resented. It was demeaning. Yet, the parents persisted. After all, what use was he going to be? Another mouth to be fed?

One day, he ran away and started working at a roadside eatery. That was when the government was running a campaign to identify child workers. Who was leading the charge of that campaign? The collector himself. Rajesh located the boy at the roadside eatery, rescued him from his fate and brought him to the ITI where he was admitted.

At this point, Sudarsan paused. He looked towards Rajesh Patil and said, 'Had it not been for this sir, I am sure, my family would have found me out sooner than later and I would have been sent back to beg.'

After that wrenching, and at the same time, uplifting experience, Rajesh took me to see the work of tribal self-help groups in the Basiktala village by the Budhabalanga River. The villagers were growing mangoes like langda and dasheri, which were sourced by Mother Dairy by the truckloads and taken all the way to Delhi. But lengda and dusheri mangoes in Mayurbhanj? I learnt that lengda and dusheri could be grafted and grown here and the weather made them flower and fruit before the crop from Uttar Pradesh hit the market in Delhi.

That is why Mother Dairy found it a great product to buy from the self-help groups and take it up north to capitalize on the off-season demand. And what were the farmers doing when the mango season got over? They had been taught apiculture and were harvesting honey. From there, Rajesh Patil took me to a rubber plantation in Jadunathpur where I was surprised to see village economies completely transformed. Mayurbhanj has 5000 acres of rubber under cultivation.

But I thought rubber grew only in Kerala?

No, sir. The climate on the foothills of Simlipal had turned out to be an excellent location for a small experiment in 1993 by the state government and the Rubber Board of the Government of India had proven to be a transformational change agent for the locals. I was learning things I had no idea of even as I belonged to Odisha and grew up in the adjoining district of Keonjhar as a schoolboy. So much had changed in forty years!

We spent the whole day going around more places where hitherto subsistence-level farmers had changed their lives with new skills and community-based agriculture.

Soon, it was getting dark and I had to move on to the next district. While saying goodbye, Rajesh Patil told me that, like me, he too was an author. His book, *Maa, I've Become a Collector*, was a bestseller in Marathi. The book had been reprinted sixty times and sold more than a lakh copies. He had attempted a translation in English. 'Could I have a copy of it?' I asked. 'Yes, sir,' he said. 'It will reach you in Bhubaneswar.'

That book, now published in English by Harper Collins, tells the unusual journey of thousands of people like Rajesh Patil who come from an India most of us have no idea of. He was born to Indu and Prabhakar Patil. His father was a small farmer in Erandol village in Maharashtra. In his book, he evocatively describes Erandol as a 'sluggish python lying motionless'. Poverty was pervasive. In that region of Maharashtra, villagers grew cotton. They borrowed money to buy seeds, fertilizers and insecticides from the same moneylenders who supplied the inputs. It was a trap. They were lending the money to buy from them and waiting for the farmers to default.

These moneylenders systematically put the farmers in debt traps that led to loss of land, alcohol abuse and sometimes, farmer suicide. There was never enough to eat from what little cultivation the family had. Everyone had to work on other people's farms or take up menial tasks to survive. A lot of Rajesh Patil's time growing up was spent in picking cotton and digging wells for a wage. He had the reputation of being a good well digger in the village. Sometimes, he hawked bread he had brought from a nearby town where his high school was.

But he was also beginning to be somewhat rudderless. When he finished high school, which no one expected him to do, he went to Pune. This is as far as his world went and it was there that he befriended a boy called Sangram Patil who changed his entire perspective, recalibrated his compass and showed him his true north. From Erandol to Dholpur House.

Folks outside the government system oftentimes have mental models about government officers. They have stereotypes of what a bureaucrat is all about. Some tend to paint them with the same wide brush. But it is fascinating to see how diverse the bureaucracy is, what kind of talent it possesses and how hugely transformational it can become in the services of the State.

Part V

Flowers Wait to Bloom

In the rank and status of a cabinet minister, I was presented with a guard of honour by armed police in every district I visited.

Sewing machine operator (SMO) trainees eat their lunch on the floor at a training centre.

In Bahadurgarh, Haryana, young Odia workers struggle every day with groundwater that is not potable.

A group of DDU–GKY trainees who became SMOs at Cotton Blossoms, Tiruppur. Odia girls make up almost a quarter of the workforce of India's garment industry capital.

Former chief minister of Odisha Naveen Patnaik meets goatherd-turned-production supervisor Basanti Pradhan.

Sumati Nayak, once a high-school dropout, now a rising star at Westside retail.

DDU-GKY trainees from Odisha at Westside, Commercial Street, Bengaluru.

Muni Tigga says a prayer before getting into the cockpit of the locomotive engine.

17 June 2016: The Day the Chariot Moved

The A-team's visit to ITE Singapore. Left to right: Balwant Singh, Rajesh Patil and Sanjay Singh, the men who made it happen.

Sudarsan, a child forced into begging by his family, was rescued by Rajesh Patil, collector of Mayurbhanj. He enrolled at ITI Takatpur.

The Skill Caravan with stories of role models, highlighting skill training opportunities to the thirty districts of Odisha.

Nursing trainee Manjulata Bhukta asks me why people tease and taunt her on her way to the hospital, raising questions of dignity for skilled workers.

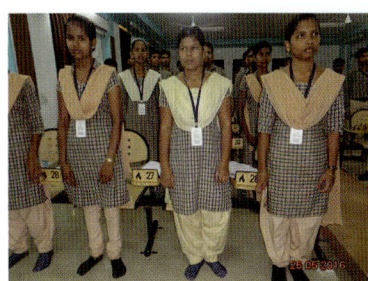 

The ITI uniform before 2016. The body language of the skill trainees says it all.

Noted Odia actress Prakruti Mishra lends glamour to the new uniform designed by NIFT, Bhubaneswar.

Balwant Singh poses with a Jeep's bonnet, recovered from a heap of scrap and given new life at the Skill Museum at ITI Cuttack.

The first state-level ITI Fest held in Bhubaneswar in 2018 was a huge success.

The Odisha Military Police Band played at the 2018 ITI Fest in the state capital, raising aspiration levels.

Dr Rajat Panigrahi, principal of ITI Berhampur, shows Chief Minister Naveen Patnaik the work done by his students.

Welder or artist? A Harley-Davidson miniature made from scraps shows how teaching design thinking changes learning outcomes and impact.

At ITI Cuttack, skill-trainee Tarini Prasad Pradhan explains the significance of the buried aircraft engine to Chief Minister Naveen Patnaik.

An all-girls welding team at ITI Jagannathpur.

The sports change agents arrive for their
training in behavioural skills at the Kalinga Stadium.
Tatwamasi stands second from my right.

Star of the show, Muni Tigga takes on audience questions on her life's journey at the launch of Odisha Skill Development Authority.

Tatwamasi teaches yoga to a group of vision and speech impaired students at the Special ITI Jatni.

Liza Rani Behera pads up at ITI Berhampur, coached by a sports change agent from Tata Strive.

Tanushri Patra in the cockpit of the Komatsu machine.

A group of young women pose in front of their Komatsu dumper, a beast that weighs 72,000 kg and stands 16 ft tall.

The government's Sudakshya Scheme gave full scholarship to girls with the result that girl student enrolment rose from 6 per cent to 33 per cent.

ITE Singapore's central campus.

The first ideation session to conceptualize the World Skill Center (WSC) held at ITE Singapore, where Bruce Poh of ITEES and Mike Chong of ADB make animated points.

Once decrepit, ITI Bhubaneswar proudly receives Bruce Poh, CEO of ITEES Singapore, led by director, DTET, Balwant Singh and Principal Jeetamitra Satapathy.

A group of ITI teachers trained at ITE Singapore ideate on the mission, vision and values of the new ITI.

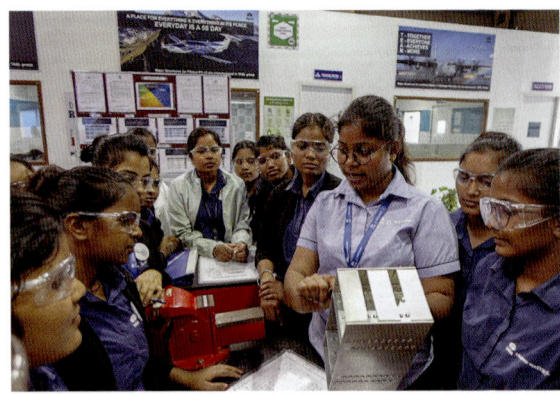

Anita Swain became an instructor at Tata Advanced Systems Limited (TASL) over a period of six years.

Damayanti Swain works on a Pilatus aircraft body at TASL, Hyderabad, where high-school graduates like her take on advanced engineering tasks.

Subasini's father worked as a private driver. She trained in plastic moulding after high school and was later employed by the Japanese company Takahata.

Gitanjali Mishra (on the bench) listens as I address a fresh batch of nano unicorns.

Sports change agent Tatwamasi with his swimming champions from the Special ITI Jatni.

Aswatha Narayana of Odisha won India the first gold at the WorldSkills Competition in Kazan, Russia.

Nano unicorn Biswajit hired his father, brother and two ITI students as his business grew.

Subhalaxmi Subudhi, who won a silver in patisserie at IndiaSkills Competition, with her male colleagues at The Leela, Bengaluru.

Prime Minister Narendra Modi blesses Pragnya Paramita Barik of World Skill Center during his visit to Singapore, where the latter was doing her internship.

A double bonus moment in Singapore where WSC trainees jostle for a selfie moment with Prime Minister Modi and Prime Minister of Singapore Lawrence Wong.

At the World Skill Center, class topper Mantu Kumar Singh presents his work to Tharman Shanmugaratnam, President of Singapore.

The World Skill Center towers over the Bhubaneswar horizon.

22

Doing More by Doing Less

ITI institutions in India, both private and government-run, come under the purview of the director general of training of the Ministry of Skill Development, Government of India. Based on their guidelines, the state governments run their own set of ITIs and the private ones, which are somewhat outside their control, do their own thing. All the government ITIs are run by the director of technical education. As Balwant Singh arrived on the scene, this was going to be his role. His office, for whatever historical reason, was located in Cuttack and not the state capital. It was housed in an obscure place on the outskirts of the city, next to an abattoir. The gory and unpleasant surroundings, in particular a pervasive odour in the air, made sure that no one important from the higher system of the state ever went there. All was good.

The situation was not much different for what was to be Rajesh Patil's set-up. His office was in Bhubaneswar and, waiting for my own office to be readied, I started working from there. But soon, a recurring theme presented itself. A mouse died under the elevator. Now, two problems ensued. One, the elevator technician had to be called to raise the elevator a couple of floors higher and hold it immobilized. Then, he needed to go down to recover the poor creature that had been in a state of decomposition for perhaps a few days. And meanwhile, the second problem pervaded the entire office—the stench that took days to go away. This became a regular affair, which was further complicated by the fact that the maintenance contract had long expired and the elevator company became elusive. This was the building that housed the State Employment Mission, the apex body for the thirty District Employment Offices spread across Odisha.

The District Employment Offices were created during the middle of the last century and played an important role, which was somewhat similar to modern-day employment portals like Naukri.com, but they had decayed beyond recognition now.

They folded into the State Employment Mission that housed a few dozen officials who were resigned to things; the decomposed rodents did not trouble them. Even though I eventually moved out of the place when my own office was ready, it was going to be Rajesh Patil's office. Cleaning up things there was the primary task on his hands, but it is from there that he had to drive the setting up of eight Advanced Skill Training Institutes. I will talk about this later in the book.

Luckier than Balwant and Rajesh was their boss, Sanjay Singh, who came in as the commissioner-cum-secretary of the Skill Development Department. His office was in the very imposing State Secretariat building. This was the 'nodal department' for all skill training that took place in the state, quite a number of them driven directly by every other department that worked in silos. Neither did the nodal department add any value to them, nor did they care about its presence.

The charter of the Odisha Skill Development Authority, and in essence my charter, was to bring every one of these entities together and move forward. But moving forward in the government has a playbook with a certain rhythm that I needed to understand first.

When a new idea catches the imagination of the system, the first thing that is done is getting the minister concerned to 'launch a portal'. A portal conveys the use of technology and it is presumed, tech means progress. It is also a low-cost, rapid turnaround effort, because the so-called portal is just a few static pages that escape scrutiny but are a good photo-op for the minsters and the bureaucrats. Most government portals in the country consist of junky information and are full of broken links. But no one is bothered because no one goes there.

Next comes the real playbook with the following three-letter acronyms: MOU, PMU, PPP and PIA. The more MOUs, PMUs, PPPs and PIAs a department can spawn, the greater their complexity. And complexity elevates the overall perception that there is a lot of activity going on and, as a result, progress is inevitable.

Once the portal is launched for whatever the undertaking, it is time to sign a few memorandums of understanding (MOU) with outside entities. These are usually made up of people keen on getting a government endorsement and ideally, a monetary contract of some kind. All MOUs are deliberately kept very high-level, with non-binding statements of interest from both sides and each MOU signing event is another photo-op for everyone.

Once an MOU or a bunch of them are signed, the next step is to set up a project management unit (PMU). This is usually run by one of the Big Four consulting companies. They have realized there is a lot of opportunity for milking the government with what is essentially a staffing business. The consulting companies quickly assemble a bunch of white-collar workers who know the Microsoft Office Suite, and there they go about making slides, Excel sheets and Word documents. Because a PMU is run contractually, the government does not need to recruit anyone directly, which is a difficult, time-consuming and irreversible process. In contrast, a PMU can be set up overnight and signal progress.

Now, the actual work needs to get done. But who does the actual work? For this, it is time to construct a public–private partnership (PPP) as a vehicle and through it, entrust it to a programme implementation agency (PIA). Now, you are all set. You do not have to do any real work. No getting your own hands dirty.

If you can smoothly move from the portal to the PIA in the government, it is deemed a lot of progress. By the time you traverse the distance, either the minister gets reshuffled or the bureaucrat and often, both. At times, the government itself collapses. And soon, it is time for a new set of players who arrive with their portals, MOU, PMU, PPP, PIA to start all over again.

But Balwant, Rajesh, Sanjay and I were not here to do this dance. We had signed up to embrace something transformative at the grassroots level. We wanted to sweat things out every day with sharp focus and clear accountability. It demanded the ability to rise above optics and cut out the many things that looked genuinely important but were going to be bandwidth guzzlers. In reality, some of these activities can be alluring because they are glamourous and easy hanging fruit but each is a distraction.

Our job was to not to confuse activity with progress. We wanted to do much of the work with our own hands; we wanted personal accountability. We also decided that we will pick out only those few things that take us towards the purpose set forth in the August event and put all energy into them. With that in mind, we embraced the idea of 'doing more by doing less'. It may sound counterintuitive, but it helps simplify things. We told ourselves, and then everyone else in the system, to focus on just three things: *'Fix' the ITIs; 'Scale up' a few but key short-term skills development programmes; and finally, 'Accelerate' the setting up of eight Advanced Skill Training Institutes.* We called it the *Fix, Scale, Accelerate* strategy. Going forward, every activity had to coalesce to make one of these happen and everyone in the skill ecosystem needed to directly identify with one of these.

23

Fix the ITI

Soon after taking up the assignment in Odisha, I had conversations with two entirely different people who happened to be my well-wishers. I will withhold one name for good reason. He thought I was being foolhardy in my pursuit of reforming ITIs. He told me that in Uttar Pradesh, the state he came from, people didn't go near many of the ITIs. 'They make country revolvers in some of them,' he said. 'What?' He went on, 'Yes, Sir. They have workshops where you have all the equipment needed for making country guns. The local gangsters get their way at night.' While the capability to forge metal did exist in an ITI, to my mind, using the facility for gun running was quite a stretch. But the concern and perhaps the disinformation spoke volumes on the reputation of ITIs in some places.

The second conversation took place in the office of Dr S. Sadagopan, founder director of the International Institute of Information Technology (IIIT), Bengaluru. This IIIT became the template for setting up several such IIITs that later came up in various parts of India. Dr Sadagopan has always been a nationally respected man with his great academic achievements and institution-building experience. When I told him about my assignment with the government of Odisha, he made a very profound statement. 'Do you realize, Subroto,' he said, 'there are two Is in the word "India". The first "I" stands for IIT and the second one, for ITI. For India to emerge strong as a manufacturing power in the world, both must be equally strong.' Dr Sadagopan elaborated on this to suggest that great design and engineering capability of a nation is of no use unless there is an equally formidable cadre of cutting-edge blue- and brown-collar workforce. In my meeting with Dr Sadagopan, the idea of fixing the ITIs got an altogether different sense of purpose. IITs were an institution. ITIs were not. What went into creating something that could be worthy of being called an institution?

During my Mindtree days, I had befriended Professor Vijay Govindarajan, a well-regarded academic at the Tuck School of Business at Dartmouth and the author of several books on strategy and innovation. He was also the first professor in residence at General Electric. Both he and I were intrigued by why some organizations went beyond simply being 'excellent' to becoming 'memorable'. This led us to a study of several organizations globally and we concluded that memorability was a function of being 'emotionally bonded' and that is what delivered sustained high performance. At the end of the study, we had posited that organizations are usually made of three distinct layers: the physical layer, the intellectual layer and the emotional layer. Physical infrastructure creates 'presence'. You build something that is so eye-catching that it grabs the attention of people. Like a fancy building of a new college campus, which springs up suddenly in the middle of a paddy field because someone simply had the money to build it. However, that physical infrastructure can be easily replicated by other money bags and can therefore soon lose its uniqueness. One fancy private school's glossy building is soon overshadowed by another that boasts of better horse stables and heated swimming pools. Such things do not create 'differentiation' over time.

That differentiation comes from building intellectual infrastructure. What makes one educational institution different from another is primarily who teaches there, what the curriculum is like, the pedagogy, the research and its publications. While intellectual infrastructure does provide differentiation, in today's world, it has a finite lifespan unless it is constantly refreshed. It does not create memorability. Great organizations, be it a school, college, a not-for-profit or a corporation, are built on the idea of memorability. They are the ones that are worth remembering.

This memorability comes when leaders constantly focus on building emotional infrastructure. This doesn't mean you don't need physical or intellectual infrastructure. In reality, you need to focus on all three simultaneously and constantly.

But here is the catch. Physical infrastructure takes the least time to build. Intellectual infrastructure takes a lot longer and building an emotional infrastructure takes an enormous amount of time and effort. Balwant Singh and his team of officers along with the principals of various ITIs started their work at all three levels in right earnest.

* * *

As a first step, we called all the ITI principals to Bhubaneswar for a two-day workshop to share how their ITIs fitted into the Skilled in Odisha vision and how their personal leadership was critical to the transformation process. At the end of the workshop mapping all three layers of institutional infrastructure, Balwant presented a set of parameters on which all the ITIs would be reviewed on a monthly basis. This was a colour-coded system; green, yellow and red to signify where each ITI stood vis-à-vis where they should be aspiring to go. Instead of making the review process a critical top-down assessment, every principal was asked to do a self-rating and that became the determinant factor for building a road map and a review process. The idea of a continuous improvement process from red to yellow to green became an exciting, purposeful journey for the principals. They had never been reviewed before and now, they felt important that they were the centre of attention.

Whenever we think of system-wide improvement, the first thing people worry about is funds. And given the context of the government, people assume that funds inevitably become the constraint. But that is no longer the case for most initiatives in any state government in India. There is enough money going around. People inside the system simply fall into lethargy or presume that their acts will be scuttled anyway. Why try? The other interesting thing is that unspent money in different heads is always available and often it is possible to be repurposed. But it needs some doing and decision-making.

As days progressed, the physical infrastructure brightened up. Balwant's starting point for review was what he called a 'clean and green campus'. It needed no funds from anywhere. Teachers and students got together and spruced up their institutes. Then, of course, money was allocated and buildings got repairs, new rooms and workshops came up, as did fresh coats of paint. Old machinery was removed, new equipment arrived. Balwant asked the principals to clamp down on students skipping classes, copying during examinations and, in some places, even paying instructors to let them pass the technical tests. Before taking a zero-tolerance view on these disciplinary issues, Balwant cautioned me that his steps could lead to serious pushback from parents. After all, most private ITIs looked the other way on such matters and let the student pass. As did many engineering colleges. I told him that we must do what is right and not what is convenient. Surprisingly, there was very little backlash.

My first very exposure to an ITI was when I had visited the one in Bhubaneswar in May 2016. There, I had met groups of boys and girls in very sorry-looking uniforms. They looked sad in them. Strangely enough, the girls wore salwar, kameez and dupattas. Clearly, with the dupatta, they were not going to be able to go near any machines on an industrial shop floor.

I asked the officials accompanying me who had designed the uniforms and how long ago? No one really knew. To me, a uniform must bring energy, joy and enthusiasm. It must make the spirit feel buoyant. It is meant to give the person identity and attract attention.

We decided to change the uniform for all ITI students. For this, we needed a new set of designs. I was told that Bhubaneswar had a campus of the National Institute of Fashion Technology. 'Let us go and talk to them,' I said. Why should we not approach a nationally reputed fashion school for designing ITI uniforms? I set up an appointment with Director Monika Aggarwal. When we arrived there, she and her team of designers were quite surprised. No one had ever asked them to design a uniform and here we were, asking it for ITI students. But they had never seen an ITI and did not quite know who went there and for what. Balwant then gave them a presentation on ITIs, explained why changing the uniform was very important to us and invited them to visit an ITI.

Dr Aggarwal fell in love with the idea. The sheer purpose of designing for thousands of young boys and girls who come from the bottom of the pyramid was uplifting. After all, why shouldn't NIFT's high fashion be accessible to those at the bottom of the pyramid?

After the ITI tour, NIFT's design team got down to design two sets of uniforms. One for the students to wear Monday through Thursday and one set for

Friday. The logic behind two sets of uniforms was simple: when we see kids from privileged backgrounds, going to name-brand schools, they have two different sets of uniforms. One for regular school days and one for the sports day. Why not the same for the ITI kids? The design team at NIFT came up with some truly fantastic designs, with the tagline 'Skilled-in-Odisha' printed on them. The effect was electric.

But we quickly realized that in doing all this, we had created a problem for ourselves. How can you change the uniform of ITI students and deny it to the students of polytechnics who also wore shabby, outdated ones? Now the brief to NIFT was expanded. But in all this, the question came up: who would pick up the tab for the switchover from the old uniforms to the new?

The one-time cost of switching over was estimated to be a whopping fourteen crore rupees. It made a lot of people nervous. But when the design book showing what the ITI kids wore now and what they would in the future was presented to Chief Minister Naveen Patnaik, he was all smiles. The state would pick up the tab. When the new uniform was produced, a group of ITI students, boys and girls, proudly walked the ramp at the at the 'Invest Odisha 2018' event. It was the state's flagship platform to attract global investments that drew industry participation from all over and garnered serious media attention.

While all this was happening, we also found that there were a few hygiene issues that needed fixing and one of them was punctuality and attendance. In order to fix that, every ITI was asked to start the day with an assembly where all students and teachers had to be present. The assembly started with the national anthem, reading the news of the day and group physical activities including fun things like dance aerobics. Videos of these were shared on WhatsApp groups that were now abuzz with different ITIs conducting their assembly in innovative ways.

In addition to the idea of assembly before starting classes, one big difference to attendance was the introduction of games and sports. A young boy or a girl comes to an ITI after passing the Class X examination. They are teenagers. Teenage is a time for play. Give a kid a playground and that kid would show up every day at school. You don't need to worry about attendance any more.

But, while every ITI had ten or twenty acres of land, not one had a football field or a volleyball court. Forget about games like cricket. ITI principals were asked to set up sports teams for girls and boys alike in every such sport. One day, a picture of Balwant Singh playing volleyball in shorts with students of ITI Talcher went viral. And then came the big one. In 2018, for the first time in the history of the state, we held the ITI Fest in Bhubaneswar where 600 students selected from different ITIs came together to compete in sports, games, music, dance and debate competitions. At the march past, the Odisha Military Police band played for them. The skill development minister and senior government officials cheered them on. The media covered the events with great enthusiasm. The number of participants swelled every year thereafter, as did the scope of competitions. Soon, thousands of youths started descending. We ran out of venues and finally, the massive Kalinga Stadium, which hosted the World Cup Hockey, had to be the new venue. During the ITI Fests, later named Skill Fests, the main streets of Bhubaneswar were closed to traffic for street festivals by the kids who put up stalls and showcased various skills.

Over time, ITI curriculum got updated, digital capabilities were enhanced, smart classrooms and computer labs popped up, students were taken to industries for field visits and they even started going to the local community around the ITI to fix domestic appliances and did other small repairs for the elderly and the poor people. With the *ten, six, four, two* formula now well understood, hundreds of role models like Muni Tigga and Nunaram Hansda were identified, they were invited back to their alma mater, their pictures adorned the walls and they shared their life stories with wide-eyed kids who saw exemplars of success in flesh and blood.

An institution that was never full, started filling up every seat. The ITIs started getting noticed by the world outside.

24

The Buried Aircraft Engine

What is common between Steve Jobs and most five-year-olds? Both have the genius ability to 'transmogrify'. It means transforming something in a surprising or magical manner. It is the ability to see an object or artefact but imagine it as something completely different. If you go back to your own childhood, your years as a preschooler perhaps, you will recall how you could spend endless time playing with sandcastles, imagining they were the real thing. Or on a long summer afternoon, bored with everything else, how you took a pencil and pretended it was an aeroplane, a flying object and went, whoosh, whoosh.

As most of us become adults, we drop this great ability to transmogrify, and this takes away the valuable inner eye. An eye that is inventive, sees what others don't and creates things of great beauty, use and value. When the world looked at a simple computer, Steve Jobs saw a Mac. When people in the Silicon Valley saw a simple mobile phone, he saw an iPhone and iTunes. This is about imagining endless possibilities whereas most of us, thanks to the assumed meaning of growing up, and thanks to traditional education, become comfortable with reductive thinking which kills the idea of wonder. That reductive thinking says, a young person trained to do welding should only be doing window grilles and not landscape art installations. Yet, the skill required to do both is, well, welding.

Decades ago, I was fascinated with the ideas of a man called Professor Yves Doz of INSEAD, France. Doz came to be regarded as an authority on the subject of knowledge management, applying his ideas in the context of what he termed as the 'meta-national corporations', with several books to his credit. During one of his visits to Bengaluru, I had invited him to deliver a talk at Wipro where I was working as chief executive of their global R&D division.

Doz explained to us that a particular piece of knowledge remaining constant, how we may look at it, how we may use it to create value out of it, can vary substantially, with vastly different economic outcome. He argued that depending on how we see it, knowledge on any subject presents itself at three levels.

At the lowest level is technical knowledge. When you see something, you focus on its parts and functionality. In the context of the ITIs, someone shows a trainee how to weld a window grille, asks to them to repeat it and then the trainee does the exact same thing that was prescribed. This is rote, and repeated over time, this has the lowest economic value addition. As a result, this has the least economic outcome and the wage-earning potential of a skilled individual.

The next level at which we can relate to knowledge is what Doz terms as experiential knowledge. Here, the holder of knowledge is not waiting for someone to prescribe what needs to be done. The holder of knowledge is encouraged to 'step into the shoes' of a potential user, a customer, and creates something novel even before being told to do so. This is the anticipative layer. Here the same skill-trained individual learns to anticipate what the world wants and then creates it. This is the layer at which Buddhadeb Bhanja was operating while seeking work near Baripada town.

But the highest level at which someone can relate to the same piece of knowledge is the existential layer, where they no longer step into the shoes of the user, they step into the user's mind and then work backwards, to create unusual new things that change perspective, add greater value and create the highest economic benefit from essentially the same knowledge. In this case, how to weld metal. Imagine someone who knows that skill of welding and uses it to create award winning sculptures, valuable pieces of art.

Decades after listening to Doz, his concept was returning to me in waves. I realized, there is another interesting angle to it. At the bottom-most layer, it is all about just plain vanilla skills. At the next higher level, you need other abilities beyond just the engineering skill. But to be a sculptor, one must understand design. Students of ITIs are considered what Nobel Laureate Mohammad Yunus famously called the Bonsai People. You keep the sapling of a giant banyan tree in a pot for the rest of its life and it will become a bonsai, a dwarf.

You do not expose an ITI kid engineering and design, art and sculpture and there you are, the giant banyan or the oak of tomorrow will soon become a bonsai.

The first time I visited the ITI at Talcher, I went to see a workshop where dozens of students had been dutifully lined up around long, dirty tables fitted with filing jigs. The moment they saw me coming, they swung into feverish action, filing pieces of metals in a synchronous, subservient way of demonstrating their learning. I did not like it. But you learn not to discourage things until you find a better way. Then, I visited the ITI at Berhampur where Principal Rajat Panigrahi was proudly showing me his trainees at the workshop and this time, I noticed small mountains of ground metal that had accumulated in the process on the ground. The powder was a byproduct of the mechanical, mindless act of filing metal by the students. I asked Dr Panigrahi what they did with the powdered metal gathering in heaps on the ground. He was surprised. No one had asked that question before.

It was just waste, he explained. It gets accumulated, goes someplace and gets dumped there. I was quite alarmed. On one hand, it was 'waste' but on the other hand, disposed the way it was, the ground metal was also harmful to the environment. 'Why can we not make things out of it,' I asked Dr Panigrahi?

In that one moment, his mind exploded. In an instant, he was breaking the glass ceilings separating Doz's model of technical, experiential and existential levels of knowledge. Yes, he told me, eyes shining, we should be converting waste to wealth. Dr Panigrahi was transmogrifying now. The next time I met him, he took me to a small room where there were clocks made from discarded cycle chains and a Ganesha made from throwaway powdered metal, which came out of filing workshops where fitter trainees toiled. Then, of course, there was no stopping as ITI Berhampur became a sought-after source of artefacts and installations made out of metal waste and other things like discarded tyres.

The day I came to meet Dr H.K. Mohanty, principal of ITI Cuttack, he was showing me around his decrepit-looking workshops. ITI Cuttack was located in a decadent part of an industrial area, straight out of the rust belt, in a shabby neighbourhood overrun by squatters and encroachers. Everywhere around the ITI, you only saw garbage and filth. It was a miracle that the ITI building still stood there. It was also a miracle that someone like Dr Mohanty ran that place.

Dr Mohanty had earned his PhD in Friction Stir Welding from IIT Roorkee. It is a solid-state joining process where the metals join at below the melting point. How did he not end up in Bengaluru or Pune, if not in the Silicon Valley or Singapore? What made people like him (and Dr Panigrahi, Pinaki Patnaik and many others) stay on in Odisha to work and live there, doing the kind of work they do? The story was the same. If you were the oldest, or the only, son, the parents wanted you to stay home. A stable government job was better than money and fame from elsewhere. Those things did not get you the sense of assurance for parents. The parents wanted togetherness; a son or a daughter who would share the responsibility of getting the younger siblings settled in life, perhaps help build the first floor of the old house that was constructed with money from the provident fund. Be there to take them to the hospital and look after them in old age. And of course, give them the grandkids to grow up with in the sunset years. In short, be around. Dr Mohanty came from a middle-class home in Kalahandi and his parents wanted him to do just that. He accepted his lot, took up the job as an ITI teacher and was the principal now, overseeing both the rot and rote. But deep within, the man was made of very different metal.

As Dr Mohanty and I were surveying the cobwebbed sheds, the ageing machines, the holes overhead that exposed a dangerously rusted roof, I saw an interesting looking artefact half buried in the soil below. It seemed as if the thing wanted to speak to me from another time in history.

I asked Dr Mohanty, what was this abandoned piece of quaint machinery that lay half buried? He did not know. Someone who had been here longer said, it was an aircraft engine.

'What?'

'Yes, sir, but very old.'

'How old?'

'Very old, sir, may be World War I.'

A closer examination showed that it was a radial engine used in aircrafts even before the first World War. The radial engine, made of solid iron, was invented in 1907 by a man named Wolfgang Walden and this piece of 'scrap' here had a serial number to it, indicating it was perhaps individually commissioned. Radial engines preceded the gas turbine engines of later times.

I was stunned. Anywhere in the world, this would have been displayed with awe and reverence in an aerospace museum. Here, it was in a heap of neglect. Where did it come from? What tour of duty did it do? When was it retired? How did it get here? For what reason? Who knows?

In India, we lack a sense of history. My mind went back to my days in Kolkata of 1985. I worked there at MMC Digital Systems, a computer hardware company the Mahindras had started and then closed down. During those days, I used to write a column for the Dataquest magazine. One day, I got a call from Dataquest's editor, Sunil Agarwal, to go visit the Indian Statistical Institute (ISI) where the first computer of India was brought in 1955.

This was called HEC 2M and it was handmade in England. Later, in 1958, came another, this time from Russia. It was named URAL. Dataquest wanted me to recreate the events around the arrival of these machines, a time when India did not know it was going to be a global IT giant in less than five decades. I visited ISI and met two people there who had some knowledge about the event.

One was Dr Dwijish Dutta Majumdar, the head of the department, and the other was Ashok Dasgupta, the peon. Both men were about to retire, taking with them the last strands of institutional memory to oblivion. They were very young when the great Dr Prasanta

Mahalanobis, father of India's five-year plan system, had ordered for these machines so that ISI could crunch the vast sets of data needed for the planning process for a newly independent India. I asked both men if I could see HEC 2M and URAL. 'No,' they said. The machines were scrapped a long time ago. Scrapped? Where? When? No idea.

Then, Ashok Dasgupta haltingly said, some of the scrap was lying under a tree on the far side for many years. I rushed there and under an old tree, within the heaps of dried leaves and layers of dirt, I found one tiny piece of what was URAL. I held it in my hand with affection and reverence. I looked at the two men and sought permission to carry it back. They shrugged, as if to say this wasn't the first time they were seeing this weird behaviour.

My mind snapped back in time to the ITI. Let us dig out this aircraft engine and keep it someplace safe, I told Dr Mohanty. Over the next few days, we recovered many such things that were no longer in use, broken, silent, but beautiful as objects of design even in their death.

Putting together the ITI Talcher, ITI Berhampur and the ITI Cuttack experiences, it occurred to me that we should be setting up a skill museum. A place where our children could understand engineering ahead of skills and design ahead of engineering. My mind told me that every ITI needed to have a museum where objects like the radial engine of yore can be showcased. Seeing them, students would be able to appreciate great design and look at skills from a different perspective.

On 4 August 2018, Chief Minister Naveen Patnaik inaugurated the first skill museum to be ever set up in an ITI anywhere, where the radial aircraft engine found its place among many other artefacts that had been previously junked. In the days to come, skill museums came to many other ITIs. They added their own special creations for others to see as well. ITI Berhampur showcased a 70-feet tall guitar, made by melting steel from metal structures uprooted by cyclone Fani. That guitar found a place in the Limca Book of Records. At ITI Bhubaneswar, Ganeshi Lal, the Governor of Odisha, personally inaugurated the Skill Museum. The word spread. Civic bodies in need of metal art for parks and public spaces to award winning architects in search of artefacts of lasting beauty came to visit and in time, commissioned artefacts and sculptures for offices and landscapes.

25

Girls Can Do Better

Right from the initial days of my skills journey, I had many defining moments with the girl-child question. The social and systemic stereotypes about girls were hitting me hard. I saw issues everywhere even when no one else did. That was because I was coming from the outside world and what was an aberration to me was nothing odd or unusual for others who lived within the system. The first problem I saw was in girl-child enrolment in ITIs. Unlike in DDU-GKY programmes where girls were the majority, in ITIs, the enrolment of girls was just 6 per cent. Yet, it was the ITIs that offered longer duration and hence, more sustainable career options. But girls were not there.

The issue was not just poor enrolment. Once enrolled, they opted for courses like stenography, computers (whatever that means) and dress design, a euphemism for tailoring. At Cuttack ITI, when I was told a batch of girls were being trained for stenography, I was aghast. Who on earth does stenography these days? For those who do not know, it is a vestige of an old past where bosses could not type. They dictated, meaning spoke out, a letter. Someone rapidly wrote it down on a 'steno-book', using symbols for shorthand of words the boss uttered, then took the steno-book and went to a typewriter. The steno then hammered out the shorthand using the typewriter into a draft printout and ran back to the boss with it, who then corrected it by hand for mistakes. Then, the stenographer again ran back, typed it all in and produced the final sheet. The stereotype of a stenographer, particularly in the private sector, was that of a subservient and sometimes efficient young woman who paid particular attention to her appearance. The typewriter and the shorthand notebook have died a long time ago, but in ITI Cuttack, they still ran a course in stenography.

While stenography was a fossil, computers were not. Except that, the girls were not really learning anything that would get them a sustainable job. While there are still some jobs available for data entry operators, they are vanishing because of technologies like bar code readers and contactless devices. For the girl and her parents, saying that she was learning computers was aspirational and it did not quite matter that no one was taking her time at ITI seriously. In most cases, it was what is popularly known as time-pass. The fashion design course ran for a year and had more tangible and predictable outcomes. At least a girl could build an extra income making dresses for neighbours and in an exceptional case, perhaps even become an Anima Sahoo.

Why was a girl learning stenography or computers or only dress design? Why wasn't she training to be an electrician, refrigeration and air-conditioning mechanic or automotive technician? Oh, those are 'hard trades', I was told. Hard trades are for boys. In any case, parents do not like girls in 'boy trades'. And, very importantly, serious employers did not like to hire girls for such jobs. But the issue of hard trade options was secondary. To begin with, the enrolment numbers had always stood at a poor 6 per cent!

* * *

Kalahandi, meaning the black earthen pitcher, is the name of a district in Odisha with its district headquarters in Bhawanipatna. Once upon a time, the district was infamous for abject poverty and recurrent famine. Many of its villagers went away en masse as indentured labour to other states. In 1985, when Rajeev Gandhi was the prime minister, Kalahandi tore the nation's conscience apart when Phanas Punji, a tribal woman, sold her sister-in-law, Bonita for forty rupees and a saree, to a man who was looking for a wife for his blind son.* When I was visiting Kalahandi in May 2016, it was no longer the face of famine.

It was known has *Bhatahandi,* the rice pot. Thanks to sustained development efforts, government

---

* Mohanty, Debabrata. 'How Odisha Turned Food Surplus.' *Times of India*, 25 June 2022. Available at https://timesofindia.indiatimes.com/city/bhubaneswar/how-odisha-turned-food-surplus/articleshow/92463724.cms.

investment in irrigation and agriculture, it had become one of the top rice-producing districts of India. Today, it has a university, a government medical college and of course, the ITI in Bhawanipatna. The ITI being the oldest among them all.

When I reached the ITI, I was accompanied by Dr Brundha D. She was a medical doctor who had joined the IAS and was now the district collector. I was always encouraged to see women as district collectors because the entire district knows who the collector is and revers that person. A successful woman like her was a powerful icon for every girl in a district. As Dr Brundha and I looked around, I saw practically no girls in the classes. Instead of asking the principal why that was, I asked the boys in the class a different question. How many of you have a younger sister at home? Two-third of the hands went up. For the record, unlike coastal districts where the sex ratio was dropping, in tribal districts, the ratio was much better, even healthy in many places. I turned to the principal and told him that the World Girl Child Day was round the corner. Every year, it is celebrated on 14 July. This Girl Child Day, every boy was to bring a sister to the ITI. The girl was to get a free run in the workshops. She could touch machines, ask questions and wander around. Feed her well at the canteen. Now, I told the boys, 'Each one, get one'. For those who did not have a sister, they were to bring their 'rakhi sister'. In villages, the girl next door is also considered a sister. When I visited the same ITI after a gap of almost five years, the girl child enrolment had crossed 20 per cent.

Many things in life are governed by the idea of priority. Change is the child of priority. It is amazing how much inert potential exists everywhere, waiting for it to be labelled as priority.

In places like Kalahandi, we did not just want to increase girl-child enrolment. We wanted to break the 'soft trade, hard trade' mould. This required a concerted effort to raise the awareness by holding up role models among young women who had come to an ITI and had broken through the gender divide. The search led to the discovery of great, inspiring stories from across the state. A riveting film was made on the theme and distributed over social media.

My star search had led to the discovery of Muni Tigga at one time. Now, as the evening sky starts unravelling blinking lights one after the other when you train your eyes to find the first one, we saw them everywhere.

We found Sunita Nayak who was running a Suzuki Service Centre where she was the workshop manager, overseeing the work of twenty men. We met Siromani Horo, once a loco pilot and now monitoring process equipment at Rourkela Steel Plant. We found Harapriya Bhoi at TRL Krosaki Refractories, where she was taming heavy machinery. We met Snehalata Pradhan who was working as a draftsman (Sorry, that title needs changing. Seriously!) and Persis Pradhan who worked in the finance department of Mahanadi Coal Fields. Suddenly, it was a starlit sky.

* * *

In 2016, when we thought of fixing the ITIs, one of the goals was to get more girls to come in and to get more of them to opt for the hard trades and do the 'dangerous' stuff that were assumed to be male preserve. We needed to break the gender stereotype. By 2024, girls constituted a third of the total student intake in government ITIs in Odisha and, by then, most were opting for trades like electrician, refrigeration and air-conditioning mechanic and welder. It is in that backdrop that my visit to Barbil, in the iron belt of Keonjhar district, becomes interesting.

Barbil, with its sister town of Joda, is home to one of the world's greatest iron ore and manganese reserves. The two are mining towns. The government ITI in Barbil did not have any particular claim to fame other than being a better than average ITI, until one day in 2022, when Principal Debashish Bisi was visited by a man named Manoj Choudhary who was an assistant manager, Human Resources, from JSW Steel that was given mining rights in the area.

Chowdhary wanted to recruit girls from the ITI as per an unusual mandate from his bosses. Debashish Bisi was an ardent believer in girl power and JSW's desire to hire girls in their mines got him very excited. He lined up twenty and of these, fourteen were selected. But finally, eight joined. Mining is not for the faint-hearted, girl or not.

The eight girls were sent to work as electricians, drilling machine operators and one of them, Tanushree Patra, to drive a Komatsu 785 dumper truck. Tanushree weighs 48 kilograms and is five feet and four inches tall. In striking contrast, the Komatsu 785 excavator weighs 72,000 kilogrammes and stands more than sixteen feet tall. The tires of the excavator are taller than her. She handles the 1200 hp, off-road dumper truck with 101.6 US tons of iron ore in one go. The Komatsu 785 is an intelligent equipment and costs half a million US dollars. It has more lines of software code embedded in its engine than perhaps a small plane and is capable of being an internet node. In short, it requires sophisticated handling and not brute force.

Tanushree's mother came from Nuamundi and her father was from Joda, both iron ore towns, Tanushree was born in 2003. After a few years, her sister arrived. At this juncture in their lives, her father abandoned the family for another woman. Her mother raised the two girls all by herself, selling *bhoga*, temple offering devotees buy to offer to God, from a portion of the small dwelling that was her shop. When Tanushree finished schooling, everyone told her mother not to educate her any further. After all, like any other girl at fifteen, she would need to be married off soon. Why waste efforts sending her for higher studies?

Neither Tanushree, nor her mother were buying this argument after seeing what a man could do to wreck his family. This is when her mother learnt about the government ITI in Barbil.

Mother and daughter did not quite know what an ITI meant but were told by the Principal Debashish Das that after paying an admission fee of just Rs 100, all subsequent costs would be picked up by the government. Tanushree got enrolled.

Around the time I got to know Tanushree, I also got to know Rukhsar Khatoon, her contemporary at the same ITI who joined JSW's 'she-brigade'. Unlike

Tanushree, she had both parents at home. Her mother stitched dresses for people in the neighbourhood and her father sold *manohari* items, trinkets, on a cycle. After marrying off the older two out of the six girls, there wasn't much left to think of providing a future to the younger ones. Rukhsar says, she wanted to study science at a college but that was out of question. While everyone seemed to get ahead, she and her sisters were going to get left behind. With a sense of failure, she came to the ITI so that at least she would land a job somewhere. After studying electrical trade for two years, she joined JSW, where she was further trained at their Vocational Training Centre for two months before becoming an electrician in the mines where she maintained transformers. When I last spoke to her, she had been shifted to drilling operations where she handled core drilling machines.

Tanushree and Rukhsar are not alone. They are part of a cohort of six girls who are called the 'Iron Girls of Odisha'. Yet, there is a part of the story that does not get reflected in the enthusiastic reportage of the media and adulation they routinely get. These girls worry about their future, they wonder where the gross salary of Rs 20,000 a month would take them in their lives.

If they need to get better jobs that assure them of better wages, they now need a diploma from a polytechnic. The good polytechnics worth their salt are mostly run by the government and require regular attendance in class.

* * *

The state government had come up with a scholarship scheme under the name Sudakshya that picked up the entire cost of a girl's education at an ITI (later extended to the three-year polytechnic course as well). This included her hostel expense and a top-up kitty to help her settle down in a new place of work after the course got over and the girl took up employment. The financial benefit was delivered through a direct bank transfer to every student. In the ensuing years, the intake of girls steadily increased. By 2024, one in every three students in an ITI was a girl.

But that increase had only so much to do with generous scholarships. A lot was contributed to by the principals of ITIs who made it their mission to put more girls behind machines. One such man was Dr Rajat Panigrahi.

Youth who enrol at an ITI come from the bottom of the pyramid. These kids, for their academic performance in high school or their family's financial reasons, cannot pursue higher education. At some level, they are considered as losers. Dr Panigrahi's job was to instil pride in them, put them through rigorous training and enable them for a job by the time they were eighteen or nineteen.

Dr Panigrahi had many challenges along the way. One of them was attracting girls to come to an ITI. Given the thrust, it was but natural to give extra attention to the girls who were already enrolled at an ITI because they were the ones become role models for the other girls.

In this backdrop, Dr Panigrahi was having consistent problems with Didi Sethi who, despite repeated warnings, was irregular with her attendance. One day, Dr Panigrahi threw the girl out of the ITI because she was simply not getting the message. The day after Didi Sethi was thrown out, Dr Panigrahi had an unexpected visitor. It was her mother. She barged in to his room and what followed was a tirade of accusations.

Who did he think he was, the woman shouted. If attendance was such a big deal, her daughter should be going to a proper college than come to an ITI. 'And whatever may be the reason, you principal,' she yelled, 'you have ruined my daughter's life just the same way my mother has ruined my sister's life. My sister is now a millstone round my neck for the rest of my life. You have added another millstone to that.' An already startled Dr Panigrahi was now quite flummoxed with that accusation.

It turned out that the woman's younger sister had been given away in marriage at a very young age because her mother, a slum dweller, saw a young girl as a risk. Soon after her marriage, the girl's husband started abusing her and one day, he simply threw her out and went away with another woman. The girl came back and had now become a liability, an additional mouth to be fed. Didi Sethi's family was already struggling to make both ends meet. By throwing the girl out of the ITI, Dr Panigrahi had, in effect, made things more difficult for her. And perhaps, Didi Sethi would have the same fate as her young aunt.

Next morning, Dr Panigrahi decided to pay the family a visit on his way to the ITI. There, he started to understand the complex reason behind Didi Sethi's attendance problem.

The family had only one source of income: selling vegetables on a pushcart. Everything, therefore, revolved around the cart in the household. Someone took the empty cart early in the morning to the local wholesale market and brought it back laden with vegetables. Another member of the family then sorted them and arranged the vegetables neatly, readying the cart to be taken to the locality where the vegetables were hawked. When the cart returned and this time with unsold vegetables, it had to be tidied up, rearranged so that in the afternoon, it would go around the locality one more time. Once the cart returned at night, it needed to be washed and readied for the early morning trip to the wholesale market the next day. Every adult in the family had an assigned task associated with the cart. Didi's task was to clean it and rearrange it when it returned from the market after its morning run. There was one problem in this entire algorithm. It was difficult to predict the exact time it would come back on any given day. It depended on so many unknown variables. Some days, the produce sold quickly, some days it didn't. Some days, weather played truant because it rained. Some days, there were too many sellers. Then, of course, there were other factors like a political rally, a bandh by the local hooligans or an unexpected heatwave. Anything. Because the exact time for the cart to return was unpredictable, Didi Sethi could not show up at the ITI at a predictable time.

Now Dr Panigrahi understood the root cause and the impossibility of her performance. The clock of the ITI and the one in Didi Sethi's home were tuned to different frequencies. He took her back with him and rearranged her schedule at the ITI. She was told to attend only the theory classes in the morning and go back home to wait for the cart to return. Then she could come for the afternoon shift of the ITI when she could take her practical lessons at the workshop.

With this new arrangement, Didi Sethi eventually completed her two-year course. She was picked up by Enfield India, where she assembled Bullet motorcycles.

Around the time that the Didi Sethi saga was unfolding, Dr Panigrahi was invited by a local juvenile shelter home for girls. A juvenile shelter home is run by the government, or under government supervision, for youth under eighteen years of age who may come there for a variety of reasons. These could be abandonment, rescue from trafficking or for brushes with the law. When they turned eighteen, the inmates had to fend for themselves. The girls there had no idea what an ITI was. When Dr Panigrahi explained that an ITI was a place where students came after their high school and learnt vocational trades, the girls were crestfallen. Most of them had not finished high school.

As Dr Panigrahi returned from the shelter home, their disappointment haunted him. Suddenly, it struck him, he could still take them in for a one-year course in painting. Not painting as in art. This was a course for painting buildings, automobiles and other machinery. For this trade, eighth-class pass was okay. The issue, however, was, what does a girl do after learning the trade? Without figuring that out, he sent for them and the girls arrived at the ITI.

Any system is designed to create hurdles for someone who does not look familiar to it. The shelter home girls did not quite fit in. The regular students and teachers avoided them. Dr Panigrahi had created a problem in trying to solve one. Anyhow, the girls started learning how to use painting equipment. Then, out of nowhere, the girls solved it by themselves.

One fine morning, without asking anyone for permission, the girls started painting the walls of the ITI. Where once dirty walls stood, sprang neatly painted ones. Their assimilation and acceptance were over. Today, some of them work at automobile plants in Pune and Gujarat.

* * *

Five years after my first visit to ITI Bhawanipatna, I returned to find five-fold increase in girl-child enrolment. They were everywhere. High energy. Learning and working shoulder to shoulder with the boys. We sat down to review the placement data of students and, to my disappointment, I found most of them were not taking up employment after finishing their course. Why was this happening?

The principal explained to me that the Sudakshya Scheme was a big boost for girls to enrol at an ITI. The tuition, the uniform, the hostel board and lodge were all picked up by the government. For the parents of young girls who had just finished school and were unlikely to go to college for whatever reason, this was perfect in the interim until their marriage was fixed in a couple of years. At home, they were a risk because they were sixteen, perhaps seventeen years old. At the ITI, they were kept busy. It was a safe place. By the time they graduated, the family had enough time to find a suitable match and get them married. Problem solved.

Whether it was Didi Sethi's story or that of the Kalahandi girls, who learnt welding, turning or how to become a qualified electrician at the cost of the government but were merely on their way to wedlock and childbearing, it is sobering to realize that the social development trajectory is a complex thing that often escapes policymakers and assorted well-wishers of the poor.

We build models that may apply to us and we go on to simply superimpose them on others without understanding the entire picture in their context. Policy planners, decision-makers and even activists oftentimes seek easy solutions, linking an apparent problem with an apparent solution. The world does not work precisely on the cause-effect principle. Every problem, if it is worth calling a problem, is complex. Complexity nests in what we call 'systems'. These systems, several of them working at the same time, have inter-connected dependencies. Unless we understand them in their totality, we cannot come up with solutions that deliver the intended result, solutions that are sustainable.

My leadership lessons were largely honed in the corporate sector. I had prided myself for my ability to understand 'systems' at work. But only when exposed to the significantly bigger challenges of government that must work with social forces, deeply ingrained ideas and beliefs, I learnt to be humble. I learnt to accept that the so-called leadership interventions are often simplistic and even naive.

Along the journey however, every day was beautiful and every day brought disappointment. Sometimes, those disappointments brought frustration. But, dealing with frustrations, each time I reminded myself what Mother Teresa had beautifully said. 'God does not require us to succeed. He only requires us to try.'

26

A Skill Anthem, a Boy Rapper and the Caravan

We needed to build excitement that something fresh, young, beautiful and vibrant was happening. We needed to make skill development and vocational training aspirational. The 'Skilled in Odisha' brand needed a visual identity to catch everyone's imagination. Through an engaged process, we zeroed in on the global ad agency Leo Burnett and coincidentally, the chief creative officer, Raj Deepak Das happened to be from Odisha. When he learnt about the project, he flew down to see me. The son of a government doctor in Odisha, he had studied in vernacular-medium government schools. After high school, he was rudderless for some time, unsure of where he was headed. His parents were quite concerned. Then, he got himself a seat in the Garden City College in Bengaluru.

After his studies in Bengaluru, he joined MICA, once known as Mudra Institute of Communications, Ahmedabad. Then magic happened. A brilliant career at leading agencies overseas and India, saw him emerge as the trailblazing chief creative officer of Leo Burnett. Raj Deepak took personal responsibility to visually interpret the idea of Skilled in Odisha.

The common misconception is that branding is a very modern and corporate concept. In reality, branding is an ancient tradition. It was the sovereign, historically the monarch who created flags, emblems and insignia, whether in peace or war, to provide identity, seek alignment, invoke authority and deter enemies. In post-Independence India, major transformative initiatives of the government like the family-planning programme were conveyed through the inverted red triangle that told every Indian, *Hum Do, Hamare Do.*

The cooperative movement of the National Dairy Development Board under the leadership of Verghese Kurien created the Amul brand, with the Amul girl who has transcended generations as an endearing embodiment of all things good about milk and butter. The 'God's Own Country' and the 'Incredible India' campaigns, credited to NITI Aayog Vice Chairman Amitabh Kant were through the government's initiatives as well.

Raj Deepak Das and his team got to work and after several iterations created a memorable logo. The logo was accompanied by a skill anthem, '*Ye toh hunnar hunnar ki baat hai*' where the singer tells young boys and girls of ITIs, 'You are no different from those who go to the moon. You are made of the same stuff'. Next, we roped in rap singer, Samir Rishu Mohanty, who is half-Japanese and half-Odia to compose a song that created a flutter in the hitherto staid government system. We engaged Nilamadhab Panda, the man who directed *I am Kalam*, to make a film to glamorize vocational training in the eyes of the youth. He made a short film with leading Odia cine actress Prakruti Mishra who was shown doing all the tough trades in an ITI in the film, hitherto considered boys only. At the closing of the movie, she rides out on a Bullet motorcycle to prove that girls do better.

So far so good, except that building a brand or creating excitement does not work if communication remains a headquarters focused agenda. We needed to take it to where it mattered the most: the districts.

During the early days of the journey, I made three discoveries: the role of the district administration, albeit the collector, had not changed since I grew up in Odisha as a boy. In fact, it had expanded manifold. My second discovery was the rise of grassroots leadership beyond the elected representatives like the members of Parliament (MPs) and the members of the Legislative Assemblies (MLAs). Once elected, the voters seldom see their MPs. They are given to Delhi. People look up to their MLAs more closely but their day-to-day life is really intertwined with their panchayat. The panchayat samiti is the fulcrum of self-governance and the chairman of the panchayat samiti plays a very direct role in local self-governance. While the idea of panchayats and panchayat samitis are very old, they really did not play a huge role in the affairs of the government when we grew up. Their presence was benign. Now that was no longer the case. Without the concurrence of 6798 panchayats, you could not push any agenda of the government. And the third discovery for me was the unbelievable rise of the women self-help groups (SHGs) that now dotted the entire state. They were organized under the women and child development department (WCD) and even as they were meant to be a catalyst for economic upliftment of women, in reality, they had blossomed into a powerful political force in the state with an astounding 70 lakh members organized into 6 lakh SHGs. We needed to take the message of skill development to the district administration, the panchayats and the SHGs. To make the skill story heard, we needed to get the attention and involvement of the collectors of all the thirty districts and very importantly, that of the 6798 panchayat samiti heads and at least some of the 6 lakh SHGs. These were the people who were the closest to our target group.

***

On 15 July 2017, coinciding with World Skills Day, the chief minister flagged off a Skill Caravan from the Special ITI for youth with vision, hearing and motor movement problems. The caravan, consisting of specially equipped buses, carried officials from various skill departments and role models chosen from the ten, six, four, two drive. They carried information material and set out to reach all the thirty districts of the state over the next fortnight. The caravan moved on four different routes to cover the entire state. Along its path, stopping to engage with high school students, their teachers. We showed them Prakriti Mishra's film and played Samir Rishu Mohanty's rap song that electrified the audience. It stopped at every skill training centre on its path where the panchayat samiti functionaries and SHG members came to discuss the skills agenda. To some places, the Skill Caravan took along an inflatable, air-conditioned, mobile Dolby theatre, something I had never seen in my life before. Skill icons were feted wherever the caravan stopped. They spoke to audiences about their life's journey.

I was simply amazed at the outpour of excitement everywhere. In many places, villagers broke into traditional song and dance. SHG members received us with tilaks and threw flowers and rice on us. School children came in droves. The local press, particularly the digital media, simply lapped it up for its sheer novelty.

People usually think the government is a boring place. That a bureaucrat is a sedate and unadventurous, albeit a dull creature. In getting on with our task, we needed to break that image as much as change the mirror and sometimes the wall itself.

In my mind, the caravan was just a metaphor for what lay in front of us. It was going to be a journey without an end.

27

Bringing the Opera to the Rainforest

Often in our lives, events that seem random and unconnected may come to shape our destiny. This is so very difficult to comprehend. As Steve Jobs famously said, 'You can only connect the dots looking backward.'

Consider this as a classic example.

Ahmedabad, Prime Minister Narendra Modi's city, was hosting a skill event. A part of the extravaganza was an elaborate skill exhibition. The exhibits included a demonstration of alternate reality/virtual reality (AR/VR) equipment for enhancing skills. The use case was an oil-rig simulation. Imagine you are a welder or electrician or any other skilled worker with a role to play on an offshore oil rig on the high seas. Now think of this: these rigs are not stable platforms. They can move and shake based on the wind, the waves and the downpour. Stormy conditions may be predictable but not the kind of impact they may have in a particular given position and time due to the many variables on the high seas. You have a repair job to do on the rig and it is time critical. As you go up the rig and a sudden gust of wind blows, the platform below shakes, the level of complexity in fixing a problem becomes very different and this could also become life-threatening. How do you train someone for something like this without going through a live situation? This is where AR/VR comes in. With AR/VR, you can run simulations of a hundred such experiences on an oil rig, without getting on to the real thing, so that when you actually arrive on the real oil rig, you have the mental model built in already. You feel that you have been there and done that. This is nothing new. Pilots go through simulation training. Before you fly the real thing, they put you through mandatory simulation. AR/VR makes it possible with sophisticated computer programming and visualization techniques at a fraction of the cost of a flight simulator.

When the prime minister was going round the exhibition, he took particular interest in the AR/VR equipment on display. Everyone was quick to notice his interest and as is apt, got activated on the AR/VR trip.

The National Skill Development Corporation (NSDC), an extended arm of the Ministry of Skill Development and Entrepreneurship created as a partnership between the government and industry bodies, was asked to pursue AR/VR.

For starters, it sent a delegation to Singapore to understand AR/VR by engaging with the companies that had showcased the technology. NSDC's CEO Manish Kumar called me and asked if I would like to come along. Manish was a Tripura-cadre IAS officer who had quit the IAS to join the World Bank, where among his many achievements was working on the Swachh Bharat Mission with the Government of India. For his work with the tribal women of Tripura, he was inducted as a Mason Fellow at Harvard. I had always liked him as an outstanding, authentic leader. Now, he was the CEO of NSDC.

When Manish offered to let me tag along, I was obviously very keen. I had expected a large delegation from India. But it turned out, not many people were there on the trip, barring a few fairly junior and disinterested folks from a few government outfits. Once we were in Singapore and attended a few meetings with the various AR/VR companies, I was quick to realize that it was a big waste of my time. I had expected a solid technological deep dive with people who had designed the stuff, but the folks in Singapore were just a bunch of resellers, not the manufacturers, far less the designers. They simply peddled the gizmos. The technology used was basically high-quality video game stuff but nothing more. It was all based on proprietary software and cost millions of dollars. I was disappointed.

At the end of the two-day visit, and somewhat as a filler, there was an option to visit a certain skill institute called ITE. I was told, Prime Minister Narendra Modi, during his 2015 visit to Singapore, was shown this place. Almost everyone on the delegation prioritized sightseeing over visiting the ITE. Having seen Singapore's attractions many times in the past, I decided to go to ITE, not expecting too much.

Accompanied by Dr Vandana Bhatnagar, chief programme officer and Jyotsna, deputy head of corporate planning and strategy at NSDC, I went to ITE. Little did I realize, from this point on, everything was to change forever for our skill development journey in Odisha.

ITE, is shorthand for Institute of Technical Education. It was started in 1992. In Singapore, the vocational and technical education system is similar to ours but, of course, with vastly different outcomes. ITE is at the bottom of the technical and vocational training (TVET) hierarchy. It is meant for students who have completed Class X and want a two-year course in an industrial trade or services to get an entry-level job in a manufacturing or a services company. This corresponds to the two years our students spend at an ITI. Above the ITE, are the polytechnics that take students who are academically a notch above, for a three-year course and beyond the polytechnic are the engineering institutions like the National Technical University.

The ITE of Singapore differed from our ITIs by a lightyear for many reasons. Two examples would suffice. ITE has just three campuses, each built at an outlay of a billion Singapore dollars. ITE is an example of what I call maximalist thinking. The second reason is perhaps even more telling. ITE produces a workforce that, at an entry level, lands a student an annual salary of S$34,000. By way of comparison, the student who graduates from a polytechnic gets S$36,000 and the freshly minted engineer from NTU begins at S$48,000. The wage level speaks volumes about what goes into preparing an ITE student for life. At the core of ITE all three layers of great institution building that I had discussed earlier in Chapter 23 were evident. It is indeed a great combination of physical, intellectual and emotional infrastructure that has made ITE an internationally respected, memorable institution.

Upon our arrival at ITE's central campus that day, we were received by Bruce Poh, the chief executive of ITE Education Services (ITEES), the international consulting arm for ITE and his much younger deputy, the chief operating officer, Lim Boon Tiong. They made a small presentation and then gave us a walking tour of the main campus of ITE. Bruce Poh explained that the core of ITE philosophy was 'hands-on, heads-on and hearts-on' skill training. You do not create a world-class workforce by just allocating budgets, constructing large buildings and dumping machines in them. You must approach it with respect and loftiness and love.

The ITE Central campus offered courses through four schools. These were the School of Design and Media, School of Electronics & ICT, School of Business & Services and finally, the School of Engineering.

As I walked around, I was mesmerized. At one place, young boys and girls were working on an aircraft engine. At another, they were working on a robotic assembly line. There were many labs with super sophisticated equipment that I had never seen before. The design studios were breathtaking. The place was ahead of most engineering colleges on India. Then there was the massive open-air performance arena, the vertical gardens all around the high-rise campus, the basketball courts and cafeteria. It was the Disney Land of skill development.

Many years prior, I had seen one of the most captivating movies of my life. The name of the movie was *Fitzcarraldo*. In it, a maverick man, straight from the heartland of the Amazon River, where people of the rainforest lived in poverty and squalor, comes to Rome and watches the opera. He is bewitched. It becomes his life's dream to one day take the opera to the rainforest so the inhabitants can watch it. He does not have the means, but he becomes so obsessed with the idea that he almost loses his mind. Along the way, he meets some unusual benefactors, builds seemingly absurd plans and while executing those, comes across hurdles of unbelievable magnitude.

The staggering story has been told by the internationally acclaimed director, Werner Herzog. It is a must-watch for anyone who wants to understand what dreams are made of. The making of the film, on location, was so fraught with dangers and setbacks that a documentary was produced by the name, *Burden of Dreams*. The visit to ITE had now placed a burden of dreams on my shoulders. I needed my fellow pilgrims to come and see the ITE. It was the opera of Rome. I told myself, if only we could take the opera to the rainforest. Just once.

28

Zheng HE and the Art of Collaboration

After that eye-opening visit to ITE Singapore, I was a possessed person. Somehow, I had to get my A-team to visit the place. I wanted them to feel the place and the only way to do that was to get them out there. The opportunity arrived miraculously one day when I got a mail from ITEES that they were holding a three-day leadership event during August 2017 to share the ITE story and this time, they were going to show the visitors all three campuses. Along with Sanjay Singh, Rajesh Patil and Balwant Singh, I went to Singapore.

When the four of us arrived, we began to see the place with the same pair of eyes. We sat through the many sessions that recounted the story of how ITE was created. The beginning of ITE was intertwined with the story of Singapore's independence. In 1965, independence was thrust upon the people of Singapore by Malaysia. After the British left, Singapore was a part of Malaysia, albeit the very poor part. All the natural resources were in Malaysia. Singapore did not even have drinking water. It was a place of poverty and squalor. One day, the Malaysian Parliament unanimously passed a resolution that they would not have Singapore as a part of Malaysia any longer. This was a huge setback for the people of Singapore who did not want the so-called independence. They needed survival. This was the time when Singapore's father Lee Kuan Yew had cried on television. But once reality settled in people's mind, the task ahead consisted of just two words: nation building. But building with what? The country, 50 kilometres from east to west and 27 kilometres from north to south, with 18,60,000 people, had nothing.

That is when the leadership decided, if they were to build a nation, they would have to build their people. Human resource was the only resource they had. And which level were their people at then? Most were uneducated and untrained. Other than a small port, there was no industry worth the name. Singapore turned to countries like Germany and India (yes, India) to get help in training their people. In India, they spoke to the Tatas who were into steel and automobiles with a reputation for high-quality worker training. This was how ITE was started. Over time, ITE grew from strength to strength as did Singapore. But unlike India, where the skilled worker was never celebrated, Singapore did not forget her skilled workers and kept reinforcing her commitment to human resource development. In time, Singapore boasted of great polytechnics and universities, but it did not happen at the cost of ITE. Even today, the prime minister of Singapore comes to ITE and delivers a state of the nation speech from its campus.

Sanjay Singh, Rajesh Patil, Balwant Singh and I were immersed in the story of Singapore; the way in which the country valued a high school graduate, who was no different from our children of the same age, made them world-class. On the second day of the leadership event, we were taken to the East Campus of ITE where Bruce Poh was to make a presentation. We took our seats as the man went up to the podium and his title slide came up. He was going to speak on, hold your breath, not vocational skill development but, Zheng HE and the art of collaboration.

Zheng HE was a great admiral of the Chinese civilization during the fifteenth century, who had 28,000 sailors and 300 ships under his command. He floated his armada on numerous voyages across the Indian Ocean. He is credited to have advocated the art of collaboration as against the art of war as a leadership strategy and statecraft. His philosophy and doctrine have been the subject of study for generations.

Everyone in the audience had expected to hear from the chief executive of ITEES, some serious nuts-and-bolts talk on TVET and here was a man who was speaking about Zheng HE. His central point was how strategic collaboration at every level, between disciplines, across institutions and across nations was critical to human resource development. At the end of the presentation, I walked up to Bruce Poh and congratulated him. He shook hands politely as do speakers who have just made an impactful presentation and a stranger walks up to express admiration. But I wanted him to remember me. I wanted him to collaborate with us.

Before we were to head home, we sought a separate meeting with Bruce Poh. He was used to such requests and over time, had learnt to take most of them with polite non-seriousness. Non-seriousness because countless international government delegations routinely descended, got momentarily excited, spoke about big plans, sought his hand and then, everything would be gently erased from their minds as their returning flights hit the cruise altitude beyond the Changi airport. But something in that meeting clicked between him and us.

We requested ITE to train our ITI and polytechnic principals in leadership and pedagogy, but we wanted it in big numbers. Could ITE develop a custom programme for us and perhaps extend a special pricing for it? Something touched a chord. At the end, he said he would like to introduce us to a gentleman from the Temasek Foundation. It was the corporate social responsibility arm of Temasek, the $288 billion sovereign fund of the Singapore government. A portion of their profits is used by the foundation to connect Singapore's institutions with international agencies as their enabler for regional development. They were always on the lookout for interesting, innovative ideas with international partners. My own decades of entrepreneurial experience had taught me to pay special attention to words like funds, innovative idea and partnership. Together, they hold a golden combination key. This is when destiny whispers.

Bruce Poh connected us to Gerald Yeo of Temasek Foundation who was also attending the event. We had to sell ourselves, explain what Odisha was, where it was and propose an idea that he could float to his board. We put our heads together and decided to push something that would be memorable from Temasek's standpoint, even before it would be of value to us.

When our meeting took place with Bruce Poh and Gerald Yeo, we suggested that we would send 100 ITI and polytechnic teachers and officials in the skill department to ITE. We wanted them to come and learn about ITE's hands-on, heads-on and hearts-on philosophy. We would send them to Singapore at our cost. We wanted Temasek to pick up the local tab for the duration of their stay and the cost of training.

Gerald Yeo liked it, but his board needed to be convinced. They would want to know the specific goals and deliverables by all the parties, granular details about the selection process for the participants and the actual relevance of the training in Singapore to their institutes. They needed to know both the readiness of our institutes and clarity on how the training at ITE would impact the state of things in Odisha. Finally, how would we take things forward after the training? In short, a detailed project plan.

I was happy to embark on writing a plan, but it occurred to me that I just might have crossed my boundaries. This wasn't Mindtree. True, Chief Minister Naveen Patnaik had promised a free hand but sending a hundred people to Singapore wasn't certainly part of the discussion.

As we flew back, I exactly knew what I was going to do upon my arrival in Bhubaneswar. Speak to the three success managers. And then, go meet the boss.

29

Changi, Here We Come

Chief Secretary Aditya Padhi, Development Commissioner Raju Balakrishnan and Private Secretary to the Chief Minister Karthik Pandian were outliers by any standard. I wonder if an outrageous idea like sending 100 ITI and polytechnic principals and a few administrative officials to Singapore for 'leadership development' would have found a receptive hearing anywhere other than Odisha. The state had a penchant for boldness as long as it was for the people at the bottom of the rung. But then, the government anywhere looks for precedents and is wary of adverse consequences. If there a precedence, it has been done before and if such a thing can be shown on file, ideas are defensible in case of scrutiny. Precedence is a reasonably good bullet-proofing of a bureaucrat's jacket. Then comes the issue of consequences. The bureaucracy is the original master of 'what-if' analysis. If you did this for ITI teachers, what if college teachers demanded the same? And if you did this for college teachers, what would happen to government clerks? This can send any project into an infinite loop. But the three men were extremely supportive. By now, there was also a flight connecting Bhubaneswar to Kuala Lumpur and then onwards to Singapore. If all we needed to do was to foot the airfare and Temasek was going to pick up the rest of the cost, it was not a difficult sell. The fact that such an idea had never been tried anywhere else in India before made it even more alluring. It was bold. It was audacious. They liked it.

The chief minister was briefed, and he blessed the idea. But this is not how governments work. All this was track-two activity and we still needed to send the file, with the detailed note sheets, through the proper channels with multiple concerned departments including finance and anyone could ask awkward questions. Sometimes, the system that had previously blessed an idea can become cautious and reticent.

Any overseas visit by big groups of government servants is always seen as junket, it is easy to attract bad press. But we kept our fingers crossed. The files were moved through the proper channels. At one stage, Pinaki Patnaik came to me and cautioned that some people were asking how we would measure impact. I told Pinaki, for starters, I wanted these 100 people to return from Singapore, draw a loan from their own provident fund account and take their spouse and children for a visit to Singapore. That wasn't a flippant statement. It was metaphoric. Our job was to build aspiration in leaders on a deeply personal level. If the leaders do not dream of the world, how could they make their institutions world-class?

Meanwhile, Gerald Yeo and a team from ITE visited Odisha and spent time at several ITI locations to assess the situation on the ground, the commitment of the government and assess if we had the ability to convert the learning at Singapore to initiate sustainable changes. That visit went well and now we had the green light from both ends.

We identified 100 teachers and administrators. They were to be sent to Singapore in three batches. But before going to Singapore, we brought them for an intensive, pre-Singapore residential training to equip them for the visit. The Institute of Hotel Management of the Government of India was roped in to train them in grooming, etiquette and table manners. The training included an understanding of Singapore's history, culture and reasons for present technological success. They were put through workshops on group learning. There were modules on post-visit expectations from the participants.

Going back to the earlier innocuous question on impact analysis, which was relayed by Pinaki Patnaik, we made an interesting discovery. Except perhaps two or three of them, none of the 100 participants had visited Singapore before. But more importantly, 90 per cent of the participants never had a passport in their entire life.

In May 2018, the first batch took off from Bhubaneswar for Changi, and it was perhaps one of my life's most exhilarating moments. In time, all the three batches completed their Singapore visit and we got the entire group to sit together for two days to think through what they saw there, what they heard, how they felt and what they would now do to change things. These two days were intense. At the end, the groups presented the mission, vision and values of the new ITI.

MISSION
Transform Society through Skilled Professionals
VISION 2020
Our physical, digital and intellectual **infrastructure** would be among **the best in the country**
At least a third of our graduates will be **women**
We will provide the environment to create **great entrepreneurs and globally employable ITI graduates**
We will **forge industry partnership** at an **international level**
Our students and teachers will be **warriors of the planet** to lead sustainability
VALUES
Human Centricity
Discipline
Integrity
Team Work
Creativity

30

Tilting the Scale

My recollection of a place called Telkoi goes back to 1969 when my eldest brother Debi Prasad, a freshly minted IAS officer, became subdivisional officer of Keonjhar. Telkoi was a block under his jurisdiction. One day, he took me with him on his tour to Telkoi by jeep. Along the way, he told me the significance of the place and why we were going there. Telkoi, he told me did not have an all-weather road. During the four months of monsoon, it was completely cut off from the district headquarters. The only way to communicate with the cut-off Telkoi block was to use the courier pigeons of Odisha Police. The block had a predominantly tribal population who lived on two staple harvests from the local forests: mangoes and jackfruits. The ate them in every form, from small raw ones to kernels and seeds. Along the way, many suffered from diarrhoea. In the entire block, there was just one Primary Health Centre. Meanwhile, the government was trying to get the local folks to cultivate Taichung rice to wean them from living predominantly on forest produce and suffering from the resultant malnutrition. The government was not succeeding because the tribals started sucking the milk of the rice husks even before they had ripened. Half a century after, I met a twenty-five-year-old, self-confident woman named Kalika Sahu from Telkoi at the Boeing unit of Tata Advanced Systems Limited (TASL) in Hyderabad.

I had a hard time associating Telkoi with her.

Yet there she was, a daughter of Telkoi, drilling, riveting and making aircraft body for Boeing planes. Her father used to work for Vedanta, the mining company and had since retired to tend to his five acres of land. She is the middle child among five sisters. Kalika finished her high school in arts from the Charigarh Mahavidyalaya in Telkoi and from there, enrolled in a DDU-GKY training in Keonjhar for learning 'computers', meaning call centre work.

This is when the PIA sent her, along with four other girls, to Bhubaneswar where TASL recruiters had arrived to select young girls as part of Aspire, their gender-diversity initiative. Three girls got selected, not comprehending what TASL was, what aircraft body manufacturing entailed and where Hyderabad was exactly. Of the three girls who made it, only two accepted the offer and joined. They came to Hyderabad. Kalika's friend dropped out after one year. She was homesick. Kalika has stayed on since and has risen from drilling and riveting aircraft bodies, to become a production supervisor with her own jig. Jig?

It is a group of workers responsible for a module of production. She is justifiably proud of her work. Where is she headed, I wonder and ask her goal in life. She has just one word: independence.

Along with Kalika, I met Anita Swain who comes from a small village near the Biraja Temple in Jajpur where she studied at the local school and did a high school course in science at the nearby Baruneswar Mahavidyalaya. After that, she was at loose ends for a year. In the meantime, her father came back from Hyderabad where he used to work and decided to stay back. He wanted to tend to his small holding of land and eventually set up an afternoon snack shack on the road.

Anita, like Kalika, heard about a DDU-GKY training centre in Bhubaneswar. One of her friends was heading there and she tagged along, only to realize upon her enrolment, that she was in a cohort of school dropouts.

She was disheartened. She couldn't fit in. This is when she learnt about TASL's drive nearby. She signed up, moved to Hyderabad, where she has been with TASL since 2017. Despite her family asking her to come back and get married, she has stayed focused on her career. Over the years, she has moved up the ranks. Now she is a technical trainer. TASL has provided both Kalika and Anita the opportunity to pursue a diploma course with NTTF. Anita tells me, she left her village after passing her high school. In her village, no matter what she does in life, she will always be seen as just a high school pass. Her friends got to college. Even as it may only be so in name. The TASL tag, the fact that she now trains others to build something like a Boeing aircraft body, does not mean anything to the people in her village. You simply do not get respect unless you have gone to a college, she tells me.

What does it take to be where they are at TASL? Anita says, it is personal desire to succeed and one's ability to adjust. Ability to adjust? She explains that her friend who had come with her to TASL in 2017 did not like the food or the place where she was staying in Hyderabad. She was not flexible. I turn to Kalika Sahu for her take on the matter. She says, you need three things to succeed: intent, patience and the ability to deal with naysayers.

I have a question for both women. Do their parents, family members, friends, villagers and teachers at their schools know about their work? No, comes the clear candid reply.

As I say goodbye, I have a piece of unsolicited advice to the two. Marry someone you know well; that person must understand what work you do and respect you for that.

* * *

The push for scale in skill building for trades like sewing machine operator had an impact on the ongoing efforts to attract industries in Odisha. The nodal department for attracting investments was the Department of Industries and they started strongly pitching the competitiveness of Odisha by emphasizing the huge push by the state for skill development. Earlier, the messaging was, we will give you land, electricity and subsidies. Now, the messaging was, 'Come to Odisha, we will give you the skilled workforce so you can hit the ground running.' Soon, garment manufacturers like Aditya Birla, Shahi Exports and Jockey came in and set up large units. But while all this was happening, the push for scale took us to other interesting discoveries like the inspiring work happening in places like Tata Aerospace, iMerit and CIPET that were not on the radar of most people in the state.

The visit to Tata Aerospace was truly serendipitous. My long-time friend Dr Aravind of Aravind Eye Hospital was a close friend of Masood Hussainy, executive director on the board of Tata Advanced Systems. Masood had requested Dr Aravind to get me to speak to his leadership team at Hyderabad. He had led the group's foray into aircraft body manufacturing, which had led to strategic partnerships with Boeing, Airbus, Lockheed Martin, Sikorsky and GE. When I arrived in Hyderabad, I was shown around the impressive facility where Boeing and Pilates aircraft bodies were being manufactured. During the visit, Masood told me that they hire a lot of workers from Odisha for aircraft body building. We stopped at one spot where I met Damayanti Swain, once just a high school graduate from Kendrapada, intently putting together a Pilates PC 12 aircraft body, oblivious to our presence as she must be. Later in the day, I met groups of Odia girls who were under training to do similar work. They were all from remote parts of the state. I was curious to know how Tata Aerospace found them. Masood explained to me that the work required high degree of hand-eye coordination, tremendous focus and of course the required skill. For this, they go to DDU-GKY training centres and look for girls who have the hand-eye coordination, focus and aptitude and then they come to Hyderabad where the rest is taught to them. It was a moment of epiphany for me. At DDU-GKY and similar training centres, we did not have the remotest idea that the best of SMOs could actually have aptitude for aircraft body building.

This sense of fungibility was completely lacking in our system. If someone signed up to be a sewing machine operator or a general duty assistant but had the aptitude of a higher or even different order, we did not spot it to make other pathways possible for the trainee.

We did not tell them that they could be elsewhere. In time, the meaning of *elsewhere* took us to Anudip Foundation. It was the skill training sister concern of a little-known company called iMerit.

When I was in my early thirties, working at Wipro as a mid-level manager, we used to hear about a lady named Radha Basu who had been sent from the Silicon Valley to set up Hewlett Packard's India operations. She was an exception in the male-dominated tech world at the time. Radha Basu was an icon for us and we knew that one day, she may even lead HP worldwide. After a stellar assignment in India, she returned to the US and left HP. In time, she set up iMerit that today has more than 5000 employees who create tech products and serve customers in the area of data-centric artificial intelligence. iMerit boasts of customers like eBay, Johnson & Johnson, Microsoft and Trip Advisor. Even as I had always admired Radha Basu during my IT industry days, I had never met her until one day when I was invited to inaugurate Anudip Foundation's training centre in Bhubaneswar. The centre was located in the unlikely area called Jharpada, which is famous only for the largest jail in the state. When I arrived there, my first delightful surprise was meeting Radha Basu herself! It was a fan boy moment. She and her husband had set up the Anudip Foundation a decade ago, initially to help rural youth in the Gangetic plain to get trained in IT and find work. In time, they had expanded operations all over India. Likewise, iMerit had pioneered the employment and upskilling of Anudip Foundation's graduates in cutting edge AI work, being a rare tech company with over 50 per cent of its workforce being women.

And here she was, in person. But even greater than the joy of meeting Radha Basu was the eye-opening experience of what Anudip and iMerit were doing in Jharpada. Anudip had mobilized high school graduates, screened them for aptitude and provided them additional computer skills. Now, these young folks, mostly girls, were employed by iMerit and were training computers to learn! If that sounds abstract, consider this:

A leading autonomous vehicle company of the world whose name iMerit does not disclose, has to continuously train its vehicles. An autonomous vehicle is a nothing but a bank of computers that drive a vehicle in place of a human driver with the help of multiple cameras, sensors and AI. In cities like San

Francisco, driverless cars like Waymo are already in service that pick up and drop passengers. Driverless trucks are in beta deployment as well. Similarly, cars like Tesla and Mercedes Benz and others at the top end have degrees of autonomy built in. You can drive a Tesla on the highway without holding (controlling) its steering stick (not a wheel any more) and the car can do all that a driver does and sometimes better. This is deep tech with deep complexity. But these machines need to learn what may be intuitive to a human being in crucial situations. Imagine a human being driving a car at a busy intersection. The car has moved, an empty jerrycan flies across the road, driven by a gust of wind. The driver will notice it instantly and carefully avoid the object, skirting it to move forward. But what if it is a toddler? The reaction will be entirely different. The driver will hit the brake hard, even at the risk of taking a collision from the car behind. The volume and speed of the jerrycan and a toddler can be the same. How does the car, in the blink of a camera, see and know the difference? Machines will need to learn human-centric decision-making and not just respond mechanically to a situation based on cold data and set algorithms. iMerit trains machines to be smart like human beings.

For this, it builds tools and thousands of scenarios and then makes machines to learn them. The young women and men in Jharpada were working on precisely that!

Like iMerit was reinventing skill development, there was CIPET, a Government of India organization that works in the area of plastic technology. They have a campus in Mancheswar and a larger one in Balasore.

CIPET runs free, six-month-long courses in plastic technology. One of the employers who hire their trainees is Takahata in Nimrana, Haryana. There I met Subasini, the daughter of a private car driver. She runs super sophisticated machinery that make automotive plastics for car companies. There are dozens of Odia workers in Takahata.

What makes Takahata special is this Japanese company is a signatory to United Nation's Sustainability Goals (SDG) for 2030. A big part of this is women empowerment. Takahata is on its way to ensure more than 50 per cent of its workforce will be women in the future and more significantly, workers like Subasini, Class X pass, can grow to positions like the general manager of the plant. The company prides itself for creating pathways for that to happen for its workers. But for starters, unlike the footwear company in Bahadurgarh, Takahata treats its workers with care and respect. Subasini and her friends get a good salary, food, quality accommodation and commute to the factory in company buses.

* * *

Fix, Scale and Accelerate. That was the core of the overall strategy we had chosen in the beginning and the *fix* part was clearly starting to gather great momentum. Very importantly, the leadership on the ground was now an active part of the vision community and in fact, they were leading it. Our job was to step back and be the enablers. The *scale* part of the strategy was for moving the needle for the short-term skilling programmes like DDU-GKY, both in volume and quality. After we visited places like Bahadurgarh, Tiruppur, Bengaluru and Trivandrum and made contact with both employers and our youth, the first set of people to respond positively were many of the PIAs themselves. To begin with, they started paying more attention to the well-being of our trainees at the training centres. They started asking us to visit the training centres and encourage their own employees to motivate the trainees. They took us to their star employers to help them build stronger connections and show our sponsorship. The leadership team at Odisha Rural Development and Marketing Society (ORMAS) that was responsible for running the DDU-GKY programme started outreach in far-flung places to seek out role models amongst their alumni—this was a rub off of the *ten, six, four, two* initiative we had first started in ITIs and polytechnics. In large cities around India, events were organized to get skilled workers together, honouring role models and celebrating skills. The biggest such event took place in Tiruppur where thousands of Odia workers joined in for day-long events like sports and musical performances.

* * *

In the years to come, our job would be to locate companies like Tata Aerospace, iMerit and Takahata, expand the scope of outstanding PIAs like CIPET and constantly work on bridging the information asymmetry that prevents girls like Damayanti and Subasini from soaring high.

Part VI

Things Fail, Things Work

31

Mission Aborted

As of 2024, there were 14,312 ITIs in India and 2579 polytechnics. Of these, more than 12,000 ITIs are privately run and the number of privately run polytechnics is 1735. Some of the privately run ITI and polytechnics are absolutely fantastic, better than many government-run ones. A vast majority are mediocre to average and a good many are simply rackets. The first private ITI I had visited near Sambalpur had left me completely shattered. There were hardly any machines in the so-called workshop, two decrepit classrooms and two students in a dirty, shabby room which was the 'hostel'. The husband-and-wife team that ran the place told me it was empty because all but these two students had gone home to help their families harvest the crops. Any roadside auto-garage would inspire more confidence that this private ITI. A few months after, I had visited the government ITI at Subarnapur. It had low enrolment. When I asked the principal the reason, he said that the private ITI nearby was luring away his students with an offer to get them a certificate without the need for them to clock attendance for Rs 14,000. An ITI is a skill training institution. The curriculum is based on 70 per cent marks for practical work at the examination. How could anyone qualify without going through the rigours of workshop practice if attendance is trivialized? The net impact is that the 14,312 ITIs in India and the 2579 polytechnics churn out lakhs and lakhs of students every year who are not job-worthy.

In the backdrop of all that, when I took charge in 2016, I was briefed about an ongoing project that the state had initiated the year before in collaboration with the Asian Development Bank (ADB).

ADB is not just a bank but a development catalyst and it engages with countries in the Asian region on infrastructure and allied projects. It gives participating governments low-interest loans and expert consulting on long-term projects with the objective of social development. It brings collaboration opportunities for such projects through its vast partner network. Sometime in 2014, ADB and the Government of Odisha had signed an MoU to fund the setting up of eight Advanced Skill Training Institutes in various parts of the state. It had an outlay of about Rs 1200 crore with a 250-crore upfront investment by the state and the balance provided by ADB as a long-term, low-interest loan. The idea had its genesis in the fact that most students who came out of vocational training offered by ITIs and polytechnics were unemployable.

Based on studies, it was estimated that the state produced almost 1,00,000 ITI and polytechnic students every year. A vast majority of them were not fit for employment. In the end, the students who were not worthy of employment became a social liability. Hence, ADB and the state came together with the idea to set up the eight ASTI as finishing schools that would offer one-year courses in various disciplines in the public–private partnership mode. These ASTIs were planned to focus on specific domains. For example, the ASTI located near a manufacturing cluster could offer manufacturing-related courses. Near seaports, it could focus on logistics and so on. As setting up of modern, well-equipped ASTI was going to be resource-intensive, the proposal was that the government would fund the entire cost of the land, building and the machinery with the ADB loan and then private partners could run them, based on agreed curriculum and quality norms, in a revenue-sharing mode.

In addition to serving the purpose of a finishing school, an ASTI would work with the local, existing ITIs and polytechnics in a hub-and-spoke model to raise the trainer quality of these institutions.

The eight ASTI were to be part of Odisha Skill Development Project (OSDP) which was to be a society under the Societies Act. When I arrived on the scene and Odisha Skill Development Authority was created, OSDP was merged with OSDA. Though a lot of work had already been done with expert help from ADB, from an overall project plan to choice of location, things were going very slow. That is the nature of the beast when it comes to most projects run with multilateral agencies that often have the same level of bureaucratic processes. For large projects, particularly in the green field areas, it is a time-consuming process.

Among many challenges on the government side, is the frequent shift of officers who handle these projects and sometimes the government itself changes. In case of Odisha, the saving grace was that the government was stable but officers came and went. Without steady leadership, a large project like this was a non-starter.

With the merger of OSDP with OSDA, things began to gain speed and eventually, ADB and OSDA were ready to conduct roadshows to attract leading employers and private-sector training agencies to come forward to bid for running the eight ASTIs.

Considering that the government was to bankroll the project and was willing to provide the land, building and machinery, we had expected a deluge of interest from different training agencies. The larger expectation from ADB and the Odisha government was that leading TVET organizations from countries like England, Germany, Switzerland, Australia and Korea would come forward, create joint ventures with local partners and grab the ASTIs. But contrary to the assumption the experts had made, there were no takers. This was a classic example of great vision, sophisticated planning based on sleek assumptions whereas the ground reality was vastly different.

International training organizations showed little interest because of their perceived risks associated with India. There were a few reputed, national-level training organizations in India but they were far too stretched to take on something new. Large employers showed no interest at all.

The traditional players that did the DDU-GKY and PMKVY kind of skill training did not have the deep expertise needed to set up and run something as sophisticated as an ASTI. This was also a time when DDU-GKY and PMKVY centres were opening in a frenzy all over the country and these were easier avenues of making money. Running an ASTI would require rigour that many operators simply did not have. It was a frustrating quagmire for both ADB and us. At the end of the last roadshow in Delhi and after a number of extensions to the last date for bidding, Sanjay Singh, Rajesh Patil and I came to the conclusion that we had a dud on our hands. It was a setback on many levels.

The entire ADB team, and in particular, Senior Social Sector Specialist Mike Chong and Senior Project Officer Vikram Harsha Annamraju had put in a lot of effort in the design of the project plan. More importantly, they had become emotionally invested in the idea. At the state-government level, the rolling out of the ASTI was part of the mission and vision shared by the chief minister when OSDA was presented to the world in June 2016. Consequently, when the core team at OSDA had drawn up the *Fix, Scale and Accelerate* idea, it was the ASTI piece that was the essence of our 'Accelerate' strategy. All of us had lived and breathed the vision of the eight ASTI, we had spoken about it passionately in every forum and now it was a non-starter.

It hurt. Yet, we did not quite know how to take it forward. But this wasn't the first time I was going through such an emotion. My first start-up, a company called Project.21 that I had set up when I was 28, had folded up after three years of blood, sweat and tears.

After its failure, I joined Wipro where I spent a decade. This was a company where chairman Azim Premji encouraged risk taking, failure was not looked down upon. Then came a time when I co-founded Mindtree that had a very similar culture. We learnt to let go of ideas, projects and even line of business that would not take off, despite the best intentions of leaders. Whenever such setbacks were imminent, I remembered Peter Drucker. He used to say, don't try to solve every problem. Go, seek opportunities. The deadly embrace of a failed idea can be hugely energy sapping. Instead, one must seek newer opportunities that create new energy in us.

The mission to set up the eight ASTIs had to be aborted. But the saving grace was that there was so much else going well and more had to be done.

I called Sanjay and said, let us move on. He replied, 'Yes Sir. But I am not sure I am ready yet.'

32

Nano Unicorn

My very first book, *The High-Performance Entrepreneur,* was about how to build a start-up from scratch, how to genetically engineer it for survival, success and scale. I wrote it way back in 2006. It has been two decades since then. While the world has changed dramatically on all fronts, the essence of entrepreneurship and what works and what does not in the start-up world remain largely the same.

While writing *The High-Performance Entrepreneur*, I was looking for material to validate my own experience on the subject of entrepreneurship and came across seminal research by Babson College in the United States. The Babson research pointed towards a very striking fact: only 4 per cent of all start-up companies succeed. They sprint ahead while 96 per cent fail. Babson calls these 4 per cent companies as *gazelles*. Babson research defined gazelles as those that stay in business beyond five years, with at least twenty employees. This brings home the tough fact that entrepreneurship is a lethal game. In some ways, it mimics nature. Look at the conversion ratio between the number of buds in a mango tree to the number of flowers, to the number of small mangoes to the number that would stay to mature, to the number that would go to market. The paradigm that best illustrates the journey of a mango is that of a funnel or an inverted pyramid. At the top are the entry-level numbers that rapidly decline as you go down the funnel or the inverted pyramid. A tiny fraction makes it to the end. Most people who have an opinion on entrepreneurship but who have never started a business miss this fact. Overall, to have more gazelles, you need to seed the starting point with more tiny enterprises, accepting that high mortality in entrepreneurship is a given.

Now we come to a salient point and this one is about the critical need for job creation in countries like India. How are jobs created and what roles do start-ups play in this?

Contrary to popular belief, the greatest job creators are not the government or big businesses anywhere in the world. The government is like a monster. If you allow the monster to expand, you will have to feed it more and more. Any economist would tell you, governments that create more government jobs are likely to create long-term national liability. Creating government jobs means you spend money on an employee for a work life of forty years and then pay pension for perhaps another forty years. The pension can also be extended to a surviving spouse and that may be for another ten years. Where does the money come from? It is largely the taxpayer who foots all the future bills.

And what happens in case of large companies? Take for example the Fortune 500 companies. In most cases, the CEO is rewarded by shareholders for shrinking the workforce: bring tech in, automate more, outsource, do whatever. Shareholders of big businesses frown on increasing payroll costs. Every new CEO focuses on cost-reduction as the first item on the agenda. A lot of that is done by freezing new hires and shrinking the current workforce.

Thus, large number of jobs are not created by the government or large public- or private-sector companies. Even in developed economies, small businesses, often the mom-and-pop shops, create more new jobs. The myopia I see among policymakers, financial institutions and academics is in their efforts to increase the 4 per cent success rate of start-ups to 5 per cent or 10 per cent or 15 per cent. A better goal would be to significantly increase the number start-ups so that, even with the static 4 per cent at the end, the actual number of eventual successes goes up. Now we need to get this entire construct in the context of hinterland India and skill-trained youth.

When I had started my entrepreneurial journey, the word 'unicorn' meant a mythical horse that had a horn and it had wings to fly. An unusual and highly coveted animal. No one thought of it as a business. But, by the time I was moving out of my entrepreneurial career in 2016, the unicorn had emerged as the new symbol of ultimate entrepreneurial aspiration. In Internet terminology, a unicorn is not a magical horse with a horn and wings. It is a start-up whose valuation touches a billion dollars. The term was coined in 2013 by Eileen Lee as a metaphor for rarity. By June 2025, globally the number of unicorns was 1434 and 117 of them were in India.

That placed India at the third rank globally, thanks to the exploding opportunities in tech, tech-driven services, finance as much as the overall mass and velocity of Indian economy.

Had I not joined the government, I would be a devout worshipper of unicorns. I would have just gloated in the fact that a bunch of freshly minted engineers and MBAs and sometime college dropouts can get together, start something with great promise with a killer idea, get the funds at a fantastic valuation and become unicorns. We absolutely need them. But truth be told, they do not create millions of jobs. If someone counted the number of direct jobs created by India's 117 unicorns, it would be a disappointing exercise other than counting food delivery and such other gig-economy company employment numbers.

Now that I had crossed over to the government and seeing life on the grounds, I realized, India needs more unicorns for sure but to create millions of jobs, we need thousands of *nano unicorns*. To me, a nano unicorn meant a tiny entrepreneur, someone in the likeness of a gazelle, one who creates perhaps one full-time job besides the entrepreneur and another which may be part-time or seasonal in the first couple of years of its existence. Then it grows some more and eventually survives for five years and over this time, builds the capacity to employ twenty-five people perhaps. But here is the question: is it possible to create enabling conditions whereby a state like Odisha, or for that matter a country like India, could create a groundswell for nano unicorn start-ups?

The question becomes significant because, whether we want to create an Infosys or a small roadside garage by Soumendra Das, in the first few years, the hurdles and the complexity faced by both are quite comparable. As is the failure rate. With little or no control over the 96 per cent failure rate, the real trick becomes, not to bemoan it. Expand the size of the funnel. Instead of grieving the death of ninety-six start-ups in a 100, seed a thousand start-ups so that instead of four success stories, we could have forty.

In my first year in skill development work, I met many nano unicorns but, unfortunately, their stories were not told to those who mattered the most. I met Maheshwar Rao on the outskirts of Paralakhemundi in Gajapati district. Gajapati was once known for left-wing extremism, illegal Ganja cultivation and girl-child trafficking and not entrepreneurship. Maheshwar Rao was a man in his fifties. He had been a postal employee all his life and the entrepreneurial bug had bitten him just a few years prior. He put in his papers, took out his provident fund money, bought a small piece of land and started a free-range poultry business.

Free range?

How on earth did he learn that language?

When I asked him that question, he called his son and asked him to show me videos on free-range chicken farming on YouTube. With YouTube, the information asymmetry was gone. What someone knows in Pune, someone can know in Paralakhemundi. Then he showed me around his farm. I noticed he had a kennel with a few pedigreed dogs. He explained to me, a Labrador pup sells in anywhere from Rs 5000–6000. A German shepherd pup fetches even more. With minimal investment, now he is also a dog breeder.

Besides, the dogs are good to have on his tiny farm which was truly in the back of the beyond. They give him security.

Then, I noticed that he had also set up a greenhouse.

What was he growing there? It was the month of May. He was growing tomatoes. Tomatoes in May? He told me, in winter, there is no point growing tomatoes. Everyone grows them, the supply is more than the demand, prices fall, farmers get angry. Often, they throw the tomatoes on the highway as a protest against low prices. Maheshwar Rao grows them in a greenhouse in May and sells them off-season. They fetch five times higher prices and the wholesalers pre-book his produce.

Okay, okay, I get it.

Maheshwar Rao gave me a live lesson on the four Ps of marketing strategy that would have made the great Neil Borden, a prominent academic who articulated the concept of 'marketing mix', very proud. Borden's ideas, later distilled by E. Jerome McCarthy argued that all marketing strategy was all about getting the product, place, price and promotion right.

Another day, another place. On a trip to Jajpur, even though it was getting dark and we had to go to the next place, the project director of the District Rural Development Agency (DRDA) accompanying me asked if I would like to stop by to meet an interesting young man. I agreed. We pulled off the highway with the intent to spend perhaps fifteen minutes on the detour, which turned to more than an hour. We met Surendra Sahoo, a very quiet man in his early thirties. When he was an adolescent in the Badakainchi village near Kuakhia of Jajpur, his mother grew marigolds in her little garden. The lady had golden fingers. Her plants were always generous. When the marigolds were in big bloom, she would tell him to take them to the flower sellers who sat outside the Biraja Temple. There, he befriended Babuli Rana who was a flower seller. Babuli Rana liked the boy who was always so dutiful and courteous. He asked Surendra to come along to Kolkata where he was meeting his wholesalers from whom he bought flowers in bulk. So, Surendra tagged along and saw the big world of floriculture and grafted plants.

West Bengal, the fourth largest marigold grower in India, produced 63,440 tonnes of flowers. His eyes opened up. After finishing school, he opted out of higher studies and a consequent job queue. He rented an acre of fallow land nearby, the land on which I stood, and started growing marigolds and tuberoses. It was getting dark. He took me inside a small structure on his farm, probably built by farmhands. It had solar lighting. Inside, I was getting constantly distracted by the fishtank with all kinds of colourful fish. I asked him how he got involved with this hobby.

Hobby? He said, it was no hobby.

One of the marigold sellers in West Bengal told him, there was good money in selling ornamental fish. What do you need to get started after all? A small space, a tank of water and a few breeder fish as a starter kit. That is it.

What do nano unicorns like Maheshwar and Surendra have in common? The ability to quickly learn new skills from unusual sources and to seize opportunities.

After meeting Maheswar and Surendra, I realized the huge potential that exists to replicate them by taking the idea to future nano unicorns in the ITIs. For that, we first needed a mental model that delinked what a young person may have studied in school and college and what the person could do in life as an entrepreneur. Just because a kid studied the electrical trade did not mean she could not be a creative economy entrepreneur, an organic farmer or whatever else.

Second, we needed to give the individual access to a small amount of money for which the funder would be happy to see a 4 per cent success rate. It couldn't be a bank. A bank would collapse if 96 per cent borrowers failed and became 'non-performing assets'.

Third, we needed to create a network of mentors whose personal journey would be a useful narrative, whose proximity gives them access to guidance and sense making. In short, people like Babuli Rana for every Surendra Sahoo in the making.

33

100, 300, 1000

Though Chief Minister Naveen Patnaik had repeatedly told me that I would have a complete free hand, that I could bring in any number of experts, in all the eight years that I served the state, I brought in only one individual from my past life. And no, it wasn't someone from Mindtree or the software industry for that matter. It was a banker from State Bank of India who was about to retire. Her name is Gitanjali Mishra. We had studied together in college.

Gitanjali, like most bright kids of our times, made it to the civil services but she chose to opt out and work for the State Bank of India instead. Once, while she was posted in Tirupati, I asked her why she wasn't trying for a posting in Hyderabad. She was quite offended. Firstly, she wasn't going to ask anyone for a transfer. Secondly and more importantly, she liked the rural postings because they gave her a chance to work with the hitherto unbanked. What good was her life if she wasn't making a difference to these people? Her principled stand on both counts had stayed with me for decades.

As the idea of the nano unicorn began to take hold of me, I felt the need for someone who could anchor a programme to create a hundred nano unicorns as a pilot project, then to step it up to 300 and eventually take it to 1000. With 1000 templates of both success and failure, we would have enough narratives to take to the ITI and polytechnic kids and say, 'Hey, you could also be doing this!' I gave Gitanjali a call and asked her to work with us for a couple of years to launch 100, 300 and the 1000 nano unicorns.

Headhunting in government isn't usual, but as an exception, you could do a 'search and select' hiring of a consultant for a specific timeframe, as long as the conditions were transparent. But doing that usually becomes a tricky affair with fixing the compensation.

That said, if you hired someone who has just retired or about to retire from the government or the public sector, it is simpler. You get the person at the same pay last drawn, minus the pension, and no one can question that.

Gita Mishra came on board and along with Balwant Singh, Rajesh Patil and Pinaki Patnaik, we got to work.

The starting point was to go to the ITI in every district. We asked the principals to nominate some of their second-year students and even a few ex-students to write a one-page 'dream sheet' in which they had to tell us what they would do if someone gave them one lakh rupees, interest free for a year, without any collateral. We said, if we liked the story, we would have the kid present it and if we liked the kid, we would then send them to a two-week, residential, mini-MBA programme where they would be taught business basics. At the end of the two weeks, the kid can redo the dream sheet and if we liked it then, we would get an impact funder to write a cheque of one lakh to start the business.

The principals asked how they would nominate anyone. How would they know who made the cut? We told them to look for the smart, intelligent troublemaker in the class. A kid who had a touch of irreverence. Had a bit of a chip on the shoulder. Someone who took the lead, tried out new things and new ways of doing things. Others in the class must like this kid and look up to them as a leader. If the kid's parents owned a small shop or took their farm produce to sell in the market as against those who were employees somewhere, even better.

As we saw in Chapter 14, the first task of an angel investor or for that matter a venture capitalist of the Silicon Valley is to be a good talent scout. It takes knowledge, skills, attitude and unbelievably great intuition. It is part art, part science and mostly witchcraft. We were asking principals of ITIs to become talent scouts.

Good going so far, but where was the money coming from? If 96 per cent of people were to fail, were we smoking weed? The plan was simple.

First, call it a pilot project. This phrase is usually disarming to the worst critics and naysayers in the government corridor.

Second, do not use government money. We went to a few wealthy individuals and like-minded private-sector companies as sponsors. We told them that the government would provide the platform, the oversight and all the money needed for infrastructure and training costs. The sponsor would give the money to the nano unicorn with the promise to return it at some point such that the same money would fund another potential nano unicorn. The sponsors were chosen such that they saw the end goal: harvest 100, 300 and then 1000 stories.

Not just 'success' stories but *stories* of entrepreneurial journeys that could give many different perspectives on how to get started, relevant to a skill-trainee at the bottom of the pyramid.

The nano unicorn programme took off. As it shaped up, it was at once uplifting, disappointing, encouraging, discouraging but above all, it was beautiful. At the end of the second year, Gitanjali Mishra walked around like a mother goose with a clutch of ducklings that followed her everywhere, quack, quack, quack.

34

And Then Flowed the Narratives

Did you go to a polytechnic and get good marks there to finally scavenge plastic bags? That was the stinging question from Naresh Behera's father, who was a hydraulic technician taking care of the many forklifts in the Rourkela Steel Plant. Naresh Behera's father was venting his deep disappointment when his son, along with his friends and associates, mounted a fifty-six-day clean-up camp on the banks of the Koel River, which skirts the steel city of Rourkela. Naresh's father would rather have his son apply for a regular job with a steady income. But no, Naresh wanted to start a business and that too, a business that saves the planet! He was not showing any interest in pursuing a regular job like his father who had spent his entire life at the steel plant.

I had met Naresh at the beginning of Covid when the nano unicorn programme had gone into doldrums. While every business had gone into hibernation, the small ones were on ventilators and many were simply choking to death. At that time, there was little point in training new nano unicorns, but Gitanjali Mishra had asked me a very pertinent question—what do you do for those who were selected before the pandemic?

It was going to be impossible to get them into a residential venue as we had done before but at least we could run online training for them, she argued. I was not quite sure it would work out but agreed to give it a try.

The twenty-second batch of nano-unicorn training was kicked off. In the introductory session, each nano unicorn gave me an introduction to their business idea. By now, I knew the variety of businesses skill trainees opted for over the years fairly well. Electrical store, farm equipment repair, carpentry unit, fashion design, air conditioner repair. But when Naresh Behera spoke, I fell off my chair. First, it had to do with the name of his business: Gadget Reviver. The twenty-three-year-old, freshly minted diploma holder from Rourkela, wanted to set up a business in a place like Rourkela, to salvage e-waste, repair devices and recycle them.

Then, he told me, with the air of a Zen monk, everything living and non-living has value; it is left to us to recognize it.

It all started when Naresh was in Class VIII. It was his summer vacation. Everyone was doing something or the other—attending math classes, enrolling at a cricket academy, rollerblading, whatever. He was idling at home. His mother said, 'for heaven's sake, go out and do something.' Our man went off to a mobile repair shop nearby and signed up as an apprentice. The repair shop guy took him in, taught him to fix things and got him started. He also gave him some money for the work he did.

When he finished his high school and joined the Rourkela Polytechnic, he chose mechatronics, but by the side, chased electronics as a hobby. He built pico satellites and sounding rockets. He was clear, he was going to be an entrepreneur someday and focus on sustainability. That is how the nano unicorn idea was a big thrust forward for him. In his own words, the training gave him a 'structure' and the money was a 'boost'.

Post Covid, when Gadget Reviver took shape, he organized his business as a set of three 'verticals' (in his words). The first one was a training business. He skilled youth like himself in repairing mobile phones, laptops, desktops and LED products. Then, he started a service business. He fixed computers, ATM machines and even breath-analysers used by the Railways for loco pilots. Finally, he started his business of selling various electronic products.

By 2024, Gadget Reviver had annual revenue streams touching Rs 10 lakh. Very interestingly, he had set a creative and ambitious repayment goal for the money given to him: he would make compounding repayments, starting with Rs 500. Each time, his repayment had to keep doubling and that is what he did until his entire loan was returned.

* * *

Biswajit Mahanta was born in Lahunipada in 1986. Never mind if you do not know where that is. It is one of the blocks of the mineral-rich Bonai subdivision of Sundargarh district. It has 18,000 households, both rural and urban. That number is important to the story, as we will see later.

In his younger days, Biswajit's father had wanted to study at an ITI. The man was selected twice but, on each occasion, the letter of admission was delivered to him by post long after the admission was over. Eventually, he took up a small-time job nearby and a little bit of farming to raise his family with two sons.

Biswajit explains that in his father's times, the postal service was very slow. It wasn't like what it is today. Unlike his father, Biswajit was born at a time when postal services had improved and his admission to the ITI at Rourkela, at a distance of sixty kilometres from where he lived, did happen on time. Post his training in air-conditioning and refrigeration, he was doing small things here and there. What could you do in a place like Lahunipada with technical expertise in air-conditioning and refrigeration? One day, his teachers called him, told him about the nano unicorn programme and asked him to apply. The idea of the mini-MBA training and the collateral-free loan instantly pulled him in.

I first met him when he was in training and remembered him as a very shy, somewhat introverted person. He wasn't like Naresh who you couldn't miss in a crowd. After his training got over, with the money in hand, he went to Lahunipada and started Hari Om

Electricals, a catch all for fixing anything that needed fixing in that place. There was an electrical goods shop but more than that, he did all kinds of repairs by going to many different places. Now, he needed extra hands.

He pulled in his father, transferred all the knowledge he had picked up from his nano unicorn training and got his old man to run the shop. Then, he sent for his younger brother who had migrated to Theni in Tamil Nadu in search of work. Now, the entire family was in business. He was ready for electrical wiring contracts for the many new houses coming up nearby. He needed more hands, this time, technically trained hands. He hired two youngsters from ITI. Then Covid happened. For nearly two years, there was hardly any work. But with his carefully saved surplus money from the business, he made sure that his employees were paid their salaries even as business had come to a standstill.

In 2024, when I spoke to Naresh, he told me, 'I used to be extremely shy, I was very afraid. I used to go from place to place to do small work. Then the nano unicorn training programme happened. It transformed me. The money was important no doubt but it was the training that changed me completely.' Then he told me, 'Subroto Sir, you had told us in our training that every business has a soul. It has eyes and ears. It is watching you; it is listening to you. Treat it with respect. Be sensitive. And that is what I am practising every day.' Listening to Biswajit, I had tears in my eyes.

Biswajit's business is growing. But will it be enough for him to sustain his momentum? Of course, he tells me. There are the 18,000 houses in the block. And then there is the subdivision. People are building new houses all the time and every house today needs electrical wiring. Right?

* * *

At the age of eleven, Kamini Kanchan, started learning to make small handicrafts and sewing from a neighbour who sold them to 'Fancy Goods Stores'. At that early age, she started thinking of owning her own business one day. After her dress design training in ITI Bhubaneswar, she went to Sainath University where she earned a diploma in fashion design.

In 2018, when the nano unicorn programme was open for enrolment, she received a call from her employability skill teacher at ITI, a man named Lakshman Swain. Swain suggested she should apply. After being selected, she underwent the mini-MBA that shaped her basic knowledge in business. At the end, as she was putting together her business plan, she decided that she would seek higher margins by greater value-add to things she would make. While many reduced their knowledge of sewing and dress making to making petticoats and blouses, she had her eye on bridal wear.

Soon after she started her business with the Rs 1 lakh loan, customers started coming in. It was mostly by word of mouth. Her hopes were high. But one day, Odisha was hit by Cyclone Fani. When natural disasters happen, we seldom realize how badly they can impact tiny businesses. Her workers went away to fix their roofs in their villages and did not come back.

But somehow, Kamini managed to withstand Fani. The business started taking shape again. She was quick to understand that she need not make everything herself, she could source things like hand embroidered sarees and dresses by commissioning job-work. Everything was going per plan but then Covid-19 came like a huge bolt from the blues. For two years, life became hell. It wasn't about the business and its survival. It was about a loan shark. After she received her one-lakh, zero-interest loan, someone she knew, coaxed her into taking another loan of three lakh from him with the obvious intent of reaping a big return from her business success. Now, this person, unsure of Kamini's future, started breathing down her neck.

He turned up every now and then and abused her. Demanded the money forthwith. Or else . . .

At twenty, you may be skilled. You may even know how to survive a natural disaster. But you are not equipped to handle harassment by people double your age. Especially if you are a woman.

During the nano unicorn training days, she had met a retired banker who became her mentor. That individual gave Kamini a lifeline. Kamini got a loan against the mentor's fixed deposit in a bank as a guarantee. With that, she repaid the man harassing her. Kamini took it as a personal challenge to square up the loan to the bank within a year, so that her benefactor's fixed deposit became unencumbered.

When I met Kamini in 2024, her business had flourished. She was billing two to three lakhs a month. She had a GST registration. The proprietorship business was now structured as an LLP. She had rented 4000 square feet of space at Rs 50,000 a month. There were ten workers, a steady wage bill of a lakh and a half every month.

But her hard-earned success frequently draws unwanted attention. People come and tell her to part with her business. She is told, you are a 'small child', you are a girl; what do you know about scaling a business?

Kamini says, every now and then, she is made aware by men, that she is a small child and a girl. They make condescending comments, sometimes they show unwanted sympathy and sometimes, a veiled threat.

And setting up a business isn't just about capitalizing her technical or business skills. It involves dealing with nasty things that life does not prepare you for.

Consider this: as her business grew, she needed someone to look after the day-to-day things so that she could focus on getting customers, manage sourcing and create business-to-business linkages for bulk orders. She hired a distant male relative at a hefty salary of Rs 50,000 a month. He did nothing. On the other hand, when he saw cash coming into the business, he asked for more money.

Six months later, Kamini got rid of him. *Fired him.* It was ugly. Now her own mother counselled her. She said, 'You are a small child, you are a girl. Why do you have to get into all this? You and I are just two people and we do not need more than Rs 25,000, may be Rs 30,000 to get by every month? Why should you run a business?'

Then the other day, while Kamini was away from work, the electricity guys came and disconnected the power line. Why did that happen? Well, the landlord had not set up the electrical connection as a commercial line. The landlord now told her it was her problem.

Every now and then, surprises and setbacks like these, that have nothing to do with her core competence, keep hammering on her entrepreneurial spine. For now, Kamini Kanchan is a brave, proud woman, and her entrepreneurial journey continues.

35

The Change Agents

Tata Strive was the brainchild of Subramanian Ramadorai who had an illustrious career as the chief executive officer and managing director of TCS. Thereafter, he was invited by the Government of India to be adviser to the prime minister of India and be the chairman of National Skill Development Agency as well as the National Skill Development Corporation. The former created policy and the latter was set up as a joint venture of the government with industry bodies to facilitate and implement various policies. Ramadorai had brought his erstwhile colleague Anita Rajan from TCS to assist him when he came to Delhi. Then, a time came when he decided to call it a day and went back to Mumbai. Anita Rajan went back as well. The two felt there was an unfinished agenda for them in the area of skill development. They saw their assignment in Delhi leading to some significant policy changes and creation of frameworks for skill development. Yet, they felt they needed to build a model skill-training institution that would be a living example of excellence and serve as a prototype for others. That is how Tata Strive took shape.

Anita Rajan sought out a meeting with me in Bhubaneswar soon after I took charge and came across to me as an extremely humble and grounded leader. She presented the great work she and her team had been doing on a not-for-profit basis, earning only so much that was needed to build and maintain an excellent institution.

After a long meeting, I asked her how open she would be to explore something Tata Strive had never done before. Then, I went on to explain what I had in mind. It would not earn Tata Strive any money. Instead, I was asking her to co-invest.

The genesis of the idea went back to the time our older daughter, Neha, had applied to an organization called Teach for America after finishing her college in the United States.

Teach for America (TFA) is a non-profit organization that recruits academically gifted students with a sense of idealism and desire to serve inner-city schools in fifty-two low-income communities that did not attract good teachers. Many of these schools were in poverty-stricken inner-city areas of places like New York, Detroit and Los Angeles. Because good teachers did not go there, students did not do well. It was a vicious cycle. The two-year assignment with TFA with a subsistence salary was seen as a real-life leadership development opportunity for the TFA aspirant and a vehicle of change for a system that was seen a write-off. Towards the end of my tenure at Mindtree, I was delighted to know that in India, the TFA model was replicated as Teach for India and, in fact, I had hosted a workshop for them at Mindtree Kalinga.

Now, I wanted Anita Rajan to implement something that I had loosely coined in my head as 'Teach for Odisha'. The idea germinated in my mind during my visits to the ITIs and polytechnics of the state to realize that these are equipping their students with just the raw technical skills.

Most students lacked 'life-skills'. These were necessary to be employment worthy in a fiercely competitive world. In my mind, life-skills were not just 'soft-skills'.

I had made a mental list of what these skills could be. Leading the self. Working with teams. Understanding and managing money. Exposure to total quality management (TQM) principles. Sustainability. Innovation and design thinking. And the fundamentals of entrepreneurship.

But I knew, there were two challenges in implementing such an idea. The existing faculty, themselves never exposed to these concepts, could not be expected to take the lead. Second, it simply would not work if we brought in the current flock of external training organizations that would not have the perspective to design what I had in mind. We needed people in the mould of Teach for America who would be there in the ITI for a full two-year period. They should be visible role models who exemplify leadership. These individuals had to be *change agents*.

Would Tata Strive, on our behalf, select capable, idealistic young women and men who would be willing to take up a posting in a remote place for two years to work with our youth from the bottom of the pyramid, many of whom saw themselves as failures? Kids who did not make eye contact, did not speak up, did not have worthwhile ambitions and did not see a role model at home or any place else? Would Tata Strive do it, as a mission, and not just a business opportunity? Would Tata Strive be open to do this experimentally, as a pilot project, and, in effect, share the cost? Anita Rajan did not think twice. She said yes to the idea.

It touched a chord somewhere. She saw it as an opportunity to make a big difference by trying something no one had done before.

The one thing that discourages people from experimenting with completely new ideas and interventions that have no precedence in the government is the process of floating tenders. Anything you want to do with public money, has to go through the tendering process. In it, usually the lowest bidder becomes the winner of a project even as it may not have the capability to execute or deliver quality. In order to ensure that cost alone does not determine win ability and quality is not sacrificed, there is a process called quality-cum-cost based system (QCBS) of procurement. Through it, even as there is a tender process, the government can separate the wheat from the chaff by first looking at qualitative aspects such as knowledge of a domain, approach to execution, quality and referenceable capabilities. It is this short-listed group that then participates in the cost comparison. Though not a guarantee of the best outcome, it is a good compromise in many cases.

However, this system typically works where a great degree of clarity exists and an idea is not completely experimental. The idea of putting change agents in the

ITIs was an experiment. It had never been done before anywhere. Even a QCBS system could not ensure that we got the best-qualified partner. I asked Anita if Tata Strive would do a 'pilot', a small but scalable project, something like a prototype. It would have a three-way construct. The government would make its ITI system available as a platform for the experimental intervention. As far as cost goes, OSDA would seek private, philanthropic funding to pick up half the cost of the project and Tata Strive would pick up the other half by accessing funds from various Tata organizations through their corporate social responsibility initiatives. The experiment would cover only five ITIs in the first phase, to be tested with five more in the second phase and, if that went through successfully, we would open it up for all the ITIs across the state. At that stage, with the lessons internalized, we could settle the framework and a model of engagement that lends itself to the QCBS approach.

Soon enough, a three-way MoU was signed between the government, like-minded philanthropic sources and Tata Strive. Tata Strive was ready to send change agents, selected and trained by them, to the initial set of selected ITIs for a two-year tenure.

The change agent was to work as an integral part of the ITI system and not see themselves as an outsider, far less a consultant. That mindset was critical to be accepted by the principal and teachers. A detailed curriculum was designed to build a basket of 'life-skills' for the students to make them feel bold, confident and active. Tata Strive and OSDA would work together closely to create the programme oversight necessary and for handholding the change agents. We were all very excited about the pilot programme. When the first set of five principals were sounded out, they were very eager to testbed it. However, there was resistance from an unexpected quarter.

Most ITIs did not have full-time trainers, as is the case everywhere else. To meet the training requirement, a few trainers were usually drawn from the locally available talent pool, often of very poor quality and no real training. These were called contractual assistant technical officers (CATO) and part-time guest faculty instructor (PTGFI). Some of them had been in the system for years with the hope that someday, the government could be pressurized to absorb them as permanent government employees.

The government did periodically select assistant technical officers through a competitive process but many of the entrenched individuals could not get through it because they were overage or simply stayed away from the selection process because they knew they would not make it.

As the pilots got rolled out, some of the CATO and the PTGI community got worried and worked up because they perceived the change agents as blocking their chances of getting regularized by the government. They did not comprehend that the change agents were not meant to do technical training and even as some of them did realize that, there was a fear that this was perhaps a backdoor method for the government to eventually bring in technical trainers using private players. In the process, they would be thrown out.

When the change agents arrived at the first five ITIs, they were treated with hostile demonstrations in some places. A few CATO and PGTI members also went to the high court and got a stay order. For a moment, I felt, this was the dead-end for a very idealistic idea. But for officers like Balwant Singh and Sanjay Singh these kinds of roadblocks were par for the course.

These are the bane of steering development in a democracy like India where managing the change process can often be so difficult and sometimes so exhausting that many civil servants choose not to engage with anything that is potentially energy sapping. But both officers persisted.

There were many parleys with the principals and protesters alike. The change agents, some very disheartened and scared, had to be assured that things would get sorted out, that the system would stand behind them. Fortunately, in the meantime, the stay order was vacated by the high court. We were now determined to push things forward.

Once the change agents started engaging with the students at the ITIs, the mood changed. There were activities and games, team-building exercises and creativity workshops, counselling for students and community outreach. When the students responded with joy and excitement, the teachers came forward and participated. It was not as if the change agents were doing it all. The place had pent-up energy, inert but intact. The change agents, trained not to stand apart from the technical instructors, consciously blended in and soon became a part and parcel of the institution.

They volunteered for activities outside their charter to help the teachers and principals. Trust was built. From the initial pilot, we then moved quickly to all the ten ITIs and very soon, every ITI was demanding for change agents to be sent. At this juncture, the pilot project was over and the government took over the entire cost of the roll-out.

The engagement with Tata Strive kept expanding over time. At the core of the partnership were several things. They listened deeply and respectfully, unlike many outside agencies that came with the assumption that it was the government that was the problem and they were the solution. Tata Strive's leadership, Anita Rajan downwards, always approached things with head on shoulders, feet grounded but eyes on larger possibilities. They were a great balance between process and empathy in their approach to programme design. Over time, the success of the engagement extended to several other fields. One such was the idea of introducing what we called the sports change agent.

* * *

It started one day with a phone call from Vishal Dev, the principal secretary to the government for several key departments and that included sports and youth services department. He sounded very concerned. The department ran an exclusive residential sports academy.

The primary goal of this academy located at the state-of-the-art Kalinga Stadium was to bring in promising sports talent from the thirty districts, give them all the facilities and groom potential stars who could win medals at national-level sports events. These students spent most of their time training on the sports field and alongside, studied the usual subjects taught at the high-school level. Understandably, the focus on academics was secondary. What worried Vishal Dev was the fact that while a number of students did excel in sports and got the medals and recognition at various levels, not everyone got there. It was the nature of the beast. This became a double whammy for most students. Having placed sports at a higher level than academics for years, these students were now at a disadvantage. What Vishal Dev wanted to know was whether OSDA could design any skilling initiatives for them so that they could find a different path leading to employability after moving out of the sports academy? It was a problem to be solved.

But I saw a tremendous, albeit different, kind of opportunity here. To me, these students were not candidates for rehabilitation.

They were indeed the solution to a bigger problem we had in educational institutions. Schools and colleges were required to have the so-called physical training instructors (PTI) but most did not have one. These students could very well fill that gap. But beyond filling the gap, many other professional paths could open up. With burgeoning interest in fitness, there was a huge demand for gym instructors, fitness trainers and so on.

I had always bemoaned the fact that every ITI and polytechnic in the state sat on large tracts of land that they never used. Cattle roamed there. No playfields. After all, ITI kids were meant to be fitters, welders and electricians. Who cares about physical fitness? Whereas, more than the other kids going to usual schools and colleges, these were the ones for whom physical fitness was so critical because they needed the kinaesthetic capability to work on shop floors, essential for their job readiness. We needed our young boys and girls in ITIs to play. But for this to happen, we perhaps needed a sports change agent. Someone close to their age. Someone fun. Someone who would say, come let us play. I spoke to Anita and we decided to try out the idea of creating a cadre of sports change agents. They already had the sports training. We needed to additionally equip them with facilitation skills. A special training programme was designed for them to become trainers.

A group of sportspersons, who no longer saw winning in national games a possibility but were both gifted and passionate about their sport, were selected for the trainer programme. It was specially designed to help them go beyond the fundamental, competitive drive to achieve personal success to that of grooming others to use sports for holistic development. This needed understanding of how to motivate, coach and facilitate.

With this, a new initiative called it Khelo ITI was kicked off. In the beginning, like any new idea being tried out for the first time, the first set of sports change agents met with varied levels of acceptance. In some places, the principals did not see any value in them; they did not give them the time needed to make the students play. To them, completing the syllabus itself was a challenge. Where was the time to play? And why play?

The second category of principals were passive and let the sports agents just be there, nothing surprising about that. And then, there was a third category who saw them as a great addition to the ITIs. Soon, the success stories started emerging out of these. Some of them went beyond what any one of us had ever imagined.

* * *

Omkar Tatwamasi, once a star volleyball player, was sent to the Special ITI in Jatni, near Khordha. The Special ITI, as the name suggests, was for specially abled students who wanted to get vocational education. The ITI had orthopedically handicapped, hearing and vison impaired students. Omkar's first reaction was wrenching. He had grown up as a sportsman. He was always around with people who had great physique. And here were hundreds of students whose identity was defined by what their body could not be. Seeing them, on his very first day, he became aware of his own handicap. How was he going to work with such students? For example, he did not know how to communicate with the hearing-impaired ones, he did not know sign language. He had never seen so many orthopedically challenged individuals in one place. He had no idea how to engage them in physical activity. Working with the vision impaired was yet another challenge.

He felt out of depth, but the place brought out a sense of commitment, of a determination that he never knew he had in great measure. No one at the Special ITI could guide him on how to get started. He turned to YouTube. He researched what kind of games and sports the specially abled could play, what equipment was needed.

He reached out to people outside the ITI. Meanwhile, he started learning sign language from the Tata Strive change agent who had been there for a while. Tatwamasi started observing and analysing the psychological aspects of working with people who could not hear, see or were mobility-impaired. Soon things began to change. His students began to blossom. One day, an orthopedically challenged past student came by and he was very taken by what he saw. He told Tatwamasi about para-athletic championships, something Tatwamasi had not heard about. After that encounter, everything changed for him. He researched about para-athletics at the state and national levels. He was now possessed. His goal was not just to make the students of the Special ITI play but to make them win. His passion created a tidal wave of energy among the students. At the next state level para-athletics, they won one gold, three silver and two bronze medals. Then, he expanded to cricket for the vision-impaired and trained a batch of orthopedically challenged students for para swimming. How did he do that when the ITI did not have a swimming pool? He took the students to the nearby village pond. In time, two of his charge represented the state at the nationals and returned with two silvers and a bronze medal.

Tata Strive engaged with us as a partner on several other fronts. When the government started a PPP-based urban transport system called Mo Bus, it brought in private operators to run the buses on a build-own-operate basis. The drivers and conductors of these vehicles came with the baggage of driving private buses; they were reckless, unregulated and their attitude was coarse. When Mo Bus started its operations, Arun Bothra, an outstanding police officer who was given the charge of the initiative, needed to build a sense of purpose in them. As a first step towards changing their mindset, he redesignated them as pilots and guides, from drivers and conductors. He figured out that on a given day more than a lakh of commuters would ride

Mo Bus in Bhubaneswar city. A commuter boards a bus for a specific reason. Someone wants to get to work on time. Someone wants to rush back home after work. Someone is on the way to the hospital perhaps and someone else could be a tourist who is here to explore the city. To a typical bus conductor or a driver, these are simply passengers who generate revenue and many of them, perhaps a nuisance.

Arun Bothra wanted the pilots and guides to see every single ride as a touchpoint for the delivery of citizen services by the government. This needed a change in the way the Mo Bus crew saw themselves: rough men, foul-mouthed, rash, aggressive, combative versus becoming ambassadors of the city.

With help from Tata Strive, we trained more than 600 of the initial staff of Mo Bus on leadership skills, conflict resolution, self-care, customer orientation, empathy and ambassadorship through intense, role-play based, experiential learning. It was a moving experience for me to see many of them tear up at the end of the two-week workshop because they, mostly half-schooled, were never part of any formal learning session or training. No one had ever cared for them. No one had made them see a larger purpose in their everyday work of ferrying people mindlessly. No one had made them feel wanted.

36

Everyone Loves a Competition

October 2017

Sanjay Singh returned from Abu Dhabi like an excited schoolboy who has just seen New York City for the first time in his life. Abu Dhabi had just hosted the WorldSkills Competition which is considered the Olympics of the skill world. After the devastation of World War II, there was a massive challenge of reconstruction in most of war-ravaged Europe. At the same time, there was a huge shortage of skilled workers. People realized that youth had to be attracted to skills in greater numbers and one way was to celebrate the idea itself. In 1950, a man named Francisco Albert Vidal led the first skill competition that was held in Madrid with only two countries participating: Spain and Portugal. Thereafter, it became a global movement, meant to honour excellence in skills for youth up to the age of twenty-three.

Until the WorldSkills 2017 event, India had never ever won a medal on a global stage. That year, Mohit Dudeja from Delhi broke that jinx to bring India her very first silver medal in the patisserie skill category. The run-up to the WorldSkills Competition follows a process. First, contestants compete at the state level. Those who excel, compete at the Regional Skill Competition and finally, the best of the best go to IndiaSkills Competition. The gold and silver medallists from the national-level competition go on to represent India at the WorldSkills Competition.

After returning from Abu Dhabi, Sanjay said that if we were to make skills truly aspirational, we had to be seen at the WorldSkills Competition. I had no idea about the WorldSkills Competition before but the way Sanjay was describing it, I was getting drawn because at the back of my mind was the need to raise the respectability of the skilled professional in the eyes of society. Unless our skilled youth got significantly higher social recognition, they, their parents, their teachers, the government officials would not find our efforts to be of any significance.

And nothing creates instant energy in everyone as the idea of a competition. It is a tried-and-tested method that never fails. One of my favourite tricks while raising our two daughters when they were small, was to often make them compete for inane things whenever they were bored, with the lure of 'two first prizes'. It instantly made them energetic. Who can count backwards from 100 the fastest? Who can finish the glass of milk first? Here, take a sheet of paper and crayons and let us have a competition for drawing a mountain with a rising sun. Name the maximum number of countries and their capitals. Count the highest number of red cars between now and the next five intersections. It worked every time. And it works at the level of a country too. An entire nation goes crazy at the idea of a competition in any which category because it becomes a metaphor for patriotism. It is captured in movies like *Lagan*, *Dangal* and *Chak De India*. Nothing raises the human spirit like a competition.

Yes, we needed to compete for the WorldSkills, I told Sanjay. But how? An idea occurred to me. I asked Sanjay if we could bring Mohit Dudeja to Bhubaneswar. I needed to see him to build a template of the future. Often, people think that a government is a bureaucratic, unimaginative maze, where people are not excitable; they do not think outside the box or jump into weird ideas. But look at this. Sanjay Singh produced Mohit Dudeja in my office just after a few days. It was a fan boy moment for me. I spent an hour listening to the story of a twenty-one-year-old who dropped out of his BBA course in Delhi, barely two months into college, went off to Bengaluru and learnt how to be a pastry chef. Because that was what he wanted to become in life.

I took extensive notes on how he trained, how the process of selection happened from the state, to the regional and national level. All the while imagining how we could produce winners who could take the India stage and perhaps someday, the world stage like this handsome, soft-spoken but surefooted young man sitting before me. Post this, Sanjay, Balwant, Rajesh and I put our heads together. The next one on the horizon was the 45th WorldSkills Competition in Kazan, Russia, in August 2019. The starting point for us was to get our act together for a state-level skill competition first.

Azim Premji had once told me, if you want to strive for something truly big, make a public commitment. On 27 February 2019, at a press conference held at the venue of Institute of Hotel Management, we announced Mission 123 to the world.

In forty-four years in the history of WorldSkills Competition, India had never won a gold. Mission 123 meant that at the next WorldSkills, Odisha would get India its first gold, two silvers and three bronzes. Mission 123 caught everyone's imagination.

As a run-up to Mission 123, we held the first state-level skill competition. The inaugural event took place at the historic Barabati Stadium in Cuttack. The venue, built on the ramparts of a fort built in 987 CE, was particularly significant because it symbolizes Odisha's valiant past. We flew in Mohit Dudeja to hold him up as the benchmark for our youth. It was followed by a spectacular dance performance with a hundred dancers, choreographed specially for the occasion by the famous danseuse and Guru Aruna Mohanty. When we had asked her to produce something never done in Odisha before, she suggested an aerial act by a dancer who would descend from the sky. This required engineering with ropes and pulleys. The engineers in charge of the Barabati Stadium would have none of that. What if something went wrong? So much for the urge to build something monumental, to create history, to push the boundary of imagination? A lot of cajoling and a bit of soft growling from my end settled the matter. The aerial ropes and pulleys were installed. On the inaugural evening, the lights dimmed and from the darkness, a dancer appeared from the sky above, with a lit-up Skilled in Odisha logo in hand, the audience gasped and then exploded in joy. We needed to signal to everyone that from now on we would pull all stops to raise the bar.

Suddenly, every ITI, polytechnic and other skill-training institutions became aware of the WorldSkills Competition. 5000 competitors descended in Bhubaneswar for the state-level competition. The entire arena, with exhibits and the various competitions, was open for public viewing.

Thousands of school children were brought in to see the event and understand what goes into vocational training. Everyone could see welding, electrical engineering, fashion design, health and wellness, plumbing, auto-body painting, bricklaying and dozens of other skill activities happening in real-time.

In the evening, Union Minister Dharmendra Pradhan personally came for the valedictory. Cultural troupes from various skill institutions put up their shows, the place was swinging to rap music. The media descended in droves and suddenly, skill was everywhere.

In time, we sent the largest contingent to the eastern regional competition in Patna. It was a clean sweep with Odisha at the number one place in overall medal tally. Now, came the preparations for Delhi.

States like Tamil Nadu, Karnataka, Maharashtra were synonymous with industrial growth and hence, skill development. We knew we were walking in the shadow of giants. Historically, these states dominated in skill events. To break into the big league, we paid meticulous attention to every small detail including the uniform for the team. During the opening ceremony, when the Odisha contingent marched past the flag at the Talkatora Stadium, I got a text message from Union Minister for Skill Development, Dharmendra Pradhan. He was thrilled to see the youth from the state, stand apart from everyone else with their smart outfit. At the end of the competition and to everyone's surprise, Odisha won the second highest medal tally, only slightly behind Maharashtra. We had arrived at the national scene. The contingent returned home to a hero's welcome.

Participation at the IndiaSkills Competition was a moving experience for the government officials of the state. As they learnt about the personal stories of many of the winners, they felt proud of their contributions. The idea that skills can be an instrument of human transformation was getting reinforced again and again.

The youngest medal winner from Odisha at the IndiaSkills Competition was seventeen-year-old Sanjaya Pradhan. He had bagged a silver at the nationals. A small, shy, village boy—yes, a boy—he could easily pass off as someone couple of years younger. The stubbles weren't out yet. From ITI Nayagad, he had made it to the Odisha Skills and then all the way up to the regionals in the electrical trade. How he could do that baffles me till date because he came from a newly started, small ITI on the outskirts of Nayagad. It did not yet have proper faculty and infrastructure. Nothing he was taught there could have made him shine the way he did. When he qualified at the regional level, we wanted him to get coached at the Schneider Electric's advanced training facility in Bengaluru in preparation for IndiaSkills. He said he couldn't go there. I needed to know why. Because his mother wouldn't let him. I decided to go and meet his mother at Nayagad, a distance of two hours from Bhubaneswar.

There, I met Laxmi Dei, a young village woman, no more than perhaps thirty-five or thirty-six, who was more scared than happy to meet me. Slowly, she opened up. And then I got to know why she wouldn't let Sanjay go. She had been married off early in life and bore two children. Unfortunately, her husband had an untimely death.

The older one was a girl who had since been married and gone away. Now Sanjay was all she was left with. She wouldn't let him go anywhere. She had no idea what on earth was IndiaSkills Competition. It took a long, affectionate conversation with her to explain what her son had already achieved, how the state now wants him to earn greater glory and that I would personally make sure he is safe and will return to her.

Often, we reduce skill development to machines, assessments, certifications and jobs. When you meet people like Sanjay's mother, you realize there are deeper dimensions to skill development that can only be addressed if we put a human face on it.

* * *

Subhalaxmi Subudhi's father was a driver at Cuttack Municipality. The man died when she was eight years old. Her mother left Cuttack along with her and her younger sister and went away to Digha in neighbouring West Bengal, where she had family. Subhalaxmi and her sister could not study there for an entire year because they did not know Bengali, which was the medium of instruction in the local schools. The sisters learnt to read and write Bengali and got admission the next year. Meanwhile, her mother raised them doing odd jobs and sold handicrafts on the side. She watched with fascination how her mother created things out of jute strings and beads. After she finished high school, she wanted to be an air hostess. But there was a problem, she had a pronounced stammer.

A well-wisher of hers told her not to be disappointed and study at Swosti School of Hotel Management in Bhubaneswar. This, he said, would get her a well-paying job on a cruise liner. Subhalaxmi came to Swosti and rather than learn other things, chose patisserie. She had seen her mother make beautiful, delicate things with her fingers. This came closest to that.

By the time Subhalaxmi cleared the regional competition, the government had learnt a few things about making pastries. Creating an award-winning pastry chef is a very expensive process. The best pastry machines come from Italy. Not everywhere in India can you find those. Also, pastry making requires essences and other ingredients that are extremely expensive. Many of these are imported. And here is the catch: you learn by mixing mistakes with your recipe time and again before you can create a seven-tier wedding cake that melts in the mouth. Mohit Dudeja had told us, to be able to compete at the national level, Subhalaxmi would have to work at the best pastry training school in India, in Bengaluru, where a month's training would cost probably upwards of Rs 15 lakh.

We sought special permission of the government for her to get trained in Bengaluru's Lavonne Institute of Baking Science and Pastry Arts. The file was put up and sent for approval and it came back under forty-eight hours. Subhalaxmi was flown to Bengaluru. And from there to Delhi to win a silver medal.

Leela Hotels' talent scouts lapped her up and the last I met her was at the Leela Palace Hotel in Bengaluru where she was a working her way up to be a pastry chef.

In 2020, *Indian Express* announced the list of Devi Award winners of Odisha for the year, celebrating outstanding women achievers from different fields. The chief minister handed over the awards. On stage, along with other winners like Jnanpith award-winning novelist Pratibha Ray, leading medical entrepreneur Dr Sujata Kar, Director of Regional Medical Research Centre Dr Sanghamitra Pati, was Subhalaxmi Subudhi.

After the national-level competition, the Government of India takes over further training and exposure for the gold and silver medal winners to be ready for the WorldSkills Competition. From the Odisha team, we had three participants who went on to represent India at the WorldSkills Competition in Kazan, Russia. To everyone's delight, Odisha's Aswatha Narayana, won India's very first gold in water technology. He stood there on the podium draped in the Indian national flag. We were in raptures. An engineering student at the C.V. Raman University, his real-time project in Kazan was to set up a water treatment and purifying plant involving knowledge of science and engineering for detecting minute chemical particles in water and to make it contaminant free. Water technology is among the most complex areas and was considered the preserve of nations like Germany, China and Singapore.

Back home, we huddled together to discuss how do we encourage skill institutions to routinely produce stars like Aswatha. A new policy paper was prepared and steered through the cabinet. It provided for previously unheard-of amounts of prize money for the winners, their coaches and their alma mater. Aswatha received Rs 1 crore from the government and his alma mater, C.V. Raman University was given a prize of Rs 5 crore so that it continued producing stars like Aswatha.

After Mission 123, there was no looking back. In the two successive IndiaSkills Competitions, Odisha emerged the number one state in medal tally. Each time, it brought out stories of outstanding commitment and determination of the human spirit breaking through all socio-economic barriers and stereotypes. My most heartwarming find was Kamini Kumari Ram who won a bronze at IndiaSkills 2021 in welding and then again, she competed in 2023 when she won gold. Her father had started life as a security guard and in later years, pulled a trolley rickshaw. She was the second among four siblings. After her matriculations, not able to fund higher education, she came to ITI Bhubaneswar where her friend had enrolled as a student in the welding trade. After passing out, she went to participate at a welding competition being held in the premises of the C.V. Raman College where the president, Dr Sanjiv Rout, spotted her. Impressed with her, he took Kamini in for a diploma course, waived the tuition fees, and gave her a stipend of Rs 1500 every month to meet her pocket expenses.

There, she perfected her skills before representing Odisha in the two successive IndiaSkills Competitions. After winning the gold in the 2023 competition, she was sent for international exposure to Dubai and then to Lyon in September 2024. At Lyon, she did not make it to the Top 3 but in my heart and in the hearts of many, she would always remain a superstar.

At Lyon, the Indian contingent had sixty-one competitors and fifteen of them were from Odisha. Of these, five were girls. Odisha's Amaresh Sahu won bronze in renewable energy and Suresh Gadela won a Medallion of Excellence in water technology.

From Barabati Stadium to Lyon became a memorable journey, made worthwhile by the collective efforts of many different individuals. It certainly changed the way the state looked at the idea of skill development, perhaps for ever.

37

Creating Wonder

As the chariot moved along, every day there was new excitement in the air for me. Personally, these felt like the best days of my life. It was even better than those seventeen years I spent at Mindtree raising it from an idea to making it an aspirational company. When you work for the government and the going is good, the sense of fulfilment is very different. You see your report card on people's faces around, you see the needle move for them. Despite all this, for all of us in the leadership team, somewhere deep inside, there remained a void. We had not been able to deliver on the Advanced Skill Training Institute promise. The 'accelerate' piece of our *fix, scale, accelerate* strategy was unfulfilled.

On 5th September 2017, Sanjay and I boarded the Indigo flight to Bengaluru, where ORMAS had arranged a large event to honour DDU-GKY alumni and to build closer linkages with their employers in and around Bengaluru. The flight to Bengaluru takes a couple of hours and for us it was a great patch of white space-time. We got talking about what we should be doing next. Sanjay was animated. He couldn't stop talking about how Russia had built permanent infrastructure and platforms to prepare their youth to excel at the WorldSkills Competitions.

'We need something like that, sir. But we should set up something really big. Very big. Like a World Trade Center.'

I looked at him closely and asked, how about a World Skill Center?

His face lit up.

'Yes, that is what we should have,' he said.

'The World Skill Center.' I repeated the words in my head a number of times. It felt really good.

By the time we touched down at Bengaluru's Kempegowda International Airport, we had it all mapped in our minds. No, we should not be nursing our disappointment about the eight ASTIs that had to be aborted. Perhaps we should be putting our entire energy and resources into setting up just one World Skill Center. And instead of outsourcing, we should be insourcing the running of such a place.

In the software industry, there is a concept called 'take my mess for less'. It is used in the context of outsourcing of software projects. It is a sure-shot way of paving the path to failure. Often, global customers create their own mess of a large software implementation and, not knowing how to deal with it, they think outsourcing will solve all their problems. In contrast, the way successful outsourcing projects work is when the client is quite adept at a task, even excels in it. But for strategic reasons, they think someone else, with well-thought-out technology transfer and collaborative oversight, would be able do a more economically efficient job. The client has the necessary core competence and an already proven model. It is the client who teaches the outsourcing partner how to manage the operation going forward.

In contrast, what were we doing at the government? The mess of poor ITIs and polytechnics was ours. We were producing defective material and then saying, get private operators, call it is a finishing school and incentivize them to run it. We needed to fix our own system; we needed to set high benchmarks and then think of outsourcing. The need of the hour was that we *insource*. Not outsource. We, the government needed to run the place ourselves.

* * *

Our conversation on the flight to Bengaluru brought back something simple yet profound that I had learnt from the well-known architect Prem Chandavarkar. It was about the idea of reductive thinking versus the idea of wonder. Simply put, when we see anything physical, we quickly notice its forms and functionality. Imagine this: I enter a room. I immediately notice its size, I see the doors, the windows, the lighting and perhaps the placement of furniture and the artefacts in it. Unconsciously, I 'reduce' the room into dimensions and objects. Whereas, my mind should *wonder*, who built this room, where did the design idea come from, what is the significance of the various things arranged in a certain way and perhaps, what great things could be done with a space like this.

Just the same way, I look at a bridge spanning a river. I am quick to think of its size and shape and take in the fact that it helps people cross the river. I do not wonder who these people are, where they come from, where they go and for what possible purpose.

Contrast this with a true designer's mind. Given the task of constructing a room or building a bridge, the starting point would be to wonder. The mind will think about what kind of people would live there, who would use the space and how the space could bring more joy. The designer begins from the realm of wonder.

This does not mean that reductive thinking is necessarily the inferior approach. It means that before you begin with reductive thinking, first, you must wonder. Once you have created the wonder, the design flows from it and then you begin to engineer it.

The idea of the ASTI had started with a reductive approach. In contrast, the World Skill Center was an idea of wonder.

That day, it seems to me, destiny was whispering to us aboard the Indigo flight. It was telling us, do not think in a *present-forward* manner: ITI, polytechnic, failed products, finishing school, ASTI. Think *future-backward*: imagine the World Skill Center. Wonder how it can be a space for tomorrow. Think of it as an iconoclastic idea to make the youth of Odisha imagine they can go, kiss the world. Make something worthwhile for global dignitaries visiting the state in the days to come to see the expression of a new Odisha.

On the way from the airport to the city, engrossed with the idea, I asked Sanjay, 'But where should we build it?'

'We do not need to, sir', he replied. I looked at him quizzically. 'There is an eighteen-storey building that is almost ready, some construction work is still going on there. We built the place to attract IT companies to come to Odisha. The idea was to offer a plug and play space for IT companies whom we have been wooing. It has half a million square feet of space, centrally air-conditioned. It has even a helipad on the top, sir. If the honourable chief minister agrees, it can be repurposed to become the World Skill Center.'

'Who owns it?'

'I own it, sir.'

'You?'

'Yes, it belongs to IDCO.'

Sanjay, at the time, was also the managing director of IDCO.

Many people do not associate bureaucrats with innovative thinking. Innovation requires comfort with ambiguity, willingness to take failure in the stride. It also asks for intuition; the ability to create an image of the future that does not exist. It is about ideation. There is perhaps no dearth of people in the bureaucracy who can ideate, sometimes usefully so. But taking a concept from an idea to its fruition is a completely different ball game. It requires tremendous initiative, resolute action, deep personal commitment and complete ownership. But that said, in working for the government, you also learn the true meaning of the word flux. During the eight years I was there, I saw four secretaries to the government in the Department of Skill Development come and go, as did the number of ministers. When an officer is aware of the unpredictability of tenure, making a commitment is not easy at all. Constancy of purpose is the most difficult thing in the world of statecraft, because transience is drilled into a civil servant from the day the individual joins. Yet, I have been fascinated by how many officers in the government defy that. In fact, the thought that the private sector scores over the government when it comes to innovation, risk-taking, accountability and ownership is a misleading and often-unfounded assumption.

When we reached the hotel in Bengaluru, I told Sanjay two things: we needed to check if the name World Skill Center was available with the Registrar of Companies and if yes, we had to immediately block it. I was almost certain that the name would have a squatter somewhere. Second, I told him, we needed to visit the eighteen-storey building he owned the very day we returned to Bhubaneswar.

38

Something Too Large to Ignore

When I was in college, the capital city of Bhubaneswar ended where today's Mancheswar Industrial Area sits in the north. Odisha did not have any small and medium industries worth the name and the so-called industrial area was essentially given away in parcels for a song by the government to many small industries over time. Some withered. Some of the allottees sold the land. A few still stand there who pack fish, make corrugated sheets and gas cylinders and run printing press or simply use their space as godowns. Once there flowed a river and now an open drain runs through it, as do the railway tracks that connect Bhubaneswar with Kolkata and Chennai at the two ends. Mancheswar does not have heft and energy like the industrial zones in states like Tamil Nadu and Karnataka, Delhi NCR or the Pune belt in Maharashtra. Apart from the few smokestack industries that have regular activity, the place is largely listless. It is the unauthorized parking lot for long-distance truckers who need a place to berth overnight, there are small eateries and tea stalls. The signature sight of stray dogs and cattle, slums and encroachments make Mancheswar somewhat of an aberration to the otherwise beautiful Bhubaneswar city. Sanjay had brought me here to see the building he owned. In the middle of it all, I saw it, a massive building still under construction. It defied everything around it and just pushed itself up, out of the landscape of decadence that was its birthplace.

Someone in the government, at some point of time had thought that an idling five acre of government land in the middle Mancheswar was perhaps an encroachment risk. Why not create a plug-and-play space for IT and IT services companies like other states? IDCO was given Rs 240 crore to build this massive place.

Someone had imagined smart-looking professionals, laptops in hand and code in their head, getting in and out this building with its impressive glass and steel facade.

But standing in front of it, Sanjay and I were seeing the World Skill Center for students of vocational training institutions who come from the bottom of the pyramid. Not children of privilege.

No one, except perhaps the Singaporeans would think of such people being housed in a building like that. We could well imagine how the idea of using it to train fitters, electricians, welders and hairdressers would baffle people in power and even draw flak. How could the state justify repurposing this fancy building that could be a money spinner for the exchequer as an IT hub instead of being a finishing school for ITI and polytechnic students?

* * *

The meeting with Chief Minister Naveen Patnaik was over in ten minutes. I told him about the eighteen-storey building and its original purpose. I explained to him very briefly about the stalled ASTI project. Then I said, we needed to insource, not outsource the intended finishing school. We needed to create something iconic, something 'too large to ignore' that could effectively coalesce eight ASTIs into one World Skill Center. I wanted him to bless the idea so that we would formally seek the concurrence of ADB and an approval by the Government of India with detailed plans. We needed to renegotiate the entire loan because now we were selling an entirely different dream. He listened to me quietly and at the end just said three words: 'All right, Mr Bagchi.'

I had first Naveen Patnaik him on 27 March 2006, when I was the chief operating officer of Mindtree. The state was wooing Mindtree to open a centre in Bhubaneswar, and I was there to sign an MoU with the government. Following this, the state had leased twenty acres of land to Mindtree.

The campus was designed by Prem Chandavarkar. When both of us had gone to show the chief minister the artist's impression, he had taken keen interest in it and had suggested that we visit a garden of medicinal plants that he had personally conceptualized around the holy Bindusagar Tank next to the Lingaraj Temple. He wanted us to incorporate some of the elements used in his pet project. He spoke about his book, *The Garden of Life*. I requested him to come to lay the foundation stone for the campus which did.

The actual execution of the Mindtree project, however, took an unbelievably long time for a variety of bureaucratic reasons and when things were finally ready, he had come to inaugurate the campus, now called Mindtree Kalinga, in September 2015. On all such occasions, I had found him spontaneous, sometimes childlike, sometimes outright funny.

But over time, he was changing into a different man. He was becoming somewhat reticent. He no longer joked about anything. He spoke very little. His public speeches were limited to three minutes. Gita Mehta often referred to him as a monk in the few interactions I had with her after coming on board. On an average day, the monk chief minister spoke no more than fifteen or may be twenty sentences. Of these, half consisted of just 'thank you'. A quarter of the sentences he spoke were 'all right', with a drawl that sounded like *awwright*. And awwright was all we needed to build the World Skill Center. An all right from him meant, 'Go do it. Do not waste a moment. And come back when it is all done and dusted. Rest, go figure out.'

After getting the nod from Naveen Patnaik, Sanjay and I called Mike Chong at ADB and then Bruce Poh at ITEES to set up a tripartite meeting in Singapore. We knew, neither the ADB loan, nor an eighteen-storey building could create what we had in mind. Money could only buy hardware, the physical infrastructure. The World Skill Center, to be truly worthy of the name, needed the 'hands-on, hearts-on, minds-on' approach to skill development. That is what we needed for an institution that would make our youth work-ready and world-ready. And, it had to be something too large to ignore.

39

World Skill Center[*]

The first ideation session for the World Skill Center took place at the ITE Central campus on 16 May 2018. Bruce Poh, Boon Tiong and Fabian Cheong were there from the ITEES side. Mike Chong and Harsha Annamraju represented ADB. Sanjay and I briefed them about the larger skill picture of Odisha, not just limited to our ITIs and polytechnics. We explained the concept of skill development as a pathway for human transformation against looking at technical and vocational training (TVET) as an end in itself.

Thanks to Azim Premji, I was once entrusted to seek a very similar partnership with what was known as the Motorola University. The American electronics pioneer Motorola was once at risk of losing their business to the Japanese. The company recognized that the only way they could fend off competition was to embrace Six Sigma, which is an approach to total quality management.

---

[*] The spelling of center was deliberate.

Six Sigma is a highly disciplined approach to product and service quality that asks the doer to measure, analyse, improve and control (MAIC) every activity such that the rate of defect in it is brought down to 3.6 in a million opportunity to make a mistake and create a defect. After Motorola achieved Six Sigma capability, they set up Motorola University that offered know-how to other global companies. When Wipro was trying to fend off global competition in the 1990s, I was sent to Chicago to understand how Motorola had embarked on their journey and subsequently had Motorola University brought in to help us architect the Six Sigma journey at Wipro. In that process, I developed an understanding of how to forge and manage relationship with a high-profile consulting organization—what works, what does not. One of the key lessons for me was that a collaborative relationship is built on a higher sense of shared purpose that must be forged ahead of just commercial considerations.

Usually, consulting organizations only look at revenues and move from project to project with very little emotional attachment to the outcome. They trade expertise.

I wanted ITEES to see the consulting opportunity as something they would be truly proud of someday. If they are unlikely to have some degree of emotion, shopping for their competence and trying to lift and shift their success would not work.

We needed to forge an emotional connection and consciously build great personal rapport even before signing on the dotted lines.

Based on my experience in Wipro, I knew that an established leader in a field can unconsciously impose their past on you and assume that you can replicate their success if you follow their formula diligently. But in life, it doesn't work that way at all. The giver has to understand the unique place at which the receiver is. Simply put, India is not Singapore. There needs to be a lot of respect and empathy towards the receiver.

It is interesting how life continuously prepares you for greater things. Navigating a relationship with ITEES for me would not have been possible if I was a complete novice at building international collaboration.

The ITEES team was very open to explore the idea of a strategic partnership. They had previously engaged with many ASEAN countries. And that had included a few projects in India. But their typical engagement was selling their consulting expertise. They provided their pedagogy and training material along with some amount of oversight during the implementation of a project.

But we were looking for something beyond that. We wanted transference of ITE's spirit and that, in our reckoning, needed a core team from ITEES to be stationed full-time in Bhubaneswar. We needed involvement for at least a period of three years to co-create the World Skill Center. This was not something ITEES had ever done before. They wanted time to think it over. Apart from other things, it also required the approval of the Government of Singapore.

In the days and weeks and months to come, we had many consultations between OSDA, ITEES and ADB teams and very soon it was apparent that there weren't really three different teams working. It was like all of us had blended into one even as we came from our respective organizations but now had become beholden to the World Skill Center.

The World Skill Center was created as a Section 8 company, meaning a not-for-profit, autonomous, corporate entity with its own chief executive and a board of directors. This would provide it the required autonomy outside of the government rules and regulations. We kept the basic charter of the ASTI intact. It was going to be a finishing school and a hub for 'spokes' made up of ITIs and polytechnics. It was to be a place for training of trainers, creation of pedagogy. It was to be a place for assessment, certification and recognition of prior learning. With our experience at the IndiaSkills Competition, we added one more dimension: it was to be the staging ground for all skill competitions in the future. The original goal to directly and indirectly impact 2,00,000 people over a period of five years, was recast to 1,51,000.

We decided to set aside $9 million to provide full scholarship to all the students in the initial years and then progressively get to a part-scholarship, part-sponsorship and part-fee-based model.

To start with, two different schools of training were planned: one for engineering and the other for services. The School of Engineering was to focus on mechatronics, facility technologies like mechanical and engineering services, vertical transportation, air-conditioning and refrigeration and precision engineering. For the School of Services, the plan was to start two long-duration courses in beauty and wellness and hair fashion and design. In each of the categories, the World Skill Center was going to have 20 per cent focus on fundamentals, 50 per cent on advanced technology, 10 per cent on safety and sustainability and 20 per cent on employability, life skills and design thinking.

In order to create the right kind of faculty, it was planned to bring in seventy outstanding, young teachers from polytechnics and ITIs and send them to ITE for training in leadership and pedagogical capacity building. The leadership skills design was aimed at management of institution, building industry partnership, holistic student development, academic delivery, branding and design thinking. A detailed work plan was drawn with nine key process areas to be tracked during the life of the World Skill Center. Meanwhile, ITEES confirmed that they would send a team of five experienced professionals, led by a principal and four directors of academics and administration to be located in Bhubaneswar for a period of at least two to three years. These five were to be shadowed by five from our end who would eventually take over the reign. Now, we were on a roll.

Or so we thought.

The roll became a roller coaster in no time. First came Cyclone Fani that battered the eighteen-storey structure of the proposed World Skill Center. While the structure stayed intact, the cyclone shattered glass, poured in thousands of gallons of water and caused many other damages that took months and months to fix.

Then came another unexpected news. The structure was not strong enough to handle heavy equipment. It needed huge modifications and additional structural support. After all, it was designed to house IT companies, not heavy machinery. We got experts from Mumbai to retrofit load bearing capacity. But even then, it was simply not possible to house the heavy machinery for the precision engineering course in that building. It wouldn't take the vibration. Now we had to pull out precision engineering and look for some other location for it. That would mean splitting the campus. Looking for new land and face all the associated hurdles with it.

More setbacks were to follow. Covid-19 arrived. The Government of Singapore indefinitely disallowed the movement of the five experts to India. Given the pandemic, all civil work on the eighteen-storey building also came to a halt. And two critical leaders from our team were transferred. First, it was Balwant Singh who was moved out by the government as collector of Puri when Fani hit. The second one to move was Rajesh Patil, who went off to Maharashtra on deputation. Meanwhile, managing the ITEES relationship through the virtual mode was becoming a challenge. Cross-cultural issues that are normal and could have been handled in the real world, became increasingly difficult with remote working. Equipment suppliers went into hibernation with the pandemic raging. The government loaded Sanjay Singh with additional responsibilities outside of OSDA, and he needed to give time to those. Through all this, day-to-day responsibilities on the project changed hands at ADB with Harsha Annamraju handing over to Neha Saini. At the ITEES end, mercifully, Bruce, Boon Tiong and Fabian remained constant. It was Bruce who was always unruffled with the many ups and downs at our end and smoothed things over when needed.

Amidst the turbulence, two new leaders appeared on the scene and took charge of what was beginning to look jinxed, perhaps to meet with ASTI's fate. These new leaders made sure we survived the storm to land on our feet. One was Rashmita Panda and the other, Reghu Gopalakrishnan.

* * *

I met Rashmita Panda, late one afternoon in May 2016 when I reached Nabarangapur. She was the district collector. The place brought back a flood of memories from my childhood. This was part of the undivided Koraput district. Nabarangapur was just a notified area council, not even as municipality. My father worked there when I was a three-year-old. It used to be a tiny little town in 1960, with just a few houses on both sides of a narrow road running through it, which vanished almost as soon as it started.

We lived there in a small, rented house and my job was to simply watch the world go by from the veranda. Nothing much really happened there. But come dusk, every day, unfailingly, a completely sozzled tribal man showed up like clockwork, his two legs falling, rising and falling again. All the time, he loudly cursed the government for imposing prohibition. The man lumbered along challenging the powers that be that he would drink all he could because Old Man Gandhi had told him to drink and to drink some more.

This was that same Nabarangapur and I was back here after almost fifty-five years! I was received by Rashmita Panda, a young IAS officer. Instead of a typical review lined up for me, she had called in a big group of DDU-GKY trainees, mostly girls, to interact with me. She had also called a few micro-entrepreneurs, some of them were young women who had received skill training and were now running their own tiny businesses. What struck me as unusual was that she knew them by name. And they knew who she was. More importantly, they were comfortable in her presence.

Rasmita Panda's father worked for the Andhra Bank all his life and moved from place to place. By the time she finished school, Rashmita had been through five Kendriya Vidyalayas.

She studied mechanical engineering from a private engineering college in Bhubaneswar where, from the very first year, she had her heart set on the Indian Administrative Service and had started preparing for it alongside her college work. After taking her degree, she appeared for the UPSC examination in 2008. She missed the IAS but got selected for the Indian Information Service. Thanks to a litigation that went right up to the Supreme Court of India, the appointment letters for her cohort of 110 aspirants did not arrive until 2010! By the time they did, she had already sat for the UPSC test one more time and cleared her way to the IAS.

By her own admission, as a child of constant displacement, she thrived in situations where things were in a state of flux. Fani had mowed down coastal Odisha. Rajesh Patil was going away to Maharashtra on deputation. And Covid-19 was on its way. It was her kind of chaos to reign over. She was good to go.

Reghu Gopalakrishnan came in place of Balwant Singh. He too was born to middle-class parents in Kerala, where he studied mechanical engineering at the Government Engineering College in Trivandrum. It was pretty much the order of the day for most students there to take up an IT job and this is what he did. He wrote code for a software company for a year, long enough to know it wasn't his calling. Along the way, he had heard about the Institute of Rural Management (IRMA) at Anand from his architect sister. He had always hero worshipped the legendary Verghese Kurien whose brainchild was IRMA. It was an easy decision to quit the software industry and go to IRMA. Post that, he started work at the Samaj Pragati Sahayog, an NGO set up by Mihir Shah, a man inspired by the philosophy and work of Baba Amte.

The NGO worked in the impoverished Nimad region of Madhya Pradesh. Nimad, adjoining the relatively more prosperous Malwa region is home to Bhils, Bhilwa and Korku people who traditionally grew a single crop of millet.

The NGO was teaching them how to diversify into other crops and how to augment their income by raising indigenous varieties of cows and buffaloes. Reghu lived in the Nimkhera village in Dewas district where he worked on the cattle project, extended insurance and helped farmers get bank linkage. It was tough and frustrating. For everything, from setting a milk route to getting an Internet connection, he had to turn to the various government agencies. During his three-year stint, he could meet the district collector just once. In his words, every small thing was a big fight. It was energy sapping. This is the point when he realized, he needed to get into the administrative system, make it accessible and be an agent of change from the inside. Reghu took time off, went back to Kerala and prepared for the UPSC examination. That is how he joined the IAS in 2011 and then got posted to the Odisha cadre.

When he took over from Balwant and joined work, I knew he would bring a different level of empathy for the task on hand as the director of Technical Education. His being a mechanical engineer was a huge plus point.

On 5 March 2021, keeping in mind Covid protocol, the World Skill Center was formally inaugurated by the chief minister at a small ceremony. Our partners, ADB and ITEES joined virtually. After Covid eased out, the leadership team from Singapore marked for deputation joined and the first batch of trainees trooped in. Except for the School of Precision Engineering that needed a ground-up construction, the School of Engineering and the School of Services became operational. The difficult past began receding.

* * *

Meanwhile, we started our search for a chief executive to lead the World Skill Center. The position was widely advertised and we were pleasantly surprised to see an excellent set of CVs flow in from the private sector. After a prolonged set of interviews, we had a shortlist of three very impressive candidates.

But after the selection, for various reasons, they had cold feet. While all this was happening, Sanjay Singh was transferred and in his place, Hemant Sharma, a senior IAS officer, took charge.

Undeterred by the lack of a leader at World Skill Center, we moved on. Bruce and I started working closely to create two unique ideas that eventually made the World Skill Center truly live up to its name. We persuaded the Government of Odisha, the Government of Singapore and Singapore-based industries to come together to back a week-long immersion programme at ITE Singapore for the top 10 per cent students from every batch. Even more significantly, we signed an agreement to send forty of the best performers every year for a six-month long paid training at leading Singapore companies.

At this juncture, Hemant Sharma suggested that we set up a search and select process for a CEO instead of advertising like the last time and came across the CV of a lady named Alka Arora Misra. She had just retired as additional member of the Railway Board. She had also headed the Rail University at Baroda. Alka was a gold medallist from Allahabad University in economics before joining the Indian Railway Service. Post her retirement, she had been contemplating setting up a skill university with special emphasis on women.

We persuaded her to try her ideas at the World Skill Center. Though she was not aware at the time, we were also looking at her as my potential successor in due course. On 1 November 2022, Alka Arora Misra took charge. Then came yet another secretary-level reshuffle at the department of skill development. A little more than a month after that, Usha Padhee, a 1996 batch IAS officer on central deputation replaced Hemant Sharma.

She was the first woman director general for civil aviation security with the Government of India and had come back to the state. With Alka Arora Mishra and Usha Padhee at the helm, World Skill Center gained great momentum. It emerged as a significant model for both skill development and multilateral collaboration of a high order. It routinely hosted diplomats from many countries, ministers from the Central government and from other states and chief executives of lending private-sector organizations.

On 29 June 2023, seven years after joining the Government of Odisha, perhaps one of the longest stints for any outsider, I made way for Alka Mishra to take over as the chairperson of Odisha Skill Development Authority, with the additional charge of chief executive of World Skill Center. I took up the role of chief adviser to the Government for institutional capacity building for all the civil services training institutes across domains. My task was to blueprint the future of civil services training so that Odisha could completely reimagine entry-level as well as in-service training for its officers. But destiny had other designs.

In May 2024, after the general elections, the Naveen Patnaik-led BJD party lost power. The Bhartiya Janata Party formed the new government. It is customary for incumbents in positions like mine to leave as these are considered 'co-terminus' with the government of the day.

Susmita and I handed over the government house, the official car and all the trappings of being in the rank and status of a cabinet minister and returned to Bengaluru.

Part VII

Leading Transformative Change

40

How Far Can We See?

What is common between someone like Muni Tigga, Buddhadeb Bhanja, Basanti Pradhan and Sumati Nayak? Apart from the obvious qualities that make them stand apart from many, it is their unmistakable power of vision. Each had a distinct vision of a future in which they saw themselves differently from who they were at the start of their journey. While Muni Tigga was still at ITI Bargarh, she imagined herself inside the locomotive engine's cockpit, hauling a train. Buddhadeb's decision to put rupees one lakh into a welding kit when he did not have a single order is the non-trivial ability to imagine something that does not exist in the here and now. Basanti saw herself, not as a SMO but a supervisor as much as the motive force behind her larger family's well-being. Sumati clearly foresaw the important link between being multilingual and being hugely successful in her profession in an alien land. Each had the power of vision.

While each of them, children of vision, had an abiding view of their individual future, what about the collective future of a people? Now that needs a true leader. And who is a leader? American futurologist Joel Barker tells us, a leader is a person others opt to follow to go someplace they would not go by themselves. Barker argues, the most important leadership deliverable therefore is the ability to see a vision; the vison of a future that does not exist.

It is not enough for one individual leader to have the power of vision. The leader must uphold the vision for people so that a *vision community* is built around it and people begin to move towards the intended future with a meta-mind.

In the beginning, it may even appear unattainable. Sometimes, there is a mountain of inertia in everyone. The most cited reason for the inertia is paucity of resources. They have got the guns; we only have bows and arrows. We do not even have food for tomorrow, how can we walk a thousand miles? These refrains come packaged in different words every day when the voice of change makes itself heard—whether in the government, the corporate sector or elsewhere.

Even as the future may promise the people their true entitlement, they remain inert and unmotivated to pursue it. Stability and status quo sing a soothing lullaby.

As an example, the people of India knew that centuries of foreign subjugation were wrong, that colonial rule and servitude were wrong. Yet, they had to wait until a Gandhi arrived and he galvanized everyone with the idea of independence. It is the same with Nelson Mandela in South Africa fighting apartheid or Lee Kwan Yew building Singapore from nothing to becoming a leading first-world economy. What unites these leaders?

First and foremost, it is their unusually high comfort in departing from the past. However, the past can often be very alluring. Sometimes, it is like a chain around our feet. Sometimes, it is so dark and dangerous that we do not want to agitate it. However, the future requires a sharp point of departure. Like a boat needs that one decisive push to leave the shore to go someplace else. It is the leader who is required to untangle the rope from the jetty and give it that one decisive push for the boat to pull out and set sail.

In doing so, a critical need is for the leader to be comfortable with incomplete information. Long-haul human journeys do not come with a built-in GPS. No one can guarantee their point of arrival. The leader must have faith in the abiding outcome even as the course of the journey is not detailed. That is why leaders are called path creators.

In life, most people we see are path dependant. They can walk the path if you show them one. But a very small set, the leaders among people, are the ones who break new ground. They build new pathways where none exist. Along the way, failure is always a distinct possibility. But these leaders do not see failure as an option.

Even as a leader may create a new path, it is impossible to build one that truly is the shortest and a clear and comfortable bridge between where people are and where they are set out to go to. As a result, losing the way is a rite of passage. In those moments, when people following their leader do not see the road ahead or an imminent danger, it is the naysayers and the cynics who immediately stand up. They tell people, we told you so. Then, of course, there are the ones who are not visible and audible. They look committed but in reality, they are the ones who are there to subvert. A true leader budgets for all of it; that is the only way of not getting frustrated. The voice of the naysayers allows the leader the opportunity to restate and sometimes recast the narrative for the people. It creates new momentum.

But sometimes, it is not the naysayers and the ones doing subversive compliance. There is popular wisdom that comes in great dollops. Sometimes, it can halt the progress just before the tunnel bends to end. The popular wisdom says it is perhaps better to turn back. It is safer to be on the ground than the seas. Popular wisdom may say it is not too late to call it off. And sometimes, popular wisdom convincingly cites data as evidence.

For taking people to the promised land, invariably, the visionary leader must deal with a larger-than-life adversary. Sometimes, it is a despot, sometimes it is an entity like a government system or a moribund corporation that has lost its way and, quite often, it is an entrenched idea like social discrimination. The leader does not see the size of the adversary as daunting. The larger the adversary, the greater the glory.

Oftentimes, the monstrous size of the adversary is the guarantee of success. From Gandhi to Mandela to

Lee Kwan Yew, the recurring theme of a David versus Goliath is a constant over centuries of civilization.

Finally, when people follow a great vision, they move the mountains every day, they do not always see butterflies and rainbows along the way. In truth, every day brings a new sorrow; there are many things to be deeply unhappy about. For a true leader, these are not reasons to question the vision. And certainly, there is no room for cynicism. A leader cannot be a cynical visionary. The two words are mutually exclusive.

And what about great vision itself?

To start with, great vision is often a child of troubled times. A recurring image of that in my mind is the part in the film by Richard Attenborough where a racist conductor throws Gandhi, hurls his luggage out of the train on to a desolate platform in the dead of the night. The train moves on. In that moment, in the apt representation of the idea of troubled times, Gandhi internalizes the pain of apartheid and servitude.

Then, there is the idea of scale. Small departures do not need a vison; they ask for no strategic intent. If we study the history of the world, whether it is religious, political, economic, scientific or in the field of creative arts, we will notice that great vision is invariably about scale. Great vison entails hairy, audacious goals. This is for a good reason. Earlier, we spoke about building a vision community. In the journey into the unknown, it is the people that must sign up, come aboard, pull the oars, bite the wind and brace the darkness. For them to enlist, the cause has to be worthwhile and the destination something to yearn for.

You can seldom excite popular imagination with a call to climb a molehill. People want to climb a mountain.

Historically speaking, momentous, impactful vison invariably involves simple people with average tools. That combination is a truly powerful one. Sometimes, you set off with the vison to discover India but you land in the United States. That is okay. It is not a bad outcome at all. Similarly, sometimes you start with a large vision and return only partially fulfilled. Remember Mission 123? One gold, two silvers and three bronzes at WorldSkills Competition in Kazan? Well, we never got the silvers and bronzes. But no one remembers that. No one cares about it because we got India her first ever gold.

How far we can see is truly about leadership and the power of vision. While people accept that, they often wonder if visionary leadership is an exceptional thing and people endowed with such capability are born, not made. In the process, they risk disenfranchising themselves. I am sure some leaders are extraordinarily talented, they may appear to be born with great abilities. But if we observe many around us over a period of time, we begin to realize, visioning is a function of how much we practise it. When we become aware of the idea, we appreciate its power and its nuances, we gain the ability to expand the size of the vision that we create, we feel comfortable in running with it over the long haul. Until it becomes one with us.

41

Crossing Over, Making It Work

I had told you in the beginning that, among other things, I want this book to be read by leaders who want to cross over. While on a basic level, many people understand it, but perhaps, we need to talk about what it truly entails and what it is not. Crossing over is not about making a job change, it is not a cross-functional shift in a corporate sense or a change of assignment for a government servant. Nor is it a post-retirement gig. A crossover leader is embracing something radically different. The leader is not really equipped with core knowledge of the new avocation. There are absolutely no safety nets. Going forward, the rolodex of the past carries limited value. New networks must now be created, new alignments negotiated and new collaborations sought. This is the 'ctrl-alt-del' moment for an individual. It most certainly is not a second gig. Crossing over calls for burning the bridge, almost certainly there is no looking back.

While crossover leaders do not know what the future entails, they have an inner call, a deep, driving desire to make a difference. In doing so, they are comfortable with the idea that they may never come back to where they were. They well know, if they fail, they will be remembered for this one last failure and not the success and reputation that have been their past hallmark. It is what we may call, a high-risk and high-reward option that you embrace.

I think the starting point for anyone wanting to take on a crossover assignment is comfort with ambiguity. The future, by its very nature, is an abstraction. Navigating it with published data is of little use. Working with the completely unfamiliar requires deep intuition. Everyone has the built-in power of intuition but many are uncomfortable using it. More importantly, as they do not use the faculty, it becomes so latent that it ceases to be of value. Just as you train for a serious trek or a marathon, you train to be intuitive.

The narrative so far may create an impression that the crossover is a deliverer who comes from the heavens and changes things. The crossover is the central character. In reality, that is not true. The central character is always the sponsor. The sponsor may not have the knowledge or skills to deliver the mission, but they have the power to invoke you. Naveen Patnaik invoked me. Without it, I would be doing my own 'read, write, travel, teach' thing in Bengaluru or someplace else. Hence, it is important to begin with an assessment of the sponsor before crossing over. And that takes us straight to the unambiguous question of authority. We need to ask the hard question, does the sponsor have the authority?

Nandan Nilekani had summarized it well for me when I had sought his advice before taking up my assignment. Remember, what he had told me? Authority can only flow from authority.

The idea of authority goes beyond the idea of high office. It comes from the personal credibility of the sponsor. Occupants of high offices are often accidental successes; they come and go. In many states in India, the office of a chief minister has a revolving door, no one incumbent lasting there a full term. Responding to a call from someone like that to come and change things and to spearhead a seemingly aspirational and transformative initiative runs a huge risk. Transformational change requires a long view of time and enacting it is a long play. If the sponsor does not have personal credibility beyond just occupying that high office, your success would be quite uncertain and perhaps extremely difficult. Your peers will not take you seriously because the sponsor may not survive the next reshuffle. A big part of the sponsor's credibility is linked to how long that individual has been around and are they known to demonstrate constancy of purpose. However lucrative the position and lofty the assignment on offer, unless the sponsor has personal reputation, crossing over is unlikely to work out for you.

Assuming that the sponsor is solid, the next thing is to negotiate upfront, the charter, the level of empowerment, the core support framework to be made available to you and the messaging needed for you to deliver. This does not need to have all the details but the basic construct must feel good.

When Naveen Patnaik had asked me to come to Odisha, there was a high degree of mutual understanding of what was expected of me—what I would do, how I would do it, what I needed from him and his aides. There was also clear understanding on what I would not do. I was embracing the allure of public life, not politics. The fact was well respected. In all the eight years I was there, I was not required to attend a political consultation and far less a meeting or a rally. My loyalty was to the government, the agreed mission and the purpose. My loyalty was not to the political party in power or every aspect of their ideology.

Many people feel overwhelmed by the persona of the sponsor. They may be in awe. They may feel insecure about their own inexperience. As a result, they may be hesitant and consider the upfront negotiation process to be awkward, even risky. As a result, they can walk into an assignment with assumptions. Worse, with a false sense of obligation. These are fatal flaws. High stakes assignments call for a relationship of candour with respect and this is best laid at the courting stage itself.

When the chief minister told me the third time during our early conversations that I was free to bring in whoever I wanted in order to turnaround the system, I told him that was not my style. I told him that I would rather work with the existing system and the current resources. I wasn't going to airdrop whizzkids from the IT industry and smart consultants from the Big Four. It signalled to him that I was not going to be a magician, I would do things my way and the hard way.

Earlier in the book, in the chapter on *The Success Managers*, I touched upon my handlers. I am immensely grateful that I got these outstanding men who made sure that I succeeded. They were invested in me. I asked of the chief minister that they must be available whenever I may need them. It is critical to know, right in the beginning, who your success managers would be. It is better to know these people before you jump in headlong. It is also necessary to do the due diligence on them, assess their reputation and determine the mutual acceptability before entering the woods.

Then, there is the aspect of how to build a framework for the working relationship with the success managers. The very idea of having them is to minimize the need for and the urge to run to the sponsor for everything. Go to the handlers for most things. In doing so, keep in mind one important thing: never take them by surprise. You have to keep them looped in on major issues, and you must get their advice and sense their concerns. They are your success managers and they must be made to feel that way. Yet, show no subservience. You are reporting to their boss, not to them. Any show of cordiality that has the slightest smell of subservience can tilt the power equation. You go to them for advice, opinion and help but not for decisions.

The other critical factor is messaging. The sponsor must signal who you are, why you have been brought there and what proximity you would enjoy. A large part of that messaging is the legislative proclamation, the rank and status of the office etcetera, but that is not the real thing. The real messaging is in fact very subtle. Nandan Nilekani had told me, somewhat in jest, that once in a while, you have to be with the boss behind closed doors even as you are doing nothing other than looking at the painting. The world outside must know that you are alone with the boss. The system takes note of such things.

More than being a literal example, the essence of Nandan's advice was meant to be taken seriously. But all credit to Chief Minister Naveen Patnaik—he made sure the system knew that I had his complete support, that I had full access to him and that I was here to drive the government's agenda. These things can be read from many things like the speed at which the sponsor accedes to a request, getting invited to a dinner hosted for a visitor not connected to your work, the power distance in the seating arrangement on a dais at a public event and that occasional ride on the same helicopter.

But such top-down messaging can be counterproductive unless one builds a parallel channel of acceptance from the team that does the real work. In my case, it was the bureaucracy. It is important not to live on the sponsor's messaging alone. On my part, I made sure that I showed due respect to every government official, sometimes breaching protocol. The demonstration of respect must happen right in the beginning and remain consistent.

Fortunately, I was very conscious about it and the result was the total acceptance by the top leaders in the bureaucracy.

It started with a small but significant thing. In the main conference hall of the government where the chief minister chairs meetings, there is a large elliptical table. The chief minister sits at its centre. To his left, the first seat is taken by the chief secretary followed by the development commissioner and then the principal secretaries. To the right of the chief minister, all his cabinet colleagues, all of them elected politicians, are seated, in sequence of their seniority. Now, I was neither a bureaucrat, nor a politician. The system had never had someone like me before to figure where I should be seated. When I entered the conference room for the first time, Chief Secretary Aditya Padhi got up and very graciously offered me his chair, volunteering to shift one place further to the left. I refused and insisted that I take the seat after him. In that moment, Aditya Padhi protested, pointing out that my rank was equivalent to a cabinet minister and that I should be seated next to the chief minister but I held my ground. It was a seemingly small thing but every single senior officer assembled in the room took note.

In the subsequent years, whenever there was a need for a one-on-one meeting, I came to the chief secretary's office even when Aditya Padhi and then, his three successors, always volunteered to come to mine. In my mind, the chief secretary of the state had a much larger charter and so much more on hand at any point in time; that decided the protocol for me.

Beyond all this, the one big thing that led to my acceptance and made a big difference to my effectiveness, was my focus on people. When leaders take on a large transformative task, they often psych themselves with the need for demonstrating urgency to show that they are making a difference. In the process, they begin by making large policy changes, scrapping or amending the old and announcing new ones. I was clear that people must be seen as my prime focus and policy was a means to that end. My starting point was to keep real people at the centre of every conversation.

I paid close attention to them; I got to know each of them by name. I got to know their personal backgrounds. I understood their own life goals and motivations. It created the foundation of trust that makes for acceptance of the changes the leader may subsequently bring in. Humanizing the leadership responsibility, putting real people's names and faces and stories at the core of every policy is very important if one wants to create a lasting legacy.

Very early in my career, I realized that every organization is a 'system' beyond being a collection of human beings pursuing a certain set of objectives. That system has a consciousness that is greater than the aggregate of its constituents. It is in fact a living being with eyes and ears and a soul. It is constantly watching you. It is listening to your voice and thoughts. It knows exactly how you feel about it and reciprocates accordingly. Remember what I had said to Nano Unicorn Biswajit Mohanta? I always tell young entrepreneurs like him that the business you build knows exactly how committed you are to it, and accordingly, it flourishes and withstands difficulties or simply withers one day. Some leaders are selective in their commitment to the organization. Some accept it with all its pluses and minuses. The system knows it. I had great affection for my charter, my organization and the larger governmental 'system' that cradled it. In fact, I loved the government. In turn, it loved me and gave me the freedom to nudge it. Love precedes all acceptance.

When we work with a system and do so over the long haul, we need to understand its inherent limitations and issues. Persuading a system to change, sometimes confronting it, is important. It is equally important to build empathy for some of the genuine constraints it may have. Instead of being critical or becoming frustrated with it, one must be understanding. There are things the government cannot change. That should not give the hurried impression that it is stodgy or lacking an inherent purpose.

One of the things one must accept about working with government is flux. During my eight years there, I saw four chief secretaries come and go, and the secretary of the skill development got reshuffled four times. I learnt not to bemoan this process. In fact, I saw providing continuity of vision and purpose and ensuring that initiatives do not get dropped was a critical part of my own deliverables.

Likewise, there are things inherent to the way governments function. Instead of venting or putting on an air of '*I am OK, the system is not*', one has to find solutions. One has to be patient and, sometimes, abandon ideas that demand an awful lot from a system that it simply cannot provide for some reason.

One of the things that I could not make a big difference to was short-term skill development no matter how much I wanted to. After Covid, the backbone of the few good PIAs broke. In addition, for good reason or bad, many of my colleagues were not excited about the idea. Sometimes, it disappointed me but I needed to remind myself that they had as much right to impact making as me. Instead of pushing them too much, I felt it wiser to pursue things where there was a natural flow of energy. Instead of relentless pursuit of everything, a leader must know what to give up, what to trade in and how to go where the energy flows. You cannot be victorious on all fronts.

As leaders chart their course, it is inevitable that they will make mistakes, and in the process sometimes cause hurt. They run the risk of not realizing it themselves and chances are, no one flags it to them. One such event remains vivid in my memory. Coming from a private-sector background, I often obsessed with punctuality, sometimes overdoing it. Once it so happened that I had called for a meeting and among the attendees was Dipti Mohapatro, a senior officer who headed the administration function of the Capital Region Urban Transport (CRUT) bus system that ran the Mo Bus system. She had come late for the meeting by perhaps half an hour and I told her the meeting was off.

She went back without a word, understandably quite upset. The meeting was reconvened at a later date. This time, she came along with her boss, Arun Bothra, a senior IPS officer with the additional charge of CRUT. The meeting went off well.

At the end, when everyone got up to leave, Arun asked if he could have a few minutes with me. In the conversation that followed, he brought up my last meeting with Dipti Mohapatro and how I had sent her back for arriving late. He said it was unfair on my part. That it wasn't her fault at all. It was *my* office that was to be blamed because she had not been informed by them in time. She had to rush at the last moment leaving her work when she learnt about the meeting. As a result, she was late. I had, without getting into details, simply sent her back.

I thanked Arun for his forthrightness and as soon as he left, called Pinaki Patnaik. I asked him where the CRUT office was. The next thing I did was to arrive at the CRUT office unannounced, with a bouquet of flowers and apologized to Dipti Mohapatro for my rude behaviour.

When people come from outside, they start by building a large set-up for themselves. Particularly in the government; how many people report to you, how many physical offices you have and how much additional charge you hold are considered measures of success. In all the years, I had exactly four people with me: Pinaki Patnaik who was my officer-on-special duty, my private secretary, first Manoj Rout and then Sasank Mohapatra and Gitanjali Mishra who set up and ran the Nano Unicorn programme. In formulating policy, reviewing government programmes, implementing changes and new initiatives, I always worked with and through the respective departments. As a result, people saw that I was not building my personal empire and it made a big difference.

In addition, I focused on consciously building collaboration at scale with many large, external organizations to make change happen. This called for building a respectful mindset and always making those organizations an integral part of our journey. This involved treating them as equals, going out of the way to make them feel important, listening to them, giving them the due credit and volunteering to help with my own time and resources for their own internal initiatives so that they could become hugely successful.

If they were going to be hugely successful in their larger endeavour beyond what they did with us, our success was a given. Our relationship was based on constant communication at the leadership level. We went beyond transactions. This is how we created a fantastic working relationship with organizations like ITEES, ADB, Tata Strive, NSDC and many others who delivered the vision of Skilled in Odisha. They were not just our providers, consultants, suppliers or enablers, they were partners who became emotionally invested in us.

All my life, I have revelled in being very hands-on in everything I do. It is usually a good thing; a virtue for a leader. Yet, sometimes, we overdo it. We risk snatching the rein from our subordinates without realizing it. Our job is to listen, to empower, set benchmarks and goals and de-risk things for them. We need to enable them with the resources and the networks we bring in but not do what they should be doing in the first place. The government does a far better job than many private-sector organizations on that count. If there is a law-and-order problem in a district, the chief secretary or the director general of police do not rush in there. They let the collector and the superintendent of police handle it. They may call in perhaps just once to check, they may have a line of advice, they may clear the deck in the background and send reinforcement but no, they do not rush in there and take charge. They don't snatch the reins from the collector or the SP of the district. It is considered extreme and disrespectful.

In any position of leadership, the leader must have their own brand. Coming from the corporate sector, I did have a brand. But that brand was the table stake. Once inside the new system, that brand of the past is baggage, and sometimes it is a liability. As someone from the outside world, leading transformative change within a government set-up, I needed to build a *new* brand for myself.

For a crossover leader, the new brand needs a distinct voice. The sooner you shed your old brand and take in a new one, the better assimilated you are. You cannot live off what you stood for in your past.

It is obvious that every leader must communicate well. But as a crossover, it is important to realize that you are now delivering a different kind of message for different stakeholders and perhaps through very different channels. At Mindtree, strange as it may seem, I did not use social media. When I joined the government, I signed up on Twitter and over time, built a large enough following. I persuaded *Sambad*, the largest circulated daily in Odia language, to give me an op-ed space to write regular columns. I regularly created content so that my ideas gather hands and legs. I used these spaces, my new communication real estate, to hold up my narratives. Not the government's narrative. These made me visible. They helped me build a credible brand that was consistent with my past reputation but went beyond my work in the IT industry.

For a crossover leader, while it is important to stay focused on the agreed charter, it is necessary to be a good volunteer when the system needs an extra pair of hands. This is particularly important while working with the government. At a leadership level, the government runs with a lot thinner bandwidth than what many outsiders believe. At the same time, it has to deal with many unscripted events during which it needs people who can show up and say, I got it covered. When Covid-19 happened, most of my work in skill development came to a standstill and at the same time, the government was dealing with a protracted public emergency. I offered my services in dealing with the pandemic. I was asked to take charge as the chief spokesperson for the government on Covid-19 and this work endeared me to everyone in the state.

Even prior to Covid, without losing focus on my day-to-day deliverables, I helped wherever I could, particularly helping other government departments in creating and validating their strategy as much as engaging in public forums to articulate the priorities in skill development to create goodwill from a broader set of stakeholders. But all along, I never lost sight of my own charter. Every day, I asked myself to remember why I had been brought here for in the first place.

As we journey into the future, seeking to fix problems or pursue opportunities, a lot of people know what needs to change, what must be fixed and what new solutions would succeed. Yet, in going about implementing the ideas and executing the solutions, they overlook the process of managing change. It is because, despite good intentions, they have inadequate understanding of, and sensitivity to, managing the change process itself. As a result, it becomes someone else's journey, not the shared journey of a people. We end up achieving sub-optimal results and sometimes meet complete failure. All large-scale transformation, particularly in the public sphere, needs a deep understanding of how to manage large-scale, transformative change. More on that in the next chapter.

42

Managing Change

Our conversation on change must begin with the idea of future itself. My fascination with it started in my twenties, particularly after I entered the nascent information technology industry of India. It wasn't called software then; it was all about computer hardware. With the arrival of very large-scale integration (VLSI) technology, India was at the cusp of change, soon to leapfrog into a future no one knew anything about.

Around this time, in 1984, I started reading books by Alvin Toffler, in particular, his great work, *Future Shock*. It captivated me. Through Toffler, I was initiated into somewhat of a fluid discipline that was being spoken about at that time: futurology. It is the art and science of connecting the dots to anticipate (as against predict) what the future may look like. This was also the time when John Naisbitt came to the fore with his book *Megatrends*. In it, Naisbitt spoke about the ten most important trends of the future shaping our world as we moved into the twenty-first century. He called each of these changes a megatrend. These thinkers began to shape my awareness of what I may call 'future consciousness'. When we can anticipate the future, the next step is to step back and ask how we can prepare for it. Every future asks us to embark on a journey that is unique to a leader and in many parts, unchartered for their people.

Simply put, as leaders, we need to anticipate a future and we build our desired place in it. This is very different from making plans based on thinking that the future will merely be an extension of the present. That what we are is all we will ever be. Or at best, a better version of who we are today.

Anticipating the future, sometimes imagining it and building scenarios of what may happen, is perhaps the first task of a leader. The second thing is to look at the emergent opportunities and understand the powers of discontinuity that it may bring along with it.

During the 1990s, I was also deeply drawn to the works of Peter Drucker, perhaps the greatest management thinker of our times. From discovering Drucker, I veered towards Peter Senge at the Massachusetts Institute of Technology, whose works helped me understand systems theory. His book *The Fifth Discipline* left a great impact on me.

Senge asks us to look at things as systems, recognize the deep, subtle interconnected nature of the parts and move from cause-effect thinking to getting to the root cause of things. In the course of understanding systems thinking, I read a book titled *Presence: The Human Purpose & the Field of the Future.* which he had co-authored with Otto Schramer and two others.

Otto, as he is better known, took a systems view of the process of change and applied it with great coherence to social engineering. A big part of the work I did with the government was about social engineering.

Otto came out with an idea he called 'Theory U' and wrote a book with that title. In it, he said, all social engineering is complex and leaders who make it happen go through a pattern of personal journey as do their people. That pattern looks like the letter U.

At the core of Theory U are three distinct points of personal experience: we begin by *sensing* the environment, the issues and the interconnectedness of things. From there, we journey on to get to a place or experience called *presencing*. It is at this point that the answers to complex issues we are dealing with present themselves. Once we get the answer, we have to move on to a state called *realizing*. This is the state in which we act out our knowledge, give the benefit of our understanding to create change that stays. These three states entail deep leadership experiences that are beautifully presented in the picture here.

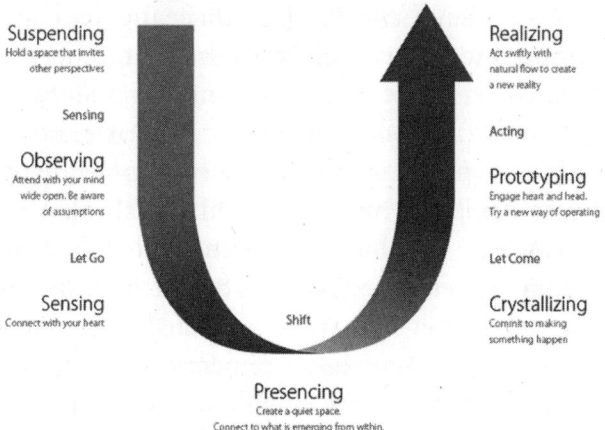

Transformational change starts at the top of the left hand of the U. This is where your journey begins. At this point, a leader must begin by suspending preconceived ideas and remove biases. This is not easy because, leaders bring past expertise, formulae of success and ego in great measure. They risk the temptation to show quick results. Replicating what has worked previously is a strong urge. But unless we suspend our past ideas and the biases, we cannot truly 'sense' the reality on the ground. No achievement of my long and successful career in the private sector could have helped me to understand the reality, as the 30 Days, 30 Districts and 3000 kilometres journey did.

Even as we can sometimes sense the environment and its underlying issues, most of us react rather than respond to them. One way we do that is to look at problems on hand and think of their apparent causes. We spring into action with solutions that do not work because we have not gone into connecting all the dots and seeking the root cause of a phenomenon. It is beautifully depicted in the story that unfolded between Dr Rajat Panigrahi and Didi Sethi. He threw the girl out because he saw her poor attendance linked to her poor commitment. He saw it as an act of indiscipline. The same Dr Panigrahi, when he visited her home, saw deeper causes behind her irregularity at class, their interconnectedness and through that leadership insight, he was able to realize his own folly in throwing her out. He needed to get to the deeper causes, in fact finally to the root cause, to come out with a worthwhile solution and not just an apparent fix. The result was profound.

Sensing is a multi-sensory act and needs honing. To start with, it is a physical act. We may or may not see things as we pass them every day during the course of our work. We may or may not hear voices as people speak. We may or may not pick up the tremor as we touch someone for a brief moment. Good leaders must begin by sensing with their eyes and ears and by learning to touch and smell and taste. Looking back, that was what was happening when I was looking at cobwebs and filthy walls on an ITI and listening to the inaudible whisper of the old instructor who was speaking about Muni Tiga. That was what was happening when

I would touch the surface of a computer keyboard in a so-called smart classroom to know it has never been used before. That is what was happening when I sat down to eat meals, to taste the gruel and the gravy, to know what skill trainees were fed in training centres.

As we listen, we forget that we have a head and a heart. The head gives us the rational space, but it is the heart that listens with empathy and love. Unless leaders have empathy and love, they cannot create hope.

The way to change people's mind is to listen to people's heart.

The process of deep listening starts to glide us down to the middle of the left hand of the U. This where we realize that we must completely let go of our past and its associated baggage. This is the one that weighs with successes no longer truly relevant, fears that may be mindless and models of constructing change that no longer work. It includes ideas that I can airdrop an elite team that I have always trusted in the past and they will fix everything.

Only when we let go does the process of deep sensing begin.

Then, we begin to listen to the inner voice of the system. We begin to get to the root of things. Otto says this is where you 'connect with your heart'. These are no trivial words. Everyone has a heart. Every heart speaks. But we need to connect to it before we can listen to its stories, ideas and guidance.

The next stop along the journey is an unusual one. It is the bottom of the U where all movement stops. All voices are silenced. We are so exhausted that we stop thinking. It is in this point that we experience 'presencing'.

Presencing is a state where your mind is so quiet that sitting at the shore of a lake, you can hear a drop of water fall in the middle of it. Remember our repeated attempts at building eight ASTIs? It was a classic example of not sensing. The more we sought to fix things, the more they were failing. Till we let go. The breakthrough idea of the World Skill Centre came from nowhere aboard an Indigo flight. Even as we were entering the plane, doors were closing, we were settling in, we had no idea we would be discussing it. Ideas that lead to truly significant, sustained, transformative change present themselves only when we are at the bottom of the U. They come from nowhere.

But the knowledge of transformative ideas is not enough. The idea must be acted out. This is where the leader begins the journey up the right hand of the U. Just as in the path to presencing you start by: 'let go', in this phase, you 'let come'.

New paths present themselves.

New collaborators emerge.

New resources are made available that previously did not exist.

But the journey up the U is not the easy one. It is the phase that signifies climbing. Metaphorically so because acting out an idea is strenuous; it needs all the sinews and the muscles of the body and the mind.

The journey up the U goes through the phases of crystalizing, prototyping and finally, 'realizing' change. Realizing change, Otto says, is about acting swiftly, with natural flow to create a new reality.

Very interestingly, the journey of the U is actually not one journey. Imagine this: The big U consists of many small U at each step. A transformative journey is, in essence, a journey of many journeys. The leader needs to be mindful of that fact.

What are the leadership imperatives needed for enacting the process of sensing, presencing and realizing in our lives? Otto talks about seven.

We need to hold the space. Listen to what life calls you to do. Listen to your own self, to others and make sure that there is space where people can talk.

Observe. Attend with your mind wide open. Observe without your voice of judgement, effectively suspending past cognitive schema.

Sense. Connect with your heart and facilitate the opening process. See things as interconnected wholes.

Presence. Connect to the deepest source of yourself and will and act from the emerging whole.

Crystallize. Access the power of intention. Ensure a small group of key people commits itself to the purpose and outcomes of the project.

Prototype. Integrate head, heart and hand. One should act and learn by doing, avoiding the paralysis of inaction, reactive action or over analysis.

Perform. Play the 'macro violin'. Find the right leaders and find appropriate social technology to get a multi-stakeholder project going.

The story of Odisha's skill development efforts was clearly a depiction of Theory U at work, every step of the way. From sensing to realizing.

43

The Transformative Leader

Congratulations, you have made it to the end of the book. Together, we undertook a journey of eight long years. Along the way, we have met so many people from so many generations, been to many lands, sometimes far beyond Odisha. Our story was woven with a common strand, the idea of transformative change. It is befitting, therefore, that we step back and reflect on the transformational leader. What are the attending leadership traits essential for change at scale to happen? As I present some of them, I want you to bind them all with four defining strands: pain, purpose, persistence and possibilities.

We start with pain, the capacity to feel pain and to be pained.

Pain reveals purpose.

Purpose needs to be enacted and this needs persistence.

It is only when we pledge persistence, that possibilities become the reality.

That is the essence of transformative change in every field of human endeavour.

A leader's feeling of pain is invariably the starting point. Without a sense of pain, a leader will not have a deep churn inside. The idea of pain is very interesting. It is not difficult to feel one's own pain. To feel a pain that belongs to other people asks us to develop deep empathy. Sometimes, these people are blissfully unaware of their own pain and are numbed by the status quo of things. They have no urgency to question it, far less come out of it. And sometimes, it is not just the pain of a people, but that of a system. A leader must have the ability to sense both.

I felt that pain with people and systems. The way Shantilata Patras of the world were being treated caused me pain as did the way the ITIs were regressing—with everything from tobacco stains on the walls to loss of identity of its people.

From a deep sense of pain emerges the purpose. Gandhi was deeply pained by the apartheid. He saw it as an act of tremendous injustice against people. No one wants to be in servitude, it is forced upon them. The transformative leader builds a sense of urgency in attempting to rectify the injustice or avenge the wrong. This becomes the purpose. And in this, a sense of urgency is very critical. This is where armchair intellectuals and activists fall short of becoming transformative leaders. In fact, these people may know more about what is wrong with the state of things and quite often know the answers, but they do not want to jump headlong. They do not want to dirty their hands. They do not climb up the U because it asks for personal commitment, sacrifice, embracing failure and constant negotiations with followers, naysayers and lay stakeholders alike.

The purpose, by itself it is not complete without a set of goals. These goals are not just the leader's goals. These are goals that belong to the people we are seeking to stir. But knowing the inertia and the apathy, people do not wake up by themselves.

Purpose wakes them up.

But as I have said it before, reducing it to climbing a molehill makes them go back to their state of stupor. A transformative leader shows them the mountain. It has impossible written all over it. Without a degree of impossibility, dreams do not become worthwhile.

And who really executes the dream? Transformative change is not delivered by any one leader. Once galvanized, it is the people who take over the task of pulling the chariot.

These are ordinary people with simple tools that bring about great change.

As a student of leadership, I have been fascinated with the depiction of how great leaders deliver lasting change with ordinary people and simple tools. This is beautifully presented in movies like *Gandhi*, *The Ten Commandments* and *Braveheart*. Gandhi takes on the British Empire with poor peasants, Moses takes on the mighty Pharoah and William Wallace wages war against the English with his ragtag bunch of fellowmen.

Contrast this with the refrain you may have heard from many leaders—about how they are surrounded by such useless people. Ah, if only I had a good team, they bemoan. These leaders cannot deliver a revolution.

Pursuing a larger-than-life purpose, something seemingly unattainable yet aspirational, requires one to pick up the cudgels against the enemy. Invariably, at that point in time, the power equation is in favour of the other side. As we saw in the chapter 'How Far Can We See', history is replete with the David versus Goliath stories. These convey a consistent message. People fear size, scale and the resultant striking power of an adversary and that makes them nervous. The transformative leader knows that the sheer size of the adversary makes it worthwhile. That adversary need not be an individual, a tyrant or a despot. Quite often, the adversary is the poor self-esteem of a people, accumulated social apathy and the asymmetry of information in a system. In fact, it is important to look for these before demonizing any given individual or a collective.

How do transformative leaders get ordinary people to do extraordinary things? For this, they need to connect with people on an emotional level and not just on the rational level. The emotional connection opens the heart to embrace the message, *be the change* and make the sacrifices necessary to move the system. The emotive connect comes from the many things demonstrated by the leader over a long period of time. It begins with what Nandan Nilekani had told me, 'Speak their language.'

Here, the language is not just the spoken word, it is how those words are used, what narrative gets built with them and the stories that get told. Sometimes, it is the words that are unsaid. Even silence has a language of its own and it better be *their* language.

Now comes the big question. Can a leader who feels the pain and sees the purpose, drive the revolution from the comforts of a drawing room? Can a leader drive change in Columbia while sitting in California?

Many people come to their village for a holiday, they drop in to see the school where they once studied. Its condition stirs them in a well-meaning way. They go to the government, ask for changes and offer to get 'involved', only to head back soon to where they came from, in time before the fancy school opens in the big city, for their own kids. Can they drive change?

Transformational leaders like Gandhi sacrificed a life of comfort to deliver on their pain and the purpose. Simply put, they were where the action was. Here, I always think of the Tata Strive change agents who made a great difference to us. I have met many of them individually. I have come to know their own stories of pain and purpose and how they have become transformative leaders themselves. Tatwamasi, who arrived at the special ITI in Khordha, exposed to hundreds of youths trying to break free from the prisons of their physical handicaps for the first time, was able to help them rise, win against their own selves and then take on the world because he was there. He was right there with them. He was no commuter-change maker.

Being there is difficult for most people because of a simple thing: it asks for personal displacement and giving up of day-to-day comforts. And it wasn't Tatwamasi alone who did that. I met another sports change agent, a young lady named Jasmin Mohanty who gave up her life of comfort, closeness of her extended family in an urban place like Puri and signed up to go to ITI Rayagada. In Rayagada, when she arrived, her principal asked her to deliver a single outcome to allow her to make his kids play. He wanted punctuality from everyone at the assembly. Jasmin, because she was staying right there on campus with the kids, made the connection. One day at a time, she won their confidence and made a deal. She would let them play, get coached by her but only if they promised to show up on time for the assembly next day. It worked magically. As time went by, Jasmin found students spend excessive time with their phones, staying awake late at night. In response, she started activities like trekking but only if they gave up their devices at lights-out time.

To be a Tatwamasi and Jasmin, transformative leaders in their own right, one has to be on the ground, day in and day out; it requires persistence. Sometimes, it is not the brilliance but the persistence of the leader that draws the world to them. Persistence is unglamourous, yet people finally take note of it and, eventually, it is the persistent leader that they opt to follow.

One of the difficulties with leadership is the urge to showcase rapid progress, visible achievements and quick wins. This is exacerbated in an increasingly polarized world of politics for elected leaders, pressures of the stock market for CEOs and the presence of social media for everyone. The cocktail that ensues gets us into a spiral of instant gratification. It is true that we need to keep our eyes on the early visible success, yet large-scale, sustainable change, something we call transformative change, asks for a long view of time. In the beginning, it may look like no progress at all. Sometimes, the wheels reverse before they move forward. This means that the leader must understand the fact that this will be long-haul; the leader must explain that to people and mentally prepare their followers. This is done when you publish the road map, show the point of departure, the point of arrival and state the time it may take as best as you can.

But this is not a one-time formality. It requires a series of periodic conversation. It is an ongoing dialogue. Only then do people internalize the idea of the long haul. You address your leaders in the conference room on the road ahead. Then you step out and talk to their teams in the cafeteria. You go home at night and write an email on the same subject in a first-person voice for the larger organization. You seek out an op-ed space in a leading daily to hold up the same narrative. Then, you do a podcast that carries your message on to YouTube. You post it on X and Insta to reinforce it, till the road ahead becomes a narrative of the people. And all the while you are communicating, you are inviting people to ask you questions. You practise deep listening, you demonstrably incorporate the voice of a silent majority as you move from one phase to the other. It is a lot of hard work.

Because transformative change is a long-haul undertaking, it is also important to conserve energy. An important part of it is to choose your battles carefully. It is necessary to know what to tackle and when and what to give up. Sometimes, one must have the courage to leave the battle to stay alive for a future war. And to know the futility of picking up skirmishes. Transformative leaders know when to confront and when to step aside. They know how to go with the energy and not lock horns with distractions along the way. All problems need not be solved, but all opportunities must be intently examined and only some doggedly pursued.

Transformative leaders are ideologically driven. It is the source of their conviction. A big problem however is confusing ideology with dogma. They must know when to be flexible, when to embrace change. They must allow people and events to mould them, and that plasticity is a very important quality. It is this mouldability that signals openness. People do not like to follow close-minded leaders.

The mindset of being ideologically driven without being caught in dogma allows emergence. It is the process of 'letting come' as Otto says, enabling us to allow opportunities to present themselves, to emerge from the environment. These hold the key to breakthrough ideas and greater progress.

Those who do not practise emergence and appreciate its power, cannot deliver long-acting change because things around them are constantly shifting.

Leaders who undertake transformative change must have a deep sense of self-worth. Without becoming egoistic, they need to see themselves as a valuable resource life has chosen for itself. Their work is an obligation to others.

Over the long haul, there are many challenges of course. There are days when the revolution looks dead. There are days when a trusted ally changes loyalty. Or people deliver subversive compliance. The transformative leader has to be okay with all that and be resilient, knowing that tomorrow will be another day.

Amidst it all, surprising new sources of energy emerge, and hitherto unknown alliances come forward.

A big part of this journey is self-doubt. It is normal to experience occasional self-doubt. It is even good because it keeps us humble.

And finally, the transformative leader is not an ascetic, not someone with complete Karmic detachment. They must laugh; they must make others laugh. They must have fun and they must nourish themselves with hope, faith and love.

That is when pain, purpose and perseverance come together and enormous new possibilities open up.

In Closing

We often wonder if change can survive. By its very name, it is not meant to. If that be so, how worthwhile is it to attempt to change something, particularly in the public space?

Now here is the elephant in the room. When political regimes give way to the new ones, and that too in an increasingly polarized world, how much of the ideas, effort and impact can continue? And if that itself is uncertain, why make the effort? In the same vein, I have also heard this refrain a number of times: what will happen when you are gone?

In many ways, *we* never really go away. During the eight years that I spent in Odisha as a public servant, I came close to so many people. They have left indelible impressions on me; they have changed me. You can see that in the many narratives in this book. I am sure I too would have touched some of them in ways that would now make them look at things a little differently in their lives. This process of being impacted by others and impacting others is a very worthwhile outcome. Things we build need not last forever. Ideas that we build need to go on. Our job is to create capacity in people to build beautiful, beneficial things on their own and not be burdened with the obligation to preserve our artefacts, far less to immortalize us.

But what about all the systemic changes? Would they be taken forward? I think it is a good thing for leaders to always assume so and work on that basis. Not taking a step forward is always two steps backwards.

That said, one must also have the pragmatism and the humility to accept that not everything we do is worth taking forward. They were perhaps appropriate in a certain time and space. Nothing and no one should have a claim to immorality.

As I look back in time, I feel wonderful that post the general elections in May 2024, the new government in Odisha has taken forward many things that we had co-created.

Within a few weeks of taking over, Chief Minister Mohan Charan Majhi, accompanied by Chief Secretary Manoj Ahuja, visited World Skill Center and endorsed its objectives.

The nano unicorn programme was embraced and in fact, expanded by the new government.

In June 2024, Odisha became the number 1 state in the IndiaSkills Competition for the second year in a row. Subsequently, fifteen out of the sixty-member Indian contingent at the WorldSkills Competition at Lyon were from Odisha.

On their return from Lyon, with one bronze and a 'Medallion for Excellence', the participants got a rousing welcome. Chief Minister Mohan Charan Majhi personally felicitated them in his office and continued the tradition. The generous and substantial reward and recognition scheme for the winners at the WorldSkills Competition, their coaches and alma mater were taken forward as well.

Meanwhile, the ITI as an institution continues to flourish. Ten out of the best 100 ITIs in India in 2024 happen to be in Odisha. More importantly, ITIs as an institution caught the imagination of everyone, now delegations from other states routinely visit Odisha to study how the state has transformed vocational education. Odisha was asked to present her stories at many Government of India forums.

UNESCO-UNEVOC International Centre for Technical and Vocational Training called out the great work at ITI Berhampur in the area of green skills and commended its 'waste to wealth' programme.

For the first time in Indian history, at the national level, ITIs occupied a place in the budget speech of the finance minister, who allocated a whopping Rs 60,000 crore for their modernization. I believe Odisha's advocacy of this institution had some contribution to making its relevance felt at a national level.

The World Skill Center has risen manifold in its stature since it started. By 2024, it had trained 4282 youth through its one-year intensive programmes. Of these, 160 students had opportunity to attend two-week exchange programmes, while ninety-six more went for paid internship programmes of six-month duration in Singapore. 2620 trainers from various technical institutions were trained here. Students from World Skill Center received upto Rs 3.8 lakh per annum as their starting salary and some had overseas offers starting at Rs 5.35 lakh per annum. The new government made an in-principle decision to replicate two more World Skill Centers, one in Sambalpur in western Odisha and one in Berhampur in the south.

When Prime Minister Narendra Modi visited Singapore on 4 September 2024, one of the high points of the visit was his joyous interaction with the trainees of the World Skill Center, who were interning in Singapore with leading Singapore companies. He was accompanied by his Singaporean counterpart Lawrence Wong. Prime Minister Modi later tweeted, 'It was wonderful to interact with interns from Odisha's World Skill Centre who are visiting Singapore.' The most heartwarming moment for me personally was when he affectionately touched the forehead of intern Pragnya Paramita Barik in a gesture of blessing her. In that moment, the prime minister touched the foreheads of a thousand Odia girls.

This occasion was followed by the historic visit of the President of Singapore, Sharman Shanmugaratnam, to Odisha on 17 January 2025. He was the highest foreign dignitary to ever visit the state. An important part of his visit was to see the World Skill Centre, interact with the trainees there and to endorse its second, more expansive and futuristic campus.

When accompanied by Sanjay Singh, Balwant Singh and Rajesh Patil, I had visited Singapore in

August 2017, we were introduced by Bruce Poh to S. Dhanabalan, who had been a cabinet minister of Singapore multiple times. Among the many boards he had chaired were Singapore Airlines and Temasek Holdings. At the end of a very polite conversation with him, he was frank enough to ask us, do tell me where exactly is Odisha? Looking back, we have come a long way since then.

None of this would have happened unless the chariot would have been pulled by everyone. I believe, despite the temporality of everything in life, there is a constant: change influences change. Once enacted, it has a way of leaving its signature, however small, even as it may evaporate in its current form and fade from ordinary sight. And sometimes, that signature is indelible.

In this context, there is a very interesting play of history that I want to share with you. Its poignancy has always inspired me. It is a reminder for every leader as to why we need to create value and why we must propagate useful ideas. The story is about how the world embraced the principles of total quality management (TQM) during the later part of the twentieth century.

The concept of TQM was conceived in the famous Bell Labs of the US during the 1940s. William Edward Deming is considered the father of TQM. When he took the idea of TQM to the American industry, he did not get a receptive audience. The American companies of the day did not care about his ideas because they were absorbed in their own success. It was Japan that discovered Deming. During the 1950s, Japan was trying to rise from the ashes of the World War II. The decimated nation needed to import food for its survival. The only way to survive was to import raw material, produce things and then export the finished goods so that they could earn foreign exchange and rebuild the country. But Japanese products were considered of poor quality. They had no takers.

This is when they came to Deming, took him to Japan and learnt his ideas. The rest is history. Japan learnt TQM, became a global powerhouse that took on the world with its high-quality products, from automobiles to electronics and everything else. It is only when the US automobile and electronics industry got badly hit by Japan and simply could not match their quality and efficiency, that the country discovered Deming.

The reason this story deeply resonates with me is because it reinforces that it is worthwhile to attempt new things, to be innovative and to create good. You never know where and how it would catch someone's attention and find large-scale adoption.

The vision we created, the ideas we experimented with, the way we humanized change and went about creating a future that did not exist may find meaning and use in other places and perhaps even in different spaces beyond skill development. Who knows?

All good things have the capacity to replicate but often in ways we cannot comprehend in the beginning. Our job is to be the catalyst. Our job is to trust the power of good and pull the chariot.

'But for the good leader, when his work is done, when his aims fulfilled, people will say we did it by ourselves.'
—Lao Tsu

Acknowledgements

One man who stands apart from everyone else is Pinaki Patnaik, additional secretary to the Government of Odisha and COO of the World Skill Center. Pinaki was assigned to me as officer on special duty. He kept me buoyed for all the years I was in Odisha. He was more than a colleague. Wherever I am visible to you in the book, do know that it is because he was there, making sure I was there. An outstanding officer and a great human being, I am grateful to Pinaki.

I am grateful to my long-time friend Thomas Abraham, who exorcised me for a long spell of thinking that people no longer read books. He told me, 'Your experience is valuable to others. You have an obligation to write.'

I am grateful to my editor, Milee Ashwarya, for finding me. During the course of writing this book, she was very patient with me despite my many demands on her as if I were her only author. I hope I have been worth her while.

Gratitude is due in large measure to my line editor, Saba Nehal, who looked at the book in great detail, asked a number of critical questions along the way and made very valuable suggestions, which I have dutifully incorporated. We have been a great team together.

The many photographs you see in the book were taken at different times by different people. It is difficult to acknowledge them individually. The quality varied hugely. Mayur Channagere, chief storyteller and photoentreprenuer at Agna has used technology to harmonize them and make them print-ready. I am grateful to Mayur.

I am grateful to Otto Schramer, Patricia Bohl and the Presencing Institute for their kind permission to use the pictorial depiction of Theory U and the liberal adaptation of Otto's work in this book.

I am grateful to Neha Bagchi who cleared the veil of self-doubt at a crucial stage of writing the book. It had to do with the narrative style. I do not like memoirs. I did not want to write a memoir. She helped me understand the difference between a memoir and using the memoir-style to deliver a narrative.

I am grateful to my journalist friend Goutam Das, vice chancellor of Ahmedabad University, Professor Pankaj Chandra, Dr Gautam Rajkhowa of Birmingham Newman University and Dr Bidyut Das, head of the department of rheumatology at the SCB Medical College. They read the raw draft of the book and provided me with very valuable inputs.

I am grateful to Dr Jogesh Chandra Bagchi, civil surgeon in the court of the king of Seraikella, a man I have never met and never will, for his seminal advice to serve the sovereign. I am sure he is very happy, from his place among the stars above, that eventually I heeded the Bagchi Rule.

Before I end, I must say that I have expressed my deep admiration for many people in this book, including several government officials, wherever it was due. There is an inherent risk in doing so.

I realized that fact long after I wrote 'Zen Garden', a column in *Forbes India*. It was based on a series of interviews with people such as the Dalai Lama, Jimmy Wales, Aamir Khan, Nandan Nilekani, Anu Aga and Kiran Majumdar–Shaw. The concept behind the column was to gather pearls of wisdom from a set of unusual people, most of them entrepreneurs. The collection was later published as a book by Penguin Random House India, titled *Zen Garden*. Decades after, as I look back, at least half a dozen of the fifty-plus interviewees floundered, some waded into controversy, some crossed over to the dark side and a few fell from grace.

People evolve, people change. When I admire someone in this book, I do so with accountability for facts in a given time and space.

Just the same way, I may have presented certain individuals, organizations and systems through a critical lens. In all humility, I must accept that my views may not necessarily be someone else's. In time, many may evolve and make a large, beneficial impact.

Scan QR code to access the
Penguin Random House India website